WRITINGS ON
SPIRITUAL DIRECTION

by Great Christian Masters

WRITINGS
ON SPIRITUAL
DIRECTION

By Great Christian Masters

Edited by
JEROME M. NEUFELDER
and
MARY C. COELHO

The Seabury Press

Library of Congress Catalog Card Number: 82-640
ISBN: 0-86683-914-3

Printed in the United States of America
5   4   3   2   1

The Seabury Press
430 Oak Grove
Minneapolis, Minnesota 55403

Note to the Reader:

All biblical references are to the Revised Standard Version of the Bible. Old Testament Section, copyright © 1952: New Testament Section, First edition, copyright © 1946; Second Edition © 1971 by Division of Christian Education of the National Council of Churches of Christ in the United States of America.

Grateful acknowledgment is made for use of the following materials:

Excerpt from *Spiritual Theology*, by Jordan Aumann. © 1980 by Our Sunday Visitor, Inc., Huntington, Indiana, and reprinted by permission. All rights reserved.

Excerpt from *The Life of Baron von Hügel* by Michael De La Bedoyere. Published in 1951 by J. M. Dent & Sons, Inc. Used by permission.

Excerpt from *Life Together* by Dietrich Bonhoeffer, trans. by John W. Doberstein. Copyright © 1954 by Harper & Row, Publishers, Inc. Used by permission.

Excerpt from *The Spirit is Present* by Edward Carter. Published by Alba House in 1973. Used by permission.

Excerpt from *The Art of Prayer* by Igumen Chariton. Published in 1976 by Faber & Faber Ltd. Used by permission.

Excerpt from "Contemporary Spiritual Direction" from *Studies for Spirituality of Jesuits*, XIII, no. 3 (June, 1975) by William J. Connolly, S.J. Used by permission.

Excerpt from *Abba: Guides to Wholeness and Holiness, East and West*, (ed. by John R. Sommerfeldt) by Sr. Donald Corcoran, O.S.B. Used by permission of Cistercian Publications.

Excerpt from *The Life of Evelyn Underhill* by Margaret Cropper. Published in 1958 by Longman Group Ltd. Used by permission.

Excerpt from *Mrs. Seton* by Joseph I. Dirvin. Published in 1975 by Farrar, Straus, and Giroux. Used by permission.

Excerpt from *Guidance in Spiritual Direction* by Charles Hugo Doyle, Newman Press, Westminster, MD, 1958. Used by permission.

Excerpt from *Spiritual Freedom* by John J. English, S.J. Published in 1973 by Loyola House. Used by permission.

Excerpt from *The Ecumenical Review*, "Saint Seraphim of Sarov, An Ikon of Russian Spirituality," Vol. XV, #3, April 1963, pp. 266, 267, by Paul Evdokimov. Used by permission of The Catholic University Press.

Excerpt from "Beginning Spiritual Direction", David Fleming, S.J. *Review for Religious*, Vol. XXXIII, #3. Used by permission of *Review for Religious*.

Excerpt from *Rufus Jones Speaks to Our Time*, Harry Emerson Fosdick, ed. Published by Macmillan Co. in 1961. Used by permission.

Excerpt from *Celebration of Discipline* by Richard J. Foster. Copyright © 1978 by Richard J. Foster. Used by permission of Harper & Row Publishers, Inc.

Excerpts from *The Way of the Pilgrim*, R. M. French, trans. Used by permission of The Seabury Press, Inc.

Excerpt from *The Art of Mental Prayer* by Bede Frost. Published in 1931 by The Society for Promoting Christian Knowledge. Used by permission.

Excerpts from *The Life and Sayings of St. Catherine of Genoa*, trans. & ed. by P. Garvin. Published in 1964 by Alba House. Used by permission.

Excerpt from *We and the Holy Spirit* by Leonce de Grandmaison. Published in 1953 by Fides Publishers. Used by permission.

Excerpt from *Guidelines for Spiritual Direction* by Carolyn Gratton. Published by Dimension Book, Denville, NJ in 1980. Used by permission.

Excerpt from *Spiritual Maxims* by Jean Grou. Published in 1961 by Templegate Publishers. Used by permission.

Excerpt from *Spiritual Counsels of Father John of Kronstadt*, trans. by W. Jardine Grisbrooke. Published by James Clark and Company, Ltd. in 1966. Used by permission.

Excerpt from *Thomas Merton—Monk*, ed. by Patrick Hart. Published in 1974 by Sheed & Ward, N.Y. Used by permission of Andrews & McMeel, Inc., Fairway, KS.

Excerpts from *The Elements of the Spiritual Life* by Frederic P. Harton. Published in 1964 by The Society for Promoting Christian Knowledge. Used by permission.

Excerpts from *Letters to a Niece* and *Essays and Addresses* by Friedrich von Hügel. Published in 1930 and 1928, respectively. Used by permission of J. M. Dent & Sons Ltd.

Excerpt from *Eternal Life* by Friedrich von Hügel. Published in 1912 by T. & T. Clark Ltd. Used by permission.

Excerpt from *The Spiritual Director* by Damien Isabell. Used by permission of Franciscan Herald Press.

Excerpt from *Exploring Spiritual Direction: An Essay on Christian Friendship* by Alan Jones. Copyright © 1982 by Alan Jones. Used by permission of The Seabury Press, Inc.

Excerpt from *The Flowering of Mysticism* by Rufus M. Jones. Copyright © 1939 by Macmillan Publishing co., Inc., renewed 1967 by Mary Hoxie Jones. Used by permission.

Contents

Expressions of Appreciation

Besides our own spiritual directors, present and past, we want to express sincere personal gratitude to several persons who have been true coworkers with us in putting this anthology together in its present form. Sister Donald Corcoran, O.S.B., worked as a consultant in preparation of this anthology and provided a number of important ideas. Sister Mary Aquin Verkamp, O.S.B., receives our highest gratitude for typing and proofreading the various phases of the manuscript until coming to the present text. For their assistance in translating some of the sources, we are grateful to our many friends for their willingness to translate the often difficult texts.

Introduction

In John Steinbeck's novel *Of Mice and Men,* Crooks, a black farm laborer forced by race to live alone, says to Lennie, a migrant worker:

> A guy sets alone out here at night, maybe readin' books or thinkin' or stuff like that. Sometimes he gets thinkin', an' he got nothing to tell him what's so an' what ain't so. Maybe if he see somethin', he don't know whether it's right or not. He can't turn to some other guy and ast him if he sees it too. He can't tell. He got nothing to measure by. I seen things out here. I wasn't drunk. I don't know if I was asleep. If some guy was with me, he could tell me I was asleep, an' then it would be all right. But I jus' don't know.

In our struggle to understand our spiritual experiences and hungers, to discern our vocation and to grow towards becoming holy, loving, and loved persons, there is much that we "jus' don't know."

Fundamental truth about human life and about God has been revealed in Christ and lived again and again by thousands since Christ. But the personal rediscovery, appropriation, and expression of that truth by each person, who must embrace it in a unique and individual manner, is seldom clear-cut and never easy. To do so requires an ongoing conversion and reorientation of both the conscious and unconscious personality that is always slow and at times arduous. Almost inevitably we feel the need to find help, as we frequently "jus' don't know."

Throughout Christian history many have sought individual guidance from other Christians and many have given it. While there are few historical records of the conversations of individuals seeking and receiving spiritual guidance from another person, there are written works about the ministry of spiritual direction in many forms. These include treatises on spiritual direction and discernment, homilies, journals, autobiographies, and letters asking for and giving spiritual guidance. We have turned to these sources to gather material for this book, believing that the wealth of experience of these writers/directors, by being made accessible, will inform and shape our contemporary understanding and practice of spiritual direction.

This anthology is a joint effort of an Anglican student of theology and spirituality and a Roman Catholic priest. The original manuscript was much larger, consisting of a collection of writings by some three hundred authors. The value of the present book is its selectivity and clearer focus on this ministry.

In this joint endeavor Father Jerome Neufelder made the original selection of material, identified the various authors, was responsible for the translations from other languages, and prepared the bibliography. Mary Coelho made the selections to be used in the book, organized the material, and wrote the commentary.

The selections are organized under themes that concern the basic dimensions of spiritual direction, from the recognition of our need for it to discussions of several aspects of the relationship itself. This thematic organization is based on human needs and a universality to this ministry within the Christian tradition. The source of the universality is the divine reality in the human situation as revealed in scripture and tradition. Spiritual direction aims to facilitate an ever-greater participation in the truth that has been revealed.

There have been significant differences in the practice of the ministry of spiritual direction in different ages and branches of Christianity. This becomes clearest in chapter two, which concerns the images and models of the director. Some reflect very different conceptions of the role of the spiritual director. Even the term *spiritual direction*, which we are using generically to cover all one-to-one relationships for the purpose of seeking spiritual guidance, including the early master/disciple relationships of the desert fathers, probably only came into use in the sixteenth century, introduced by Francis de Sales. Throughout the text we have pointed out some of these shifting emphases.

In choosing selections for this book we have attempted to be faithful to the voice of the tradition as found in the original larger collection of writings. In some sections of this book this has resulted in a picture of spiritual direction unadjusted to twentieth-century assumptions. We have attempted to communicate the judgment of history on the nature of spiritual direction. Although some of the later authors quoted engage in dialogue with contemporary psychology, we have not attempted to cover this dialogue to the extent that it deserves but have tried to provide a strong foundation of understanding of spiritual direction from which this dialogue may proceed.

Material for this book was also selected for its practical and pastoral usefulness for individuals called upon to give spiritual direction. We also hope that the book will be of assistance to people considering seeking spiritual direction.

Through the long process of working with the material for this book two unanticipated conclusions pressed themselves to our attention. The first is that the evidence of history challenges those efforts which reduce spiritual direction to a kind of counseling with directors claiming a type of trained professional authority in matters of prayer and meditation and the stages of spiritual growth. Such a view tragically diminishes the claim and call of God on the director/guide. We believe there emerges in this book, especially from some of the early traditions and the Russian Orthodox staretz, a much greater claim. In these traditions the guide is a model and teacher whose very life teaches with authenticity and evokes a longing for holiness. The director must be, as a person, open to the burden and gift of God in his or her own life so that he is available as a person to others as a bearer of the Spirit. However important our learning and knowledge of the human sciences, spiritual direction must always stand under the ultimate claims and ultimate mystery before which we all stand in judgment.

Our second conclusion was to see that all too frequently the pursuit of personal spiritual growth has been exclusively seen as an individual process isolated from our common human life. This isolation has become less acceptable in the age of the "global village," when an individual's life is more obviously bound with the destiny of the total human community. The critics of spiritual direction who see its temptations to a narcissistic, privileged comfort for the spiritual elite concerned only with personal salvation have truly seen its weak side and greatest danger. We must add to the lists of the content appropriate to spiritual direction the expectation that it also include an account of the way in which we have been a brother and a sister to the poor and the oppressed, the imprisoned and the captive.

Jerome M. Neufelder
Mary C. Coelho

Chapter One

THE NEED FOR
SPIRITUAL DIRECTION

Two are better than one, because they have a good reward for their toil. For if they fall, one will lift up his fellow; but woe to him who is alone when he falls and has not another to lift him up.

[Ecclesiastes 4:9–10]

"Ask, and it will be given you; seek, and you will find; knock, and it will be opened to you. For every one who asks receives, and he who seeks finds, and to him who knocks it will be opened. Or what man of you if his son asks him for bread, will give him a stone? Or if he asks for a fish, will give him a serpent? If you then, who are evil, know how to give good gifts to your children, how much more will your Father who is in heaven give good things to those who ask him! . . .

"Enter by the narrow gate; for the gate is wide and the way is easy, that leads to destruction, and those who enter by it are many. For the gate is narrow and the way is hard, that leads to life, and those who find it are few." *[Matthew 7:7–14]*

Stand in the assembly of the elders. Who is wise? Cleave to him.

[Ecclesiasticus 6:34]

For centuries, writers have offered many often compelling reasons why spiritual direction is essential. However, in apparent contradiction, we find the equally strong confidence that sometimes the Holy Spirit guides the soul directly. Reflected in the selections in this first chapter is a tension that is a fundamental dynamic of spiritual direction: that while the aid of one person to another is often essential and the influence of one person on another is at times of a transforming nature, there remains the basic freedom of each individual relationship with God. We have started with those exhortations that recognize our need for spiritual direction, and they are followed by selections that describe direction of the soul by the Holy Spirit without the aid of a spiritual guide.

In my own room I do all that a person is counseled to do there, and I find no consolation from God. The elder said: "This happens to you because you want your own will to be done." The brother said, "What then will you command me to do, father?" The elder said, "Go, give yourself over to a man who fears God, be humble before him, give up your own will to him, and only then will you find consolation from God." [*The Sayings of the Desert Fathers*]

Who is so smug and blind as to trust in his own judgment and power of discretion when the chosen vessel [Paul] confesses that he had need of counsel with his fellow apostles. We clearly see that the Lord Himself does not show the way of perfection to anyone who having the opportunity of learning ignores the teaching and guidance of the Elders. [*Conferences*]

> *John Cassian, Eastern ascetic influential in the*
> *formation of Western monasticism, 360–433*

There is nothing more harmful than trying to direct oneself . . . that's why I never allowed myself to follow my own desires without seeking counsel. . . . In the Book of Proverbs it says, "Those who have no guidance fall like leaves but there is security in good advice" (Prov. 11:14). Take a clear look at this saying, brothers. Look at what Scripture teaches us. It tells us that we should not establish ourselves

as guides, that we should not consider ourselves wise, that we should not ever think we can direct ourselves. We need another's help; we need guidance besides God's grace. No one is poorer, no one is more defenseless than a person who has no one to guide him along the road to God. Scripture says, "Those who have no guidance fall like leaves." Leaves are always green at the start; they grow quickly and are quite pleasing to look at. Then, after awhile, they dry up and drop off, and in the end, they are blown about by the wind and are walked on. So is the person who is not guided by someone. At first, he has great fervor about fasting, keeping prayerful watch, silence, obedience, and other ascetic practices. After a short time, the fire is put out and, not having anyone to guide him and support him, and kindle his fire again, he dries up, and so, becoming disobedient, he falls and finally becomes a tool in the hand of his enemies, who do what they want to with him. [*Dorotheos of Gaza, Discourses and Sayings*]
    Saint Dorotheos of Gaza, monk and preacher, sixth century

Nine things are needful for a pilgrim who has far to travel. First, he must ask the way. Second, he must choose good companions. Third, he must guard against thieves. Fourth, he must guard against excess. Fifth, he must hitch up his clothes and belt them in fast. Sixth, as he climbs mountains, he must stoop. Seventh, as he comes downhill, he must walk upright. Eighth, he must ask for good men's prayers. Ninth, he must be glad to talk about God. So it is with our spiritual pilgrimage, in which we must seek God's kingdom and His righteousness in the perfect works of Love. . . .

    Although not referring to spiritual direction specifically she continues later in the letter:

And ask the way from those who are with you and whom you see to be following Him most closely, and who are obedient to Him in all the works of virtue. So follow Him who is Himself the way, and them who have followed and still follow him. [*Letter 15*]
    Blessed Hadewijch of Antwerp, Flemish Beguine, c. 1250

Meister Eckhart said this: One who is a master at right living is better off than a thousand who have mastered only the learning of books.

Still, no one can live life fully without God. If I were seeking a master of studies, I should go to the colleges of Paris where higher studies are followed, but if I wanted to know about living a perfect life, they could not help me there.

To whom should I go? To a person with a nature that is pure and free and to no one else. Only there would I find the answer which I so eagerly seek. Why do you look among dead bones, dear people? Why don't you look for eternal life in the holy places of life? The dead can neither give nor take. If an angel wanted to find God without God, he would look for him in a pure, free, selfless creature and nowhere else. [*Fragment #8*]

> *Meister Johann Eckhart, German Dominican priest*
> *and theologian, 1260–1307*

I say that the Holy Scripture and the advice of the saints and their lives, and the experiences that we have seen, all with one voice recommend to us that we do not deceive ourselves with our own prudence, but incline our ear to the counsel of another.

> [*Hear, O Daughter*]
> *Saint John of Ávila, Spanish diocesan priest, 1500–1569*

God is completely satisfied that the guidance and direction of people be mediated through other people, and that a person be guided by human intelligence, that He certainly does not desire that we confer all our confidence to His supernatural communications, nor that we authenticate their veracity and surety until they come to us through this natural instrument of the mouth of another person. As often as He manifests some truth to a person, He confers upon his soul a particular capacity for also manifesting this to the appropriate person. Until a person does this, he usually is living without complete peace of mind, because he has not received it from another person like himself. [*Ascent of Mt. Carmel*]

The person that desires to be alone, lacking the assistance of a master and guide, will be like a lonely tree in the field that has no owner. No matter how much fruit it bears, strangers will pick it all, and it will not get ripe.

The person that is alone without a spiritual guide, and has virtue, is like a glowing ember that is alone. It will become more frigid rather than hotter.

The person that falls down by himself remains on the ground alone and does not value his soul, since he entrusts it only to himself.

If you are not fearful of falling alone, how do you dare to try to rise alone? Notice how much more can be done by two together than by one alone. [*Spiritual Maxims and Sentences*]

> *Saint John of the Cross, Spanish cofounder (with Saint Teresa*
> *of Ávila) of the Discalced Carmelites, poet, 1542–91*

I want to remind her [a niece] one more time that she must submit herself to God and I advise her to choose a wise and capable guide to help her accomplish this. She must begin this way. . . . One who has no director will have difficulty staying free of the enemy. Although she may manage to avoid them, I still do not feel she can make any progress in the spiritual life. [*Letter to Son*]

> *Saint Marie of the Incarnation, French Ursuline nun*
> *and missionary in Canada, 1599–1672*

Everybody should know this truth that no one is gifted with such prudence and wisdom as to be adequate for himself in the guidance of his own spiritual life. Self-love is a blind guide and fools many. The light of our own judgment is weak, and we cannot envision all dangers or snares and errors to which we are prone in the life of the spirit. Powerful and crafty enemies fight us—the devil, the world, and the flesh. Their deceits and temptations God points out to us through those whom he has appointed for our counsel and guidance.

> [*A Treatise on the Spiritual Life*]
> *John Cardinal Bona, Italian Cistercian abbot, 1609–74*

There is scarcely any truth of which we have naturally more difficulty in allowing ourselves to be convinced than the necessity of a director. Each one wishes to be the absolute master of his own conduct and to regulate for himself all his actions. The inclination that we have naturally for independence makes us fear subjection. The good opinion that we have of our own talents persuades us that we have no need of outside help. There is almost nobody who doesn't experience deeply within himself a great repugnance toward allowing himself to be led. Whenever a person has the spirit of enlightenment, he claims the right to make for himself some rules of conduct. He believes it would be a weakness to do otherwise. He cannot persuade himself that he has any needs great enough that they can't be remedied in other ways than by a director. Yet the saints have always been very far from these thoughts; for they have thought that there couldn't be in this world any greater wisdom than to allow oneself to be directed in all things. [*Obedience to One's Director*]

Louis Tronson, French priest and
third superior general of the Sulpicians, 1622–1700

So you ascribe all the knowledge you have to God, and in this respect you are humble. But if you think you have more than you really have, or if you think you are so taught of God as no longer to need man's teaching, pride lieth at the door. Yes, you have need to be taught, not only by Mr. Morgan, by one another, by Mr. Maxfield, or me, but by the weakest preacher in London; yea, by all men. For God sendeth by whom He will send. [*A Plain Account of Christian Perfection*]

John Wesley, founder of Methodism, 1703–91

When men are in the first fervour of penitence, they should be careful not to act on their own private judgment, and without proper advice. Not only in forming lasting engagements, but in all they do, they need a calmer guidance than their own. They cannot manage themselves; they must be guided by others; the neglect of this simple and natural rule leads to very evil consequences. We should all of us be saved a great deal of suffering of various kinds, if we could but persuade ourselves, that we are not the best judges, whether of our own conditions, or of God's will towards us. What sensible person undertakes to be his own physician? Are the diseases of the mind less numerous, less intricate, less subtle than those of the body? Is experience of no avail in things spiritual as well as in things material? Does induction lose its office, and science its supremacy, when the soul is concerned? . . .

And what is more preposterous still, a person is thus to be his own guide and instructor at the very time, when by the nature of the case he is in error and difficulty. How can a person show himself the way, when by the very hypothesis he has lost it? How can he at once guide and be guided? The very seasons I am speaking of are those, when a man is agitated, excited, harassed, depressed, desponding; the very time when of course his judgment is not clear, when he is likely to be led away with fancies, when he is likely to be swayed by inclination, when the light that is in him becomes, if not darkness, yet a meteor leading him the wrong way. But if the blind lead the blind, shall not both reason and passion, shall not the whole man, fall into the ditch?

Nor is it to the purpose to say, that we cannot be guided without the grace of God, and that the grace of God will guide us; and that the grace of God is gained by private prayer. For still God makes use of means; we must do our part; we must act, and God will guide us while we act; and the question is, whether taking the advice of others is not God's way, through which He blesses and enlightens us, and without which our souls will not prosper.

[*Sermons Bearing on Subjects of the Day*]
John Henry Newman, English theologian and cardinal, 1801–90

Everyone admits that, to get to this point [a good beginning in the spiritual life], direction is indispensable in the same way as a master's help is required for initiation into any art; but many are persuaded that they can do without any direction afterwards. . . .

1. Who has not observed this phenomenon, that in explaining a situation we clear it up; the presence of a listener stimulates us, and the necessity of making ourselves understood disentangles our ideas.

2. We are too near ourselves to see ourselves properly; another is just the right distance off. What a number of illusions deceive us which would not deceive us in the presence of others. There are those who are very clever in giving advice, yet who hesitate to make any decision in their own case. Others make the mistake of not hesitating enough.

3. Direction gives confidence and courage. Even in the most ordinary matters, every prudent person has a remote fear of making mistakes; this fear is entirely dissipated by the director's words; thus set free, we shall act with an altogether different kind of animation.

4. It is not light that is mainly wanting, but rather strength. But direction offers us this invaluable element. Respect for a witness, the authority of a counsellor to whom we shall have to give an account,

these give our resolutions a steadfastness which they would not find in our own conscience.

5. But let us leave secondary reasons and enter fully into the supernatural: direction places us under God's authority: "He who heareth you, heareth Me," and God attaches to such obedience the promise of victory: "He who obeyeth shall speak of nothing but victories."

6. This wise practice which is a safeguard, is also a lesson, a lesson we are prone to forget in riper years: "Except you become as little children, you shall not enter into the kingdom of heaven."—Our constant need is to make ourselves little and humble and docile; and direction makes us all these. [*Spiritual Progress*]

Leopold Beaudenom, French priest
and convent chaplain, 1840–1916

Behind every saint stands another saint. That is the great tradition. I never learnt anything myself by my own old nose.

[*Essays and Addresses on the Philosophy of Religion*]
Baron Friedrich von Hügel, lay Catholic
theologian and writer, 1852–1925

In a letter to his sister, Charles de Foucauld writes:

My dear Mimi:
In a city like Dijon, a very well-informed, intelligent director can certainly be found: there is no doubt about it. For the soul's life, it's indispensable. . . . If ever I see you again, my dear, I will be able only to repeat that to you again and again, because that is the key to sanctification, the means of living in interior peace, and the means of not taking a false route with good intentions. For me I have M. Huvelin and we will never depart from one another until one of us dies. You need someone who can see your daughters, to whom they can confess, and to whom you can, from time to time, also confess. Pray the Good God to direct your choice, to choose with care. In the beginning find out if it is good and really what you need. Open yourselves well and follow well the advice, consult well and comply well with the responses. All is there, one must only do that well and one has all; and if one does not do it one has nothing, because for

lack of sufficient knowledge, one takes a false route, even with the best intentions. For me, when I am in a place where I don't know anyone, I always consult the Jesuits.

I am allowing myself to go on talking to you about this; don't be astonished, it's my favorite subject. Let me speak to religious men, to religious women, to rich and fashionable people of every kind, I never have anything else to say to them. Is it on account of having made long journeys in the Sahara where the first and the most indispensable thing is a good guide? Is it on account of having read the Gospel a great deal where this doctrine is on each page? For these two motives probably, and perhaps also on account of a little of the old monastic and Benedictine spirit which is a spirit of faith, of discipline and of peace. [*Spiritual Writings*]

Charles de Foucauld, French priest, and hermit, 1858–1916

In The Way of the Pilgrim *the hermit tells the professor:*

The guidance of a director or starets who is experienced and knowledgeable in spiritual things, to whom one can open one's heart every day without hindrance, with confidence and advantage, and tell one's thoughts and what one has met with on the path of interior schooling, is the chief condition for the practice of prayer of the heart by one who has entered upon the life of silence. Yet, in cases where it is impossible to find such a one, the same holy Fathers who prescribe this make an exception. Nicephorus the Monk gives clear instructions about it, thus: "During the practice of inward activity of the heart, a genuine and well-informed director is required. If such a one is not at hand, then you must diligently search for one. If you do not find him, then, calling contritely upon God for help, draw instruction and guidance from the teaching of the holy Fathers and verify it from the Word of God set forth in the Holy Scriptures." [*The Way of a Pilgrim*]

By an anonymous Russian, c. 1860

But in all contemplative traditions, it has been found necessary that those who have attained to some depth of religious insight should to some extent guide others who seek to attain the same experience of truth in their own lives. [*Contemplation in a World of Action*]

Thomas Merton, Trappist monk, 1915–68

How do ministers, as living memories of Jesus Christ, guide their people in the concrete circumstances of everyday life? Two ways of guiding suggest themselves: . . . confronting and inspiring. It may be surprising to think of confrontation as a form of guidance, but a prophetic ministry which guides toward a new future requires the hard, painful unmasking of our illusions: the illusion that "we have arrived," that we have found the final articulation of our faith, and that we have discovered the life-style which best gives shape to our ideals. We are constantly tempted to replace the original vision with a rather comfortable interpretation of that vision. . . .

But guidance demands more than confrontation. It requires re-capturing the original vision, going back to the point from which the great inspiration came. . . . Ministers who guide step back in order to touch again the best memories of their community and so to remind their people of the original vision. The paradox of progress is that it occurs by conserving the great memory which can revitalize dormant dreams.

Thus the minister guides by confronting and inspiring. Confrontation challenges us to confess and repent; inspiration stirs us to look up again with new courage and confidence. [*The Living Reminder*]
Henri J. M. Nouwen, Dutch Catholic priest and teacher, b. 1932

Clearly, spiritual direction is urgently needed in order to give orientation to this inner search for God. How can the transition from drugs to meditation be best aided, and the pitfalls avoided? How can the young person who believes he has experienced God on LSD be helped to interpret and evaluate that experience? How can the "dabbler" who moves from one eastern method or technique to another be helped to attain stability and sobriety of spirit? What resources are available for those who are finding through Yoga and Zen valuable insights into spirituality? [*Soul Friend*]
Kenneth Leech, English Anglican priest, b. 1939

The selections that follow describe the more immediate direction of the soul by the Holy Spirit.

Peter: I really do think that this holy man would have needed someone else to counsel with him before he could become a spiritual guide for other people.

Gregory: From what I know he had no one to counsel him, but the gift of the Holy Spirit is not limited by any law. In accord with good monastic practice, a person should never attempt to become a superior until he has learned obedience; if he does not know how to obey, he should never require obedience of others. But there are occasions when the Spirit guides a soul totally from within. In such instances the guidance of the Divine Teacher makes up for the absence of any human guidance. [*Dialogues*]

Saint Gregory the Great, Benedictine monk and pope, 540–604

This, then, is what I have written to your Kindness, in order that which you had entreated to hear once for all from my poor person, you have it now in writing in order to read it, when you wish. But if you consider, providentially and for your good, that it is really the Holy Spirit who prescribes to you all this by our mediation, all will be realized from beginning to end, in the way that we have said; and all that which we have left unsaid, because it would take too long to say it, it is Christ in person who, by Himself, will instruct you concerning it. [*Theological Chapters*]

Saint Symeon the New Theologian, Eastern monk
and abbot of Studios, c. 949–1022

Be sure of this: there is no creature ever made by God who can set you free or help you; only God can do it. Run about as you will, search high and low the whole world over, you will never find the help you need anywhere except in God. If the Lord chooses to use an instrument, man or angel, to achieve this, He can; but He must do it and no one else.

Seek this help inside yourself, the depths of your soul; stop running around, stop searching up and down the countryside; be still, be calm, stay where you are, in Egypt, in darkness, until the angel comes to call you. Joseph was asleep when the angel called him.

[*Spiritual Conferences*]
John Tauler, German Dominican preacher
and mystical writer, 1300–1361

She [Catherine] was guided and innerly taught by her own gentle Love alone, without the outward assistance of any human person, priest or layman. If she attempted to get support from someone, Love caused her such intense mental suffering immediately that she was forced to give it up, saying, "O Love, now I comprehend you." When she was advised that it would be preferable and safer to place herself under spiritual guidance, and she was in doubt about what plan she was to accept, her Lord answered her within her own mind, "Totally confide in me and have no doubts." [*Life and Doctrine*]

Saint Catherine of Genoa, married woman,
hospital director, 1447–1510

He was never instructed by men in the interior life, yet he spoke of it to me with so much subtilty, such fulness and solidity, that all I have read or heard said about it, is as nothing compared with the value of his discourse to me. From my first discovery of this treasure, I contrived, as far as I possibly could, to seize every opportunity of speaking to him in private. . . .

I put him through every point of the spiritual life, both speculative and practical, which suggested itself to me, and during three days he satisfied all my questions, and gave me answers that filled me with astonishment. . . .

He told me one of the first virtues that God gives to a soul He possesses is prudence; that the supernatural light which God pours into the soul shows her more clearly what she has to do, than the sunlight manifests sensible objects; that the multitude of things which the soul, illuminated with this divine light, discovers within herself, is greater than all that is contained in the whole compass of material nature; that God with all His greatness dwells in the humble, simple, pure and faithful heart, and makes Himself known to it; that certain operations of God in the soul are miracles so great that they astonished him more than if he had seen all the dead brought to life; but that God is not sparing of miracles in favour of a soul that has attained to perfect union. As I pressed him to tell me whether he had not had a director, who had instructed him, he said he had not; that he had had no other master than the Holy Spirit; that even were the sacred books lost, he could dispense with them, God having Himself taught him enough of them for his salvation; that there are souls whom creatures cannot prejudice, God being all in all to them.

[*Spiritual Letters*]
Jean Joseph Surin, French Jesuit, 1600–1665

A letter to Elizabeth Seton from Bishop Brute, her spiritual director:

My good Mother, your poor physician of the soul does not see you much, as he does not wish to fatigue you. He has no cause to fear, knowing that the heavenly Physician, the Beloved, the Spouse, the Only Desire of your heart, is continually present: present in the love, confidence, abandon, which He inspires, abandon the most tender and most unreserved—present in the continual acts of penance, humility, dependence and resignation to suffer everything in union with Him, with His cross—present in the peace, the tranquil joy which He imparts; in the total disengagement which He teaches; in the grace of every moment, pain or comfort which He dispenses.

[*Personal Notes*]
Saint Elizabeth Seton, American founder of
Sisters of Charity, 1774–1821

A Christian person should be led to give his life to God mainly because God is the chief and, strictly speaking, the only real guider of persons. Christ is not only the Way, which He reveals to us by His teaching and example, He is also our inner Leader, the Shepherd Who provides good pasture and, by His hidden promptings and encouragement, leads His sheep in search for it. All this being true, He still providentially causes us to need the ministry of priests for the direction of our souls. He gives His own grace to this ministry, and through it He gives all necessary counsel and instruction. He is the only Hidden Master. He and He alone can speak to our heart.

[*Spiritual Maxims*]
Jean Grou, Jesuit classics scholar
and spiritual director, 1731–1803

No one really doubts that the Holy Spirit, by His hidden coming into the souls of the just, influences and stirs them up by admonition and inspiration. If it were different all external help and guidance would be useless. If any one positively affirms that he can consent to the saving preaching of the Gospel without the illumination of the Holy Spirit, who imparts sweetness to all to consent to and accept the truth, he is misled by a heretical spirit. But as we all know from our own experience these promptings and inspirations of the Holy Spirit for the most part are not discerned without the help and, as it were, without the assistance of guidance outside ourselves. . . .

It must also be remembered that those who want to follow a more perfect way are by the very fact entering upon a way of life which for most people is untried and more exposed to error, and therefore they, more than others, stand in need of a counselor and a guide.

[Letter, Testem Benevolentiae]
Pope Leo XIII, 1810–1903

I am there in order to help you to recognize yourself (to collect yourself), to find your way in the crossroads; but it is God who calls, God who formulates and who measures his demands. Direction is not an oracle rendered from the height of a tripod, it is a collaboration in which one reveals that which is in him, and the other person helps him to recognize himself there and to find his way.

[Letters of Direction]
Msgr. Maurice d'Hulst, French priest, 1841–96

Father
Before leaving I want to speak to you again, it may be the last time perhaps, for over there I shall probably send you only my news from time to time just so as to have yours.

I told you that I owed you an enormous debt. I want to try to tell you exactly what it consists of. I think that if you could really understand what my spiritual state is you would not be at all sorry that you did not lead me to baptism. But I do not know if it is possible for you to understand this.

You neither brought me the Christian inspiration nor did you bring me to Christ; for when I met you there was no longer any need; it had been done without the intervention of any human being. If it had been otherwise, if I had not already been won, not only implicitly but consciously, you would have given me nothing, because I should have received nothing from you. My friendship for you would have been a reason for me to refuse your message, for I should have been afraid of the possibilities of error and illusion which human influence in the divine order is likely to involve.

I have told you that you are like a father and brother at the same time to me. But these words only express an analogy. Perhaps at bottom they only correspond to a feeling of affection, of gratitude and admiration. For as to the spiritual direction of my soul, I think that God himself has taken it in hand from the start and still looks after it.

That does not prevent me from owing you the greatest debt of gratitude that I could ever have incurred toward any human being. This is exactly what it consists of.

But the greatest blessing you have brought me is of another order. In gaining my friendship by your charity (which I have never met anything to equal), you have provided me with a source of the most compelling and pure inspiration that is to be found among human things. For nothing among human things has such power to keep our gaze fixed ever more intensely upon God, than friendship for the friends of God. [*The Simone Weil Reader*]

Simone Weil, French philosopher
and political activist, 1909–43

The director wants to know our inmost self, our real self. He wants to know us not as we are in the eyes of men, or even as we are in our own eyes, but as we are in the eyes of God. He wants to know the inmost truth of our vocation, the action of grace in our souls. His direction is, in reality, nothing more than a way of leading us to see and obey the real Director, the Holy Spirit, hidden in the depths of our soul. We must never forget that in reality we are not directed and taught by men, and that if we need human direction it is only because we cannot, without man's help, come into contact with that "unction (of the Spirit) which teaches us all things" (1 John 2:20).

[*Spiritual Direction and Meditation*]
Thomas Merton, Trappist monk, 1915–68

Chapter Two

IMAGES AND MODELS OF THE SPIRITUAL DIRECTOR

A faithful friend is a sturdy Shelter: he that has
    found one has found a treasure. . . .
A faithful friend is an elixir of life; and those
    who fear the Lord will find him. [*Sirach 6:14, 16*]

For though you have countless guides in Christ, you do not have many fathers. For I became your father in Christ Jesus through the gospel. I urge you, then, be imitators of me. Therefore I sent to you Timothy, my beloved and faithful child in the Lord, to remind you of my ways in Christ, as I teach them everywhere in every church.
[1 Corinthians 4:15–17]

My little children, with whom I am again in travail until Christ be formed in you! [*Galatians 4:19*]

A variety of images and models have been used to describe the spiritual director. He or she is called God's usher, gardener, father, the Bridegroom's friend, Moses, the "pilot that conducts our soul through the unknown ocean of the spiritual life," and physician. These images and others reflect a range of thought about the nature of spiritual direction. Some images, such as spiritual father, *give a central, formative role to the director as the very means by which God acts in the other person, whereas other images, like* gardener, *depict the role of the director as auxiliary to direct guidance of souls by God. This is the same tension found in chapter one in which some writers emphasize the transforming influence of one person on another, whereas others place the director in a secondary role. This difference derives from the value and weight given to the human person as the bearer of divine life and action. In both situations it is God who calls and transforms a life: he may act through a person or he may not.*

Those images and models placed first in the chapter give a primary place in spiritual direction to the director's role. It will be noticed that the Russian staretz and writers of the early centuries of Christianity will be found in the first section rather than later in the chapter, where the role of the director is understood in a secondary capacity.

Christ is often the model of the spiritual director. The director is the bearer of the Word or the one who speaks "as if God had spoken."

The brother asked another elder: "Whom should one ask about thoughts? And is it proper to question someone else about the same thoughts?"

The answer of John: "You should ask someone in whom you have trust, of whom you have ascertained that he is able to give consideration to such reflections; and you should trust in him as in God. To ask someone else about the same thought is characteristic of distrust and of trial. If you have assurance that God has spoken to his holy one, what need have you of trial? . . ."

[*On Consultation with a Spiritual Father*]
Saint Barsanuphius and John, master and disciple,
hermits in Gaza, Syria, c. sixth century

Putting all things into the hands of your spiritual father, as in the hand of God, is an act of perfect faith . . . . A person who has developed a living faith in his spiritual father, when seeing him, thinks he is seeing Christ Himself. Being in his presence or following him, he firmly believes that he is with Christ and is following Christ.

[Theological Chapters]
Saint Symeon the New Theologian, Eastern monk
and abbot of Studios, c. 949–1022

Every judgment and deliberation that one has placed before his spiritual master, the disciple should leave to his master's decision, so that what the master will have approved, the disciple also will praise; and whatever he shall have condemned, he will condemn in like manner. He should not doubt that God is speaking in his master, and he should not shrink back from being subjected to him as to Christ, because the Lord will never desert one who has confidence in his master because of Him, and is submissive because of Him.

[On Monastic Discipline]
Saint Laurence Justinian, patriarch of Venice, 1381–1456

Spare no hardship in your attempt to find a teacher and guide . . . a person bearing the Spirit within him, who leads a life equal to his words, lofty in vision of mind, humble in thought of himself, of good temperament in all ways, and generally such a teacher of Christ as he should be. . . . Having found such a person, hold on to him with body and spirit like a devoted son to his father and from then onwards obey all his commands implicitly, try to agree with him in everything, and see him not as a mere person, but as Christ himself. . . . Is it ever possible to think that a person leads a Divine life, in accordance with the Word of God, if he lives without a guide, pleasing only himself and obeying his own selfish desires?

[Ascetic Conferences]
Callistus II Xanthopulus, patriarch of Constantinople, c. 1397

Since you are going in search of a good guide, you ought with great insistence ask the Lord that He guide you with His hand to such a person. Thus shown the way, confide your heart to him with every confidence, and do not hide anything from him, good nor evil; the good so that he may direct you and advise you, the evil so that he may correct it in you. Do not do anything of importance without his counsel, putting your confidence in God, who is a friend of obedience. God will put in the heart and on the tongue of your guide whatever is best for your spiritual health. In this way you will flee from both evils and extremes. One of these evils says, I do not need the advice of people, God Himself teaches me and satisfies me. Others are so subject to people alone, without noticing anything other than what is human; to them is directed this curse, wicked is the person who hopes in another person. Subject yourself to another person and you will have escaped the first danger; do not confide in the knowledge and strength of a person alone, but in God, who will speak to you and strengthen you through another person, and so you will have avoided the second danger. [*Hear, O Daughter*]

Saint John of Ávila, Spanish diocesan priest, 1500–1569

By virtue of what right does a man intervene in the community? By the authority of the Word of God.

The Lord of the Church embodies the Word by transmitting it through a human mouth; he designates for this purpose the spiritual director, giving him the necessary spiritual gifts amongst which are the discernment of spirits, and other charisms which, in the same community, he refuses to other believers who possess gifts which the spiritual director does not have. Neither one nor the other person are complete beings. It is only in giving themselves that they become complete.

In itself, the human word does not have a shade of authority. It receives it from God only. Therefore, to obey God one must obey him who is the bearer of his Word.

Also, the person who waters down the Word for purposes of announcing it is in a very dangerous situation, acting as if he would prefer to push away the Lord who compels him to speak with full authority.

Will not a man's sin get involved in his word? A grave question which requires one's constant vigilance.

He who is exercised in the word knows that his authority is entirely interior, since it has come down to him, and is credible only in a spirit of prayer. This presupposes an unmasking of self to search, with those who are under his care for the divine will.

If he can bear the title of director, it is because God operates in him, that the Lord of the Church endows him with a particular authority, due to his particular charism. He is a director in the name of God.

Certainly, the "old" man will often seek arguments for refusing to obey the Word of God. He will persuade himself that only a human utterance was revealed to him; he will deny the evangelical absolute which it contains; he will judge his director, as if he were not a poor christian, as though he no longer needed repentance or forgiveness.

Let him remember, in these rebellious moments, that the eternal truths are always afforded him in earthen vessels.

[*Introduction to Community Life*]
Roger Schutz, founder of the Taizé Community, b. 1915

The spiritual director is imaged as the spiritual father or mother who begets a divine child.

"Come, my children, listen to me: I will instruct you in the fear of the Lord." This is the voice of your faithful teacher, encouraging you to learn through his fatherly kindness. The disciple is truly the spiritual child of the teacher. The person who receives from another guidance in holiness is shared by him and is brought to life, just as the fetus of a mother is formed within her and is brought to life. For this reason Paul himself took upon himself the whole Church of the Galatians, which had fallen away from his earlier instruction and was, as it were, about to be aborted. Paul formed Christ in them anew and called them little children; and, when with pain and sorrow he corrected those erring children, he said that he was in labor in his soul because of his personal pain over those who had fallen away. "My dear children, with whom I am in labor again, until Christ is formed in you." Therefore, "Come, children, listen to me" . . . .

[*Exegetic Homilies*]
Saint Basil of Caesarea, bishop of Caesarea and organizer of the monastic movement in Asia Minor, 329–79

The power of a human father is seen in these ways, i.e., life, motion, intelligence, and affection; and the spirit given by him operates in this manner, as all know, who have studied well the nature of human generation. . . .

Just as a human father gives birth to a son, unless nature makes a mistake, who is always born in perfect likeness to his human father, so also a spiritual father gives spiritual birth to a person with a divine likeness, unless the son places an obstacle to this. . . .

[Commentary on Luke]
Saint Albert the Great, Dominican theologian, bishop, 1200–1280

Our ministry has a more excellent end and operation because it does give birth to and form this Jesus in hearts, it does give his body and his spirit to the world; it does give a new birth to the one who is born of all eternity in the heart of the Father, and in the fullness of time in the womb of the Holy Virgin, and it does give us this sort of alliance with the Son of God, whom the same Son of God has honored, celebrated and elevated with these great words: "He who does the will of my Father, is my brother, sister and mother" (Matt. 7:21).

[Memorial of Direction to Superiors]
Pierre Cardinal de Bérulle, French diocesan priest, cardinal,
and founder of the Oratory in France, 1575–1629

It must not be forgotten that the spiritual director in primitive times was much more than the present name implies. He was a spiritual father who "begot" the perfect life in the soul of his disciple by his instructions first of all, but also by his prayer, his sanctity and his example. He was to the young monk a kind of "sacrament" of the Lord's presence in the ecclesiastical community.

[Spiritual Direction and Meditation]
Thomas Merton, Trappist monk, 1915–68

It is a peculiar feature of this living Word that it is passed on, so to speak, from father to son. That is to say, the Word only reaches the baptized person via the living band of brothers and sisters who have been born of the same Word before him. This may be the role of a priest; but a lay person too can be for us the spiritual father or mother through whom the Word comes to us and by whom the new life is brought to birth in our heart. This is the normal way of attaining to an awakened heart and the practice of prayer. You do not learn this on your own. You learn it from someone else. You may learn it from the look on another's face or catch the sound of it in his heart—in a heart that lives, that radiates life and awakens others to life. . . .

Thus the life of the Spirit which is slowly germinating and growing in the junior person is sustained by the same life which in a senior—an "old one," a staretz in the literal sense—has already come to full maturity. . . .

So the spiritual father forms a living bond with the Tradition. It is now his turn to interpret the Word; and in this handing on of his experience the Word attains to new Life. [*Teach Us to Pray*]

> *André Louf, abbot of the Trappist Monastery*
> *of Katsberg in France, c. 1927*

The example of a guide's life is inseparable from his or her teaching. The guide as a person becomes a model and is the teaching or the living word.

Remembering the promise of God, along with his brother, he [Pachomius] started enlarging the monastery so that he might allow more men to lead that life. As they were in the building process, Pachomius, for his own purpose, would make it wider, while his brother, having his own idea about a monk's life, would make it narrower. On one occasion, John, who, was younger by birth, was angered at him told him, "Stop being so proud." He did not correct his brother's words at all; he heard them, and accepted them as an exhortation for spiritual change.

Being master of his own heart, the following night he descended into the cellar and started weeping loudly. In his prayer he said: "God, the weakness of the flesh is still in me; I still live according to the flesh. Pity me, for I shall die, as has been written. In spite of so much training and discipline of heart, I am still seized by anger, even if it is for what I consider good. Have mercy on me, Lord, or I will perish. If the enemy finds a place in me, however small, and if you do not hold me up, I shall become his evil instrument. For if a man lives according to all your laws and breaks only one, he is guilty of breaking all of them. I believe that, if your great mercy helps me, I will then be taught to walk in the way of the saints, reaching out to those who went before me. With your help they completely defeated the enemy. O Lord, how shall I guide those whom you call to choose this way of life with me, if I myself am not victorious myself?"

[Life of St. Pachomius]
Saint Pachomius, founder of monastic community life
in Egypt, c. 290–346

A monk ought by all means not seek to learn to practice all virtues from one person no matter how perfect that person is. One person is gifted with flowers of knowledge, another is personally strengthened with discretion, another is well established in the noble state of patience, another is advanced in the virtue of humility, another in that of continence, another is clothed with the grace of simplicity. This person excels all others in nobility of mind, that one in pity, another in night watches for prayer, another in silence, another in manual labor. For this reason the monk who desires to collect spiritual honey, should like a very careful bee, drink in virtue from those who specially possess it, and should carefully store it up in the vessel of his own breast. He should not inquire into what any one is lacking in, but only be concerned and gather whatever virtue he has.

[Institutes]
John Cassian, Eastern ascetic influential in the formation
of Western monasticism, 360–433

She [Syncletica] also said , "It is perilous for a person to teach who has not first been seasoned by personal experience. For if someome who owns a shabby house invites guests there, he endangers them by his neglected building. It is the same situation for someone who has not first built an inner abode. He causes danger to those who visit. By words one may convert them to salvation, but by bad personal conduct, one injures them." *[The Sayings of the Desert Fathers]*

Amma Syncletica, a hermit in Egypt who lived
with her blind sister, d.400

A brother asked Abba Poemen: "A few brothers live with me. Is it your desire that I be in charge of them?" The old man said to him, "No, just labor yourself first, above all, then if they want to live like you, they will take care of it themselves." The brother said to him, "But it is they themselves, father, who ask me to take charge of them." The old man said to him. "No, be their example and not their rule giver." [*The Sayings of the Desert Fathers*]

Abba Poemen, Egyptian desert father, fourth century

God also showed Ezekiel what the disposition of a master should be, and what manner of conversion he should bring about in his disciples: "Son of man," He says, "take a tile, and lay it before you, and portray upon it the city, the city of Jerusalem" (Ezek. 4:1). This means that the master should help change his disciple from sand into a holy temple. The words "and lay it before you" have special meaning, for the disciple will quickly mend his life if he is continually within eye sight of his master. The constant effect of a good model marks other souls with its own imprint, as long as they are not completely obstinate and dull. The reason Gehazi and Judas yielded, the one to theft and the other to disloyalty, was that they left the sight of their masters. If they had stayed under the guiding influence of their master's gaze, they would not have fallen into sin. [*An Ascetic Discourse*]

Saint Nilus the Elder, priest-monk in Ancyra, Galatia, d. 430

If you accept my counsel, you will select for yourself a man whose life is such that it will act as a personal model to touch your heart, one whom you will respect so much that whenever you think of him you will keep on going because of the esteem you have for him and keep yourself in check. Think of him as if he were present to you and let the love you have for one another act in you to change all that needs to be changed, while your solitude suffers no violation of its privacy. [*Golden Epistle*]

William of Saint-Thierry, Cistercian theologian, 1085–1148

You should seek a faithful and wise man who has the inclination and the personal capacity to lead you along on the way to holiness. A man whom you greatly respect rather than fear; one who does not castigate the transgressor but rather leads them to repentance; and whose life is validated by his actions rather than by mere words. He is a poor guide who gives excellent counsel but does not follow it himself.

[*Guide to Heaven*]
John Cardinal Bona, Italian Cistercian abbot, 1609–74

The director is like an angel and is an instrument of the one God.

There are others who go forth out of Sodom and Gomorrah, that is to say, from avarice, intemperance and impurity, and who have still to suffer dire assaults from these vices. They should have an angel for director and counsellor; that is to say, a man compassionate, grave and of an austere manner of life. He who allows himself to be thus directed or led will surely escape pride, avarice and sensuality, according to the words of Isaiah: "For you shall go out with joy and be led forth with peace" [Isaiah 4:12]. Or according to our Saviour: "In the world you shall have distress" (John 16: 33), and "in Me, peace."

[*Sermons and Conferences*]
John Tauler, German Dominican preacher
and mystical writer, 1300–1361

This spiritual guide should always be an Angel in your eyes, i.e., when you have found him, do not see him merely as a human person, nor confide in him as such, nor in his human knowledge only, but in God, who will bless you and communicate to you through this man, placing into his mind and on his lips those ideas necessary for your happiness, so that you should listen to him as to an Angel, who comes down from heaven to lead you back to heaven with him.

[*Introduction to the Devout Life*]
Saint Francis de Sales, French bishop and theoretician
of spiritual direction, 1567–1622

The human messengers who receive from God the duty of teaching His Divine plan should imitate the detachment of the guardian angel. When they are too reliant on their own power, trust their own insight too much, and are too fond of their own will, they force their own human judgment upon the persons entrusted to them, and thus replace the Divine working with their own human action, and the divine inspiration of the Holy Spirit with their human judgment. In this way they grab for themselves the place of God, and usurp His rights, and this must always be harmful to the personal well-being of the directed and the director. [*The Degrees of the Spiritual Life*]

Abbé Auguste Saudreau, French diocesan priest
and spiritual writer, 1859–1946

The office of a director is a subordinate, dependent one; he is no more than an instrument of the one Director, Jesus Christ. His sole work is to wait upon God, to seek to discern the Divine will for each soul, to follow the "attraits" and graces which God bestows upon souls, to co-operate with the Divine leading by aiding the soul to see, understand and follow it. Direction is not our own work upon which we invoke the help of God; it is His work which He calls us to aid Him in accomplishing. [*The Art of Mental Prayer*]

Bede Frost, Anglican Benedictine Monk, 1877–1961

The spiritual director as the bridegroom's friend.

There is one fact that the spiritual director must be certain about above all others. He can accomplish absolutely nothing if he is not given the grace to listen patiently and to say the word that will empower the Holy Spirit to shower on a person his direction. Without this gift from above, the director can only be engaged in a psychological exercise, or force on others his own theological or moral convictions. He must be very much aware that he has been sent in place of Christ, and that it is to him that he must guide those who look to him for guidance. The one who has the bride, the Church, is the bridegroom, Jesus Christ. The director must completely eliminate from himself any spirit of possessiveness, authority, or exclusive intimacy with those whom he directs. This is a delicate and complex task, for our natural inclination, and the great temptation of the pastor, is to cultivate this kind of possessiveness, this authoritarianism, and this desire for personal esteem, intimacy, and affection.

The spiritual director is only the friend of the bridegroom; he is not the bridegroom. His task is to stand in for Christ, contemplating his Person, meditating on his teaching, and interceding with him for all those who are given to him in ministry. His greatest joy should be to hear the voice of the bridegroom, to discern what is his will for those under his care. The joy of the spiritual director will be realized fully, when he sees Christ growing in those whom he has been working with to guide them towards him. Little by little he notices that he is replaced by the action of the Holy Spirit in them, so that his own ministry becomes less and less necessary for them. "He must increase, but I must decrease." [*Confession*]

> *Max Thurian, monk of Taizé, 1899–*

The spiritual director as an usher.

The instructor therefore is to behave himself toward them all according to the quality and need of each spirit, always remembering that his office is not to teach his own way, nor indeed any determinate way of prayer, etc., but to instruct his disciples how they may themselves find out the way proper for them, by observing themselves what does good and what causes harm to their spirits; in a word, that he is only God's usher, and must lead souls in God's way and not his own. [*Holy Wisdom*]

> *Dom Augustine Baker, English Benedictine monk, 1575–1641*

Moses, the Exodus leader, is a model for the spiritual director.

After he [Moses] was taught these and other important matters by the unspeakable teaching of God while he was still engulfed by that invisible cloud, and having exceeded his own ability by the aid of the heavenly learning, he again came out of the darkness. Then he went down to the people to share with them the great wonders shown to him in the vision, to deliver the divine commands, and to establish for them the sanctuary and priesthood according to the divine plan shown to him on the mountain. . . .

Whenever someone escapes from Egypt and, after getting outside the borders of the country, is frightened by the attacks of temptation, the guide then provides unexpected salvation from above. Whenever the enemy's army encircles the one being chased, the guide is then compelled to make it possible for him to cross the sea. . . .

So Moses, who eagerly wants to see God, is now taught how he can see Him; to follow God wherever he leads is to see God. God's going by signifies his guiding the one who follows, for someone who does not know the way cannot finish his journey safely in any other way than by following behind his guide. He who leads, then, by his very guidance points out the way to the one following. He who follows will not turn away from the right way if he always keeps the back of his leader in full sight of his vision. [*Life of Moses*]

Saint Gregory of Nyssa, Cappadocian bishop
and theologian, 330–95

Those who renounce the love of the world depart truly out of Egypt; they leave King Pharaoh's service in renouncing pride, vainglory, presumption and all other sins; and those who would go out of the world have great need of finding a Moses who will serve them as conductor—one who will be like the first Moses, full of gentleness and compassion. They need a guide—sweet, kindly and patient—who will make their going forth, which costs so dearly, more easy to them. [*Sermons and Conferences*]

John Tauler, German Dominican preacher
and mystical writer, 1300–1361

The director as physician.

No one ever attempts to teach any art unless he has learned it himself after much thought. With what stupidity, then, would the pastoral office be undertaken by the unqualified, seeing that the guidance of souls is the art of arts! Who does not recognize that the wounds of the mind are more concealed than the internal lesions of the body? Those who have no knowledge of the curing powers of drugs shrink from pretending to be physicians of the body. Nevertheless, persons who are totally ignorant of spiritual matters are often not afraid to present themselves as physicians of the heart. [*Pastoral Care*]

Saint Gregory the Great, Benedictine monk and pope, 540–604

A person who really thinks he is sick is easily motivated to reveal his sickness in order to obtain medical aid. If a person wishes to have a doctor or some medicine for his sickness, he cannot have the good effects of either without revealing his disease. Likewise, how can anyone enjoy relief from the diseases of his soul without a spiritual doctor or without consenting to take the medicine prescribed by him? Never fear this manifestation, for it is easier to expose your death-dealing wound to a doctor than to hide it. Calling a doctor and allowing him to see our sick body brings great consolation, banishes sickness, moves the beholder to pity, and restores our health to its former good condition. [*Spiritual Writings*]

Diego Álvarez de Paz, Spanish Jesuit
who lived in Peru, 1560–1620

The task of the physician of souls is twofold. His first duty is that of diagnosis, by which he must endeavour to discover the poison which is doing most to hinder the soul's contact with God and the shaping of his life to carry out the purpose of God. His second duty is to find out how the contact with God through prayer, which is a source of health and strength in the spiritual life of the individual, can be increased and trained. [*A Guide for Spiritual Directors*]

Reginald S. Ward, English Anglican priest, 1881–1962

Nobody has expressed more fully and beautifully the nature and the importance of the difficult art of spiritual direction than St. Gregory Nazianzen. He begins by saying: "To guide a man seems to me to be the art of arts and the science of sciences." He proves his assertion by comparing the care of souls with the care of bodies or with the duties of the medical profession, showing how much more difficult and more noble is the former because of its supernatural end and the very nature of soul and body. The spiritual director is the physician of souls, not, however, in the mere natural order; for in that case he would be more or less of a psychiatrist. He is rather the physician of souls that are elevated to the supernatural order and tending to a supernatural goal with supernatural means while still in this world and encumbered with natural difficulties and obstacles of various kinds. [*The Ascetical Life*]

Pascal P. Parente, Italian-American diocesan priest
and teacher of ascetical theology, 1890–1971

The director seen as a gardener.

It seems very necessary to me, my daughter, that one who has cleared his garden and fertilized it and sown it should get himself a good and faithful gardener; one who is knowledgeable about sowing and watering and watching and gathering the fruits of the garden at the proper time in order that they might be able to reach perfection; if he did otherwise he would be able to have little use and consolation from the garden. Now I wish to say the same applies spiritually. I say then that it seems to me, both wishing you to attain your holy and good desire and that the seed which God has sown in the garden of your soul in order that it might come to perfection and be watched and cultivated, very necessary that you find and get for yourselves a good spiritual father who is expert and faithful; and above all I encourage you to do your best to find one who is a God-fearing man and who cares for his own soul. [*Art of Living Well*]

Saint Anthony of Florence, archbishop of Florence
and pastoral theologian, 1389–1459

Rome, November 27, 1850

The less there is of your own action, the more will the good Master supply with His own, and despite the numbers [that you have to guide] and of the shortcomings of each one, everything will move ahead with ease. For when there is question of directing souls the action of God is needed. All the elements obey man, so to speak, but the Creator and Redeemer has kept the realm of souls for His own. He wants to make use of us, certainly, but only as instruments and not as movers. Let us allow Him to act. Let us be no more than a gardener who cultivates the soil; he turns it over and pulls out the weeds; but once the seed has been sown he has no more to do than to water it and to drive away the insects or other enemies of the plant.

[*St. Madeleine Sophie: Her Life and Letters*]
Saint Madeleine Sophie Barat, French founder of
the Society of the Sacred Heart, 1779–1865

Spiritual directors guide the maturation of our persons as a gardener cultivates his fruit trees according to the nature of each individual tree. [*Letters of Direction*]

Henri de Tourville, French priest-sociologist, 1842–1903

The director is described as a nurse.

A good director, he [Dom Chapman] held must be a nurse, no more. He should confine himself to the task of teaching his penitent how to walk alone and unaided. That done, he should be ready to retire into the background; only emerging on rare occasions when unusual circumstances or some particular crisis called for his assistance. Directors of this kind would be no danger to simplicity or humility, while an over-dogmatic or too eager Director, giving unsuitable or unnecessary advice with relish and impressiveness, would harm both his penitent and himself.

> [*The Spiritual Letters of Dom John Chapman*]
> *Dom John Chapman, English Benedictine abbot, biblical and patristic scholar, 1865–1933*

Sometimes the image of mother is used in a maternal, nurturing sense.

Know, that you must be mothers to those that are assigned to you and not masters. If, from time to time, severity must be employed, let it be fatherly and not tyrannical. Show yourselves mothers in encouragement and fathers in correction. . . . Why make more burdensome the yoke of those whose burdens you should carry? Why should this little child, bitten by the serpent, avoid the priest, when he ought to fly to him as he would to the breast of his mother?

> [*Sermon #23*]
> *Saint Bernard of Clairvaux, Cistercian abbot, preacher, 1091–1153*

Saint Bernard writes to Pope Eugene II, a former monk of Clairvaux:

It is true that I have been released of maternal obligations toward you, but I am not robbed of all love for you. Once you were in my womb; now you will not be taken from my heart so easily. Ascend to the very heavens or descend to the depths, you will not flee from me. I shall follow you wherever you go. I loved you when you were still weak in spirit. I shall still love you as a father of the poor and the wealthy. If I know you, you did not stop being poor in spirit when you became the father of the poor. I am confident that this change was forced on you and was not of your own making, that this honor has not displaced your earlier disposition, but has enriched it. Therefore, I will instruct you not as a master, but as a mother, indeed, as a lover. I may seem like a fool, but only to one who does not love, to one who does not feel the power of love. [*Five Books of Considerations*]

Saint Bernard of Clairvaux, Cistercian abbot,
preacher, 1091–1153

Another argument for the necessity of a director may be drawn from the nature of a director's office. His business is not that of a pioneer. It is rather to go behind, and to watch God going before. He must keep his eye fixed on God, who is in the dimness ahead. He does not lead his penitents. The Holy Ghost leads them. He holds out his hands from behind, as a mother does to her tottering child, to balance his uncertain steps as he sways overmuch, now on one side, now on another. He is not to have a way of his own. [*Growth in Holiness*]

Frederick William Faber, Catholic priest
of the Oratory in England, 1814–63

The director seen as a pilot.

Under God, they [spiritual directors] are the pilots that conduct souls through this unknown ocean of the spiritual life. If no science, no art, however simple can be learned well without a master, much less can anyone learn this high wisdom of gospel perfection, where such great mysteries are to be found, i.e., visions, revelations of both kinds, rapture, and ecstasy, which can come from God or the devil. . . . This is the reason why I hold it morally impossible that a soul could without a miracle or without a master, go through what is highest and most arduous in the spiritual life, without running the risk of perishing.

[*Practice of Mystical Theology*]
Miguel Godinez (Michael Wadding),
Irish Jesuit missionary to Mexico, 1591–1644

One noted spiritual writer has stated "that if so few persons arrive at spiritual perfection and contemplation, it may be blamed on the fact that there are too few good spiritual directors, who are by the grace of God, the pilots to guide persons in the unchartered waters of the spiritual life." [*The Christian Life and the Spiritual Life*]

Père Yves Ernest Masson, Dutch Dominican priest and scholar, 1883–1971

"As a ship having a good pilot, with the help of God will reach port without any danger, so a soul, even though it has committed much evil, if it has a good shepherd, will easily reach heaven. No matter how prudent a person may be, he will easily go off the road without a guide; so also a person having all the wisdom of this world, will easily perish if in monastic life he relies only on his own judgment." According to Saint Bernard, whoever guides himself has a fool for a disciple. [*The Ascetical Life*]

Pascal P. Parente, Italian-American diocesan priest and teacher of ascetical theology, 1890–1971

Friendship as a model for spiritual direction.

What happiness, what confidence, what joy to have a person to whom you dare to speak on terms of equality as to another self. You need have no fear to confess your failings to this person. You can also without shame make known whatever advances you have made in the spiritual life. You can entrust all the secrets of your heart to him and before him you can lay out all your plans. What, therefore, is more pleasant than to unite your spirit to that of another person and of two to form one. No bragging is to be feared after this and no suspicion need be feared. No correction of one by the other will cause pain; no praise on the part of one will bring a charge of excessive flattery from the other. . . .

Friendship is a moment quite near to that perfection which consists in the love and knowledge of God, so that a person goes from being a friend of his fellowman and becomes the friend of God, according to the words of the Savior in the Gospel, "I will not now call you servants, but my friends." [*Spiritual Friendship*]

Aelred of Rievaulx, Cistercian abbot, 1109–67

Friendship is not only a state of being open-hearted with one's brethren, it is (as we have seen) a mode of sharing and absolutely presupposes a response. It demands reciprocal trust and frankness. The gift of ourselves which we offer must be received with an attentive and respectful heart and calls for a return. Friendship is a welcoming encounter between two brothers. . . .

Some brothers experience a kind of shyness in speaking about their relationship with God, their inner life, or their personal difficulties . . . I ask myself whether any real good is served by keeping a part of ourselves secret in this way. It is not the fact of expressing in a direct and simple way what we are thinking and feeling that intrinsically constitutes "self-exposure"; that depends upon the motive that prompts us to do so. [*Brothers of Men*]

René Voillaume, French priest and Founder of the Little Brothers of Jesus, 1915–68

Chapter Three

SEEKING AND CHOOSING
A SPIRITUAL DIRECTOR

Thus says the Lord; "Stand by the roads, and look, and ask for the ancient paths, where the good way is; and walk in it, and find rest for your souls." [*Jeremiah 6:16*]

And God gave Solomon wisdom and understanding beyond measure, and largeness of mind like the sand of the seashore, so that Solomon's wisdom surpassed the wisdom of all the people of the east, and all the wisdom of Egypt. For he was wiser than all other men.

[*1 Kings 4:29–30*]

"Beware of false prophets, who come to you in sheep's clothing but inwardly are ravenous wolves. You will know them by their fruits. Are grapes gathered from thorns, or figs from thistles? So, every sound tree bears good fruit, but the bad tree bears evil fruit. A sound tree cannot bear evil fruit, nor can a bad tree bear good fruit. Every tree that does not bear good fruit is cut down and thrown into the fire. Thus you will know them by their fruits." [*Matthew 7:15–20*]

To aid in the important search and choice of a spiritual director, a number of recommendations and suggestions begin this chapter. These are followed by descriptions of the qualities of a spiritual director to aid both in the choice of a director and to extend our comprehension of the traditional understanding of spiritual direction and the role of the director. The chapter concludes with suggestions about the frequency and timing of spiritual direction, the occasions of greatest need and thoughts about changing directors.

Searching for a spiritual director:

Therefore, so that I may speak as if I had only one listener, here is what I will tell you: Brother, invoke God with persistence, in order that He might show you a person capable of guiding you well, one whom you must listen to as God Himself, while performing without hesitation all that he will tell you, even if his orders appear to you contradictory and at first have the appearances of harm. And if grace inspires in your heart a deeper trust toward the one whom you already have had as spiritual father, do what he tells you and you will have salvation. It is better for you to be called a disciple of a disciple and not to live according to your own will while gathering useless fruits from doing as you please. But if the Holy Spirit sends you to another person, do not hesitate in the least. We hear that it is Paul who plants, Apollos who waters, and Christ who makes it grow. [*Instruction XX*]
Saint Symeon the New Theologian, Eastern monk and abbot of Studios, 949–1022

Who will find this friend? The wise man tells us: they that fear the Lord; that is to say, the humble, who eagerly seek their spiritual progress. Since it is of the greatest urgency, Philothea, that you should travel with a good guide on this holy journey of sanctity, pray to God with great zeal, to provide you with a person after the heart of God, and have no doubt; for even though God should have to send an angel from heaven, as he did to the young Tobias, he will give you a guide who is good and faithful. . . .

For this reason, choose one person among a thousand, says John of Ávila. But I say, among ten thousand, for there are fewer than can

be imagined, who are fitted for this ministry. He must be filled with charity, knowledge, and prudence; if one of these three qualities is lacking in him, there is danger. I say once more to you, pray to God to give you such a person, and, when you have received him, praise his divine Majesty, remain steadfast and do not search for any other, but travel on simply, humbly, and trustfully, for you will have a most beneficial journey. [*Introduction to the Devout Life*]
Saint Francis de Sales, French bishop and theoretician
of spiritual direction, 1567–1622

The choice of the director is of the greatest importance, because like master, like disciple. Before choosing their director, the brothers and sisters will pray fervently to God to guide their choice; then they will choose with maturity, reflection and serious consideration. [*Directory*]
Charles de Foucauld, French priest and hermit, 1858–1916

The Church gives you absolute freedom of choice as to who your director shall be. Your parish priest may well be the right person and this arrangement has added advantages, but there is no question of obligation, and should you go elsewhere it involves no disloyalty or insult. The priesthood rightly contains great variety; some of us can do one job and others have different gifts. Your parish priest may be a great Old Testament scholar, a good administrator, and a fine preacher, but he may be—despite deep personal devotion—bored to tears with the technology of prayer. And this is a personal relation where trust and temperament have rightful places. Some people are happier with a close social relation in direction—inevitable with your own incumbent—and some prefer their director to be rather outside normal life—a more plainly professional relation. You have free choice. . . .

Do not fear "attractiveness" implying someone whose judgment you think you can trust, someone you find approachable and easy to talk to. Here we can apply the medical analogy exactly; your doctor must be qualified and competent, if he is also a respected friend so much the better. You do not choose him because you like the colour of his eyes yet there is no virtue in having a doctor or priest just because you hate the sight of him. . . .

But do not be too fussy. Competence is the only essential. So if the associations of ordinary life fail, consult your Christian friends or clergy in exactly the same way as you seek a dentist when you are in a strange district. If that fails write to anyone you like who is in a position to advise, if need be to the Bishop; you can be assured that you are not "troubling" anyone with something trivial. I have no direct experience of episcopal emotions, but I venture an inspired guess that a letter seeking a spiritual guide, amongst all the finances, speeches, committees, awkward churchwardens, and more awkward clergymen, would at least be a refreshing change.

[*Christian Proficiency*]
Martin Thornton, Anglican priest
and theology professor, b. 1915

Pray fifteen minutes a day, asking that God give to you the name of that person or the names of those persons who can act as your Spiritual Director.

Having been given the name of a person, ask him or her to pray about assuming this responsibility. The person you choose must want to know and guide your spiritual life as you would have it known and guided. . . .

The fact that a person is your best friend does not necessarily mean that he is your best choice of a Spiritual Director. Your Spiritual Director should be able to look at your difficulties with a certain detachment and not be unduly swayed by personal sympathies.

[*Call to Commitment*]
Elizabeth O'Connor, Protestant author and member of
the Church of the Savior in Washington, D.C., b. 1921

The director may be a man or a woman. There are times when it is advantageous for the director to be a man, and times when it is advantageous that the director be a woman. This may seem an obvious and simple conclusion but in the light of the historical development presented in the beginning of this paper, its significance cannot be overlooked. What would have been theory a few years ago is now a reality. There are many women, mostly sisters, who have been called forth by their own sisters, by priests, and by lay men and women to minister as spiritual directors. This phenomenon is quietly yet persistently changing the traditional concept of the priest as spiritual director. Because the feminine qualities of gentleness, intuition and receptivity are especially important in fostering the directee's life with God, and women more often live out of these gifts, it seems likely that the number of women called to minister in this important dimension of the Church's life will continue to increase. The quality of the Church's spiritual leadership is being enriched by their presence in this field and it offers the hope that women's contribution will find its rightful place in every facet of the Church's life.

[*New Approaches and Needs for Women in Spiritual Direction*]
Sister Vilma Seelaus, American Discalced Carmelite,
twentieth century

For a long time I wandered through many places. I read my Bible always, and everywhere I asked whether there was not in the neighborhood a spiritual teacher, a devout and experienced guide, to be found. One day I was told that in a certain village a gentleman had long been living and seeking the salvation of his soul. He had a chapel in his house. He never left his estate, and he spent his time in prayer and reading devotional books. Hearing this, I ran rather than walked to the village named. I got there and found him.

"What do you want of me?" he asked.

"I have heard that you are a devout and clever person," said I. "In God's name please explain to me the meaning of the Apostle's words, 'Pray without ceasing.' How is it possible to pray without ceasing? I want to know so much, but I cannot understand it at all."

He was silent for a while and looked at me closely. Then he said: "Ceaseless interior prayer is a continual yearning of the human spirit towards God. To succeed in this consoling exercise we must pray more often to God to teach us to pray without ceasing. Pray more, and pray more fervently. It is prayer itself which will reveal to you how it can be achieved unceasingly; but it will take some time."

[*The Way of a Pilgrim*]
By an anonymous Russian, c. 1860

It is a common complaint that it is hard to find a good spiritual director. This objection is addressed in the following selections.

It is difficult . . . to find people of a universal ability in discernment who can see clearly to an equal degree in all issues. It is not essential to have people of this kind in order to receive good direction, and there is no problem, it seems to me, with collecting from many flowers the honey which we cannot find in one flower only. [*Letter #107*]

*Saint Francis de Sales, French bishop and theoretician
of spiritual direction, 1567–1622*

But someone may say: "If good directors are so essential, why does God allow them to be so rare and so difficult to find?"

This is a common problem. However, even if excellent directors are not so easily found because of the required union of qualities necessary, still there are very many other directors who, although less perfect, have more than adequate skill in direction to help souls in a very real manner. Furthermore, even if many souls do not have suitable directors, they are not thus deficient in the means that is necessary for reaching their supernatural end, but only one that would enable them to attain a much higher degree of perfection if they had perfect spiritual direction.

*[The Theology of the Spiritual Life]
Joseph de Guibert, Jesuit teacher at
Gregorian University in Rome, 1877–1942*

The first and nearly spontaneous reaction to the idea of a spiritual guide is: "Spiritual guides are hard to find." This might be true, but at least part of the reason for this lack of spiritual guides is that we ourselves do not appeal to our fellow human beings in such a way as to invite them to become our spiritual leaders. If there were no students constantly asking for good teachers, there would be no good teachers. The same is true for spiritual guides. There are many men and women with great spiritual sensitivity whose talents remain dormant because we do not make an appeal to them. Many would, in fact, become wise and holy for our sake if we would invite them to assist us in our search for the prayer of our heart. A spiritual director does not necessarily have to be more intelligent or more experienced than we are. It is important that he or she accepts our invitation to lead us closer to God and enters with us into the scriptures and the silence where God speaks to both of us. When we really want to live a life of prayer and seriously ask ourselves what the prayer of our heart may be, we also will be able to express the type of guidance we need and find that someone is waiting to be asked. Often we will discover that those whom we ask for help will indeed receive the gift to help us and grow with us toward prayer. [*Reaching Out*]

Henri J. M. Nouwen, Catholic priest and teacher,
twentieth century Dutch

Many attempts have been made to delineate the qualities of a good spiritual director. This is a difficult task given the variety and the complexity of the human personality and the subtlety of its breadth and depth.

A good spiritual director is one who has the necessary gifts and training and who has been called forth by the confidence of others to this ministry. What usually attracts is a kind of spiritual depth and vitality which is communicated in the very being of the one called forth. He or she is recognized as a person of prayer. A director who does not pray is like a guide accompanying another through territory unfamiliar to both, thus a director needs experience not only in prayer but also in receiving spiritual direction. [*New Approaches and Needs for Women in Spiritual Direction*]

Sister Vilma Seelaus, American Discalced Carmelite,
twentieth century

With great diligence and wisdom seek to find a person adept at guiding those who are making their way toward God, who will be a faultless director of your life. He should be blessed with virtues, bearing witness by his own deeds to his love for God, familiar with the Holy Scripture, recollected, free from avarice, a good, quiet man, tranquil, pleasing to God, a lover of the poor, mild, forgiving, laboring hard for the spiritual advancement of his disciples, without vainglory or arrogance, not affected by flattery, not given to vacillation, and preferring God to every thing else. [*On Renunciation of the World*]

Saint Basil of Caesarea, bishop of Caesarea and organizer
of the monastic movement in Asia Minor, 329–79

The same amma [Theodora] said that a master ought to be unfamiliar with the desire to dominate, vain-glory, and pride; one should not be able to confuse him by flattery, nor blind him by gifts, nor overcome him by the stomach, nor control him by anger; but he should be patient, gentle and humble as far as possible, he must be tried and without partiality, full of concern, and a lover of souls.

[*The Sayings of the Desert Fathers*]
Amma Theodora, Egyptian ascetic and hermit in the desert
near Alexandria, c. fifth century

One should not question everyone, but only that person who has been entrusted with the guidance of others, whose life is exemplary, and who is himself "poor, yet making many rich" according to the Gospels. Many inexperienced persons have done damage to many unwise people, for which they will be judged in eternity. Everyone does not have the right to guide others, but only those who have been endowed with Divine discernment, according to the Apostle, namely, that discerning of spirits which distinguishes good from evil by the sword of the word. Every person has his own natural reason and discernment, either practical or scientific, but not all have discerning of spirits. Therefore the wise man of Sirach says: "Be in peace with many: nevertheless have but one counselor in a thousand." It is difficult to find a guide unerring either in deeds, words, or understanding. A person who is without error can be recognized if he has his testimony from the Scriptures both for personal practice and for understanding, and is humbly wise in the sphere of wisdom. For it takes no small amount of labor to know truth clearly and to keep away from what is opposed to grace. For the devil is accustomed to present his illusions in the garb of truth, especially to beginners, hiding his deceit in something spiritual. [*Rules for Hesychasts*]
Saint Gregory of Sinai, Orthodox Bulgarian monk, 1295–1346

It is very important that the spiritual master have prudence. I mean that he have good judgment and experience. If together with these he has learning, so much the better. But if one cannot find these three qualities together, the first two are more important since persons with an academic training can be searched for and consulted when there is a need. I say that if these learned persons do not practice prayer their learning is of small assistance to beginners. I do not mean that beginners should not counsel with learned persons, for I would rather see a spirit without personal prayer than one that has not started to walk in truth. Learning is also a great thing because learned persons teach and enlighten us who know little. When placed before the truths of sacred Scripture, we do what we should. May God deliver us from an empty piety. [*The Life of Teresa of Ávila*]

Saint Teresa of Ávila, Spanish founder of the reformed order
of Discalced Carmelites, 1515–82

Now to the end to enable the soul to make a good choice (I mean such a soul as hath freedom to make her own choice), I will set down the qualities necessary to be found in a good director, by which title I do not mean simply a *Confessarius,* that is only to hear faults confessed, to give absolution, and there an end; for the ordinary qualities of learning and prudence are sufficient thereto. But by a spiritual director I intend one that, besides this, is to instruct the disciple in all the peculiar duties of an internal life; that is, to judge of her propension to contemplative ways, and that can at least teach her how she may fit herself with a degree of prayer proper for her; that knows all the degrees of internal prayer, and can determine how long she is to remain in such a degree, and when to change it for a higher; that can judge what employments, etc., are helpful or hindering to her progress in internal ways; but especially that can teach her how to dispose herself to hearken to and follow God's internal teaching, and to stand in no more need of consulting her external director, etc. Such are the proper offices of a guide, to enable him whereto there are generally by spiritual writers required three principal qualities: 1. a good natural judgment; 2. learning; 3. experience.

[*Holy Wisdom*]
Dom Augustine Baker, English Benedictine monk, 1575–1641

St. Seraphim was above all else a staretz. The word designates a spiritual person of great maturity and possessing special gifts for guiding others. . . . Among these gifts we may mention: charity, knowledge through the heart (cardiognosis), diacrisis, discernment of spirits and hidden thoughts, powerful intercession by prayer, and lastly the gift of insight and prophecy (the ability to speak meaningfully to the spiritual state of the disciple).

[*Saint Seraphim of Sarov: An Icon of Orthodox Spirituality*]
Saint Seraphim of Sarov, Russian monk, hermit,
and staretz, 1759–1833

He must be a person of charity, of knowledge, and of prudence. If one of these three basic qualities is lacking in him there is real danger.

[*Introduction to the Devout Life*]
Saint Francis de Sales, French bishop and theoretician
of spiritual direction, 1567–1622

What qualities does one look for, then, to find someone who knows the inner journey and the pitfalls and can also see the possibilities for growth?

The most important thing to look for is the person's comfortable acceptance of himself or herself, in fact acceptance of everything that goes to make up a total human being. Spiritual direction cannot even begin unless we can share whatever is in our being, good, bad and indifferent. A counselor who makes one feel uncomfortable enough to hold things back can only give advice about surface problems, which will probably do no harm. Good advice, as Jung once remarked, seldom hurts anyone because so few people take it seriously. . . .

Before anyone can help another with this process, that person must be self-accepting. Jung has commented that this is the very essence of the moral problem and that facing the prospect makes any honest person livid with fear. In a moving and almost poetic passage in *Modern Man in Search of a Soul,* Jung writes of the absolute necessity of self-acceptance before one can go a step of the way with someone else on the inner journey. He writes: "Yet the patient does not feel himself accepted unless the very worst in him is accepted too. No one can bring this about by mere words; it comes only through the doctor's sincerity and through his attitude towards himself and his own evil side. . . . We cannot change anything unless we accept it. Condemnation does not liberate, it oppresses. I am the oppressor of the person I condemn, not his friend and fellow-sufferer." If this quality is necessary for a psychiatrist, it is ten times more needed by spiritual directors. Again and again I have talked with clergy and seminarians who had had "spiritual direction" but had never opened up the problems that were bothering them the most. . . .

But this is not all that is needed. It is equally important to find a guide who understands the structure of the human psyche or soul and how it functions. We have enough trouble finding our way in the inner world without letting misunderstandings about transference or projection, about varying personality types, or depression, or fear, deflect the only compass we have.

There is a gradual increase today in the number of clergy and Christian lay people learning to work with the techniques of Jungian psychology. It is unquestionably becoming easier to find individuals who are familiar with the symbols found in dreams and who understand how a person's dream life shows what is going on below the surface of consciousness. This skill is needed for spiritual direction. One does not have to look for a trained therapist, but it is important to find a director who knows enough to see when therapy is indicated, and who will direct one to a therapist when the situation requires it.

The last and perhaps most important credential for a spiritual director is to have taken the inner way himself or herself and still be on it. Such a director will not give the impression of having it made. If a person appears too confident about these experiences, it usually means that he or she has come to a standstill and is too blind to see the way for anyone. One can better trust a guide who admits honestly to having days of wondering about ever making it through and is still open and able to learn from experience. [*The Other Side of Silence*]
Morton T. Kelsey, American Episcopal priest
and professor, b. 1917

Although spiritual counselling and psychological counselling have fundamentally different goals, we should not conclude from this that the spiritual guide has no need of psychological knowledge. Having a basic knowledge of psychological principles relative to both the normal and abnormal personality can be extremely valuable to the spiritual counsellor. Possession of such knowledge can serve a variety of purposes. It enables the counsellor to recognize signs of serious neurosis or even psychosis. Being able to read these signs, the spiritual director knows when to refer a person to a psychologist or psychiatrist. A basic knowledge of psychology also allows a director to help a person to deal successfully with minor emotional problems. Finally, an acquaintance with psychological principles which pertain to normal personality growth obviously is an advantage to the spiritual director in his attempts to aid a person towards full personal maturity.

[*The Spirit Is Present*]
Edward Carter, American Jesuit priest, b. 1915

Selections containing thoughts on the importance of learning

The spiritual person should not be misled by saying that intelligent persons without prayer are unsuitable for those who practice it. I have counseled with many learned men for some years because of a greater necessity and I have sought them out more. Personally I have always been a friend of men of learning. Although some do not have personal experience, they do not disdain the Spirit nor do they ignore it, because in Sacred Scripture, which they study, they always find the truth of the good spirit. I hold that the devil cannot fool with illusions the person of prayer who counsels with learned men, unless this person wants to be fooled, because the devils have an enormous dread of that learning which has the companionship of humility and virtue. The devils know they will be discovered and so they go away with failure.

Often I am quite impressed with learned men, religious especially, who after the work it cost them to acquire their knowledge use it to help me for nothing more than my asking them. They are truly persons who do not want to benefit from this labor! May God never permit this to happen! I see these men obedient to the hardships of religious life, which are great, with its penances and bad food, subject to authority. This often puts me to shame, certainly; then together with all this, the loss of sleep; everything a burden, everything a cross. It seems to me it would be a great mistake for anyone to lose so much good through his own fault. Some of us who are free of these trials and accept this knowledge already prepared and served, as they say , and living our lives to our own pleasure, think that just because we spend a little more time in prayer, we are due more than those who have suffered so many hardships.

[*The Life of Teresa of Ávila*]
Saint Teresa of Ávila, Spanish founder of the reformed order of Discalced Carmelites, 1515–82

What is important for him is an adequate knowledge of the four closely related branches of theology—dogmatic, moral, ascetical and mystical. Of these we would stress the importance of the third, which should be studied not in little modern books, but in the works of the proved masters. If one is to train souls in the spiritual life, one must know what that life is and how souls may cultivate and grow in it and this means careful study of ascetical theology.

[*The Elements of the Spiritual Life*]
Frederic P. Harton, English Anglican priest, 1889–1964

If the spiritual director is a holy person he or she may mediate the presence of the Holy Spirit for the directee as illustrated in this encounter of a disciple with Saint Seraphim of Sarov.

"Father, I do not see how I can be completely sure that I am in the Spirit of God. How can I myself know His true manifestation?"

Father Seraphim answered: "I have told you, my son, that it is very simple and I have exactly described to you how people swell in the Spirit of God and how one must be aware of His appearance in us. What then do you want?"

"My desire is to understand this well," I said.

Then Father Seraphim held my shoulders very tightly and replied: "We are both together, my child, in the Spirit of God! Why are you not looking at me?"

I replied: "I cannot look, Father, because brilliant light streams from your eyes. Your face is brighter than the sun and my eyes are paining me."

Father Seraphim said: "Do not fear, my child; you too have became as bright as I. You too are now in the fullness of the Spirit of God. You would otherwise not be able to look on me as I am now."

After this he bent his head towards me and whispered gently in my ear: "Give thanks to the Lord God for His unspeakable mercy!

You have seen that I did not even make the sign of the cross. Only in my heart did I pray mentally to the Lord God and said within myself, Lord, grant him to see clearly with his own eyes that coming of Your Spirit which You give to Your servants, when You are happy to appear in the light of Your wonderful glory. . . .

"Come, my child, why do you not look me in the eyes? Look now and do not be afraid. The Lord is with us!

"When the Spirit of God comes down on a person and fills him with the fullness of His outpouring, then the human soul overflows with great joy, because the Spirit of God changes into joy all that He may touch. . . .

"Poor as we are, the Holy Spirit of the Lord now fills us to overflowing. Come now, there is no more need to ask, my child, how people may be in the grace of the Holy Spirit! Will you recall this coming of God's great mercy which has visited us?"

"I do not know, father," I said, "whether the Lord will always help me to remember this mercy of God as clearly and personally as now I feel it."

Father Seraphim answered me, "The Lord will help you always to retain it in your memory, since otherwise His goodness would not have bowed so instantly to my humble petition and would not have so quickly answered his servant, Seraphim."

> [*Conversations with Seraphim of Sarov*]
> *Saint Seraphim of Sarov, Russian monk,*
> *hermit, and staretz, 1759–1833*

Charity and non-judgment are valued

The monk must be dead in regard to his companion and never judge him at all, in any manner whatever.

> [*The Sayings of the Desert Fathers*]
> *Abba Moses, former slave, Egyptian desert father,*
> *c. fourth century*

Abba Isaac said, "I have never permitted a willful thought against my brother who has hurt me when he entered my cell. I have seen to it that no brother should go back to his cell with a thought against me." [*The Sayings of the Desert Fathers*]

> *Abba Isaac of Cells, monk and priest at Nitra, c. fourth century*

Once a brother came to an old man and said: "My brother continues to abandon me, and goes traveling everywhere; and I suffer because of it." And the old man advised him: "Bear it calmly, brother. God will see your sincerity and endurance, and will return him to you. It is not possible for a man to be dissuaded from his purpose by cruelty and severity. Devil cannot drive out devil. You will bring him back to you more with kindness. That is how God acts for our benefit and holds us close to himself." [*The Sayings of the Desert Fathers*]

I do not want confessors to place hardships on the ways of virtue, especially to those who are new converts. They should not create problems for them with any harshness. . . . On the contrary, we should use every effort to gain them to Christ by compassion and sympathy, by kindness and love. Let us go down to them as far as we can. Let our aim be to warm their hearts by the love of God, which alone can help them do great things. [*Life of Saint Philip Neri*]

Philip welcomed all who came to him for the first time as if they were his lifelong friends, and embraced them lovingly as if he had waited for them a long time. Even towards those who were hardened in their wickedness he showed the same warm welcome and invited them to confession by saying, "For the love of God, my son, confess your sins, for God Himself is waiting to forgive them." He was accustomed to say that in the early stages of conversion to God, we should be satisfied if our penitents can refrain from falling into serious sin.
[*Life of Saint Philip Neri*]
*Saint Philip Neri, Italian priest and founder of the Oratory,
a congregation of secular priests, 1515–95*

These selections illustrate the qualities of patience and gentleness. Although the first does not refer to spiritual direction, it reflects the values of the desert fathers and mothers who served as spiritual guides.

Some old men came to see Abba Poemen and said to him, "When we see brothers who are dozing at the common prayer, shall we wake them so that they will be attentive?" He said to them, "When I personally see a brother who is nodding in sleep, I put his head on my knees and let him be at peace."

[*The Sayings of the Desert Fathers*]
Abba Poemen, Egyptian desert father, called the Shepherd,
c. fourth century

Marcellus could not take his eyes off Philip, and slowly a strange feeling of wonder came upon his soul. When Philip had finished his prayer, Marcellus came near and spoke to him. Philip received him with his usual love, and invited him to come and hear the sermons at the Church of Saint Jerome. Marcellus went, and in a few days he desired to make Philip a general confession of his life. Philip not only told him the secrets of his own heart and his most secret sins, but before giving him sacramental absolution he hugged Marcellus and said to him: "My son, do not resist the Holy Ghost. God Himself wants your salvation." After this Marcellus went every day to see the saint, still wearing his fashionable clothes. But Philip did not scold him nor even refer to it. He tried only to stir up in his heart a deeper sorrow and to inspire him with the love of God. In about fifteen or sixteen days Marcellus began to feel ashamed of his wordly dress, and changed it of his own free will, and became one of Philip's most beloved disciples. This is a usual expression of Philip's spiritual method. Let us all learn it well. [*Life of Saint Philip Neri*]

Saint Philip Neri, Italian priest and founder of the Oratory, a
congregation of secular priests, 1515–95

Msgr. Brown, a priest of Southwark in England, writes about Janet Erskine Stuart.

Some very talented people must display their gifts . . . all intercourse with duller or unappreciative minds is irksome and unwelcome; they need the extraneous support of listeners impressed by their powers. Not so Mother Stuart. Ready to discuss the commonplaces of life with those who sought her counsel and help, she never betrayed the least sign of the mental arrogance that sometimes unfortunately goes with great intellect. To her nothing that concerned the needs, especially the spiritual needs of others could be trivial. Life, as she knew, is a succession of minute incidents, of small doings, of little hopes and fears, so she could never be impatient of detail where the well-being of others was concerned.

[*Life and Letters of Janet Erskine Stuart*]
Janet Erskine Stuart, superior general of the
Society of the Sacred Heart, 1857–1915

The importance of experience is discussed in the following selections.

For all that we do in life, it is better for a person entering upon a task to get a knowledge of whatever he is seeking to know from teachers than to attempt to learn by himself. This task of ours is not so easy that one can necessarily judge for himself what is best, and when a person dares to attempt something he is not familiar with, he takes a risk. Just as men, through experience and close scrutiny, have gradually found out the previously unknown art of healing, so that the helpful and the dangerous are recognized through experiments, knowledge is collected for the profession, and instruction as to what is to be observed is handed down by those who have learned before, and thus the novice does not have to decide the effects of medicines, whether a drug is harmful or helpful through his own experiments. He becomes a successful physician by learning what is known from another. In the same manner, it is not necessary to learn the healing art of the soul through trial and error. (I am speaking of the principles through which we learn the cure for all diseases touching the soul.) It is learned through the authority of the learning of one who has developed the ability through long and extensive practice.

[*On Virginity*]
Saint Gregory of Nyssa, Cappadocian bishop
and theologian, 330–95

To master any art requires time and much instruction; is it possible that the art of arts alone can be mastered without being learnt? No one without experience would go into farming; nor would someone who has never been taught medicine try to practice as a doctor. The first would be condemned for making good farmland infertile and barren. The second would be condemned for making the sick worse instead of better. The only art which the uninitiated try to exercise, because they think it is so very simple, is that of the spiritual way. What is so difficult many consider easy. What Paul says he has not yet grasped (cf. Phil. 3:12), they claim to know thoroughly, although they do not even know this; that they are terribly ignorant.

[*An Ascetical Conference*]
Saint Nilus the Elder, priest-monk in Ancyra, Galatia, d. 430

Saint Isidore of Pelusium wrote a letter to the monk Luke advising him to consult those who have already cultivated and dug in the divine vineyard.

You have taken upon yourself a heavy yoke, you who have had no part of a yoke until now. But there is a danger that you may grow faint and fail in bearing the yoke of the cultivation of the Lord. Then you would be seen to share the lot of the man who undertook the building of a tower, having only minimally considered and tested his abilities and strength beforehand. So, if you are really intent on becoming a good monk, do not begin calculating how you shall live by your own judgment or desire to have your behavior appear to be good to yourself alone. Rather, submit your mind and personal counsel to those who, in life, and time, and labor, have already cultivated and dug in the divine vineyard before; from them you will easily learn this duty thoroughly. It is clearly ridiculous, that we obtain teachers of the mechanical and menial arts, and we still blunder here and there, while we commit the divine science to ourselves as though it were something base and worthless. [*Letter #260*]

Saint Isidore of Pelusium, Greek priest and theologian of the monastery at Pelusium, d. 440

Do not seek counsel from a person who does not lead a life similar to yours, even if he be very wise. Entrust your thoughts to a person who, though he lacks learning, has studied the work in practice, rather than to a learned philospher, who only speaks out of his speculations, with no practical knowledge. What do we mean by experience of things?

Having experience means not merely to approach things and look briefly at them, getting no deep knowledge of them, but through a long acquaintance with them to discern clearly by experience their usefulness and their dangers.

A thing can often look harmful from the outside, but inside is full of benefit. Conversely a thing frequently seems to be helpful, while inside it is full of danger.

Therefore accept the counsel of a person who has himself experienced all and knows how to decide patiently what needs to be discerned in your case, and can indicate what is truly helpful to you.

[*Book on Contempt of the World*]
Isaac of Nineveh, bishop of Nineveh, monk and teacher,
c. sixth century

But if anyone tries to practise it [the Jesus Prayer] by himself, merely from descriptions in books, he cannot escape illusion. In any description only an external outline of the work is given: a book cannot provide all the detailed advice which is supplied by the staretz, who understands the inner state that should accompany the Prayer, and so can watch over the beginner and give him the further guidance that he needs. He who practises this method of prayer without a guide to help him, is, of course, left with only the external activity and the various physical exercises. . . .

Inner prayer brings salvation. But in our inner prayer we stand in great need of experienced direction, so long as we are still praying by our own efforts and labour. It is precisely during this period of practicing inner prayer that those who lack a skillful hand to guide them are mostly liable to go astray. [*The Art of Prayer*]

Theophane the Recluse, Russian bishop and abbot, 1815–94

The following selections offer suggestions about the responsibility for initiative in seeking spiritual direction, the frequency of direction, and occasion of special need.

However you choose, or whoever you choose, as your director, you must make the first move, and in direction, whenever you want particular help you must ask for it. Whatever priests may do in the name of evangelism, it would be arrogant and quite intolerable for them to say to anyone, "I think I ought to be your spiritual director!" Priests must be, in practice, self-effacing and reticent. It would be impossible and against all etiquette for a doctor to stop you in the street with "My word you look ill, you had better come to my surgery." It would be as bad for the family doctor, however much of a friend, to call occasionally just to be sure you were quite well. And there is nothing worse than the sort of priestly possessiveness that is for ever popping in to see if "everything is going all right!" That attitude only shows up lack of trust, lack of manners, over-anxiety, and lack of love. Therefore you must make the first move—always. . . .

> [*Christian Proficiency*]
> *Martin Thornton, Anglican priest and*
> *theology professor, b. 1915*

As soon as the soul enters upon the passive purgations and mystical prayer, she has more than ever need of a learned and experienced guide, from whom she has no secrets, though from every other she should conceal the favours of God. [*The Ways of Mental Prayer*]

> *Dom Vital Lehodey, French Trappist abbot*
> *and theologian, 1857–1948*

The actual usefulness of the director and the need to submit our private inspirations to him vary greatly as time goes on. We need a director most during our years of formation. Later on, when we are well established in our vocation, we may feel we have received a new call from God to a life much more closely united to Him, a purer, more mortified, more apostolic life. Perhaps, too, we may pass through an intense spiritual crisis. Such a crisis might take the form of misfortune, illness, extraordinary temptations, dereliction; or it might be a yearning for more conscious union with God, for a simple, delicious, intoxicating, absorbing union that presses us to pray without ceasing, to humiliate ourselves deeply, and so on. In these various instances we need continuous and rather explicit guidance. We shall gain much by submitting to it, for it is morally indispensable.

> [*We and the Holy Spirit*]
> *Leonce de Grandmaison, French Jesuit priest*
> *and theologian, 1868–1927*

Having found an adequate guide somehow: Use him. Remember it is a two-way relation, do not be apologetic, you cannot be a "nuisance"—unless you are downright foolish. It is sometimes just a little difficult to decide precisely when, and when not, to consult a director. The medical analogy helps here too; you do not rush off to the doctor with every slight cold or headache—direction is not "submissive" and you must stand before God on your own two feet—but do not wait until pneumonia is firmly set in. If we bring in the dentist, we have the idea of the regular periodic examination, which is a normal practice in direction and a very sensible one. But do not feel tied to such an arrangement, and you must still make the request—every time.

Last but by no means least, seek direction in prayer when things are going well; when you are cool, calm, and collected—or rather recollected. Prayer is a positive adventure not a negative duty. Human nature, and the unfortunate "medieval-medical" equating of direction with confession; all lead to the idea that you put off consulting a priest until you are in the throes of serious aridity, trouble, or sin. It is much easier for a priest to help you when all is well, and such guidance lived out in prayer will hold you in good stead when difficulty or trouble arise. All parish priests have seen the frustration and fear in those who suddenly seek consolation from prayer and religion in bereavement; the callous but true answer is that they should have got down to the matter twelve months earlier. If you are on a sinking ship in the middle of the ocean, it is a bit late to learn to swim. Look on prayer in terms of adventure and proficiency at least as well as devotion. Do not wait for disaster. [*Christian Proficiency*]

Martin Thornton, Anglican priest
and theology professor, b. 1915

The Spiritual Director must be in enough contact to know the currents and movements in the life of the directed. This is a person for whom he is responsible before Christ. Like teachers, spiritual directors will be judged with more strictness. There will be exceptional times when contacts may be as often as once a day, and times when they need to be made only once a month or once every three months. . . .

The matter of frequency should be spoken of in terms of the greatest flexibility. So much depends upon the particular individual—his or her temperament, stage of spiritual development, and other circumstances. One who is just entering seriously upon the spiritual journey often will feel more need of spiritual counselling compared to the person more advanced in the ways of the Spirit. But even persons relatively far advanced will at times desire an increased frequency of dialogue with the spiritual counsellor. This could come about for various reasons, for instance, when the Spirit seems to be leading to a new kind of prayer, or when particularly critical decisions have to be made. But if the frequency of spiritual counselling can vary so greatly, it seems reasonable to maintain that the seriously committed Christian will see the basic desirability of such guidance. He will not assume the attitude that spiritual guidance never has any place in his life. [*The Spirit Is Present*]

Edward Carter, American Jesuit priest, b. 1915

Spiritual direction has no limitations on it. We never totally outgrow it; and so it does not become outmoded according to the progress we have made in the spiritual life. The need is present throughout our lives because we are Christians who journey by faith. The regularity or intensity of spiritual direction in our lives does vary, and the advantage of recognizing its continuing importance will allow us to seek it as a matter of course during such moments of greater need.

Spiritual direction is one of the ways we most immediately touch the Incarnation in our own lifetime. For us to ever approach it lightly or to reject it as of no value is to find ourselves undermining the deepest roots of our Christian faith. [*Beginning Spiritual Direction*]

David Fleming, American Jesuit, Co-Director of the Institute of Religious Formation at Colorado Springs, twentieth century

Thoughts concerning changing spiritual directors:

Spiritual directors should give freedom to people and support them in their desire to seek growth. The director does not know the means by which God may wish to honor a soul, especially if that soul is no longer satisfied with the director's counsel. This dissatisfaction is indeed a clear sign that the director is not helping the soul, either because God is making it advance by a road different from the one along which the director is guiding it, or because the director himself has changed his method. These directors should themselves advise people to change. To do otherwise comes from foolish pride and possessiveness or some other personal need. [*Living Flame of Love*]

Saint John of the Cross, Spanish cofounder (with Saint Teresa of Ávila) of the Discalced Carmelites, poet, 1542–91

The first thing it is necessary to pay attention to is the choice of this spiritual director, for many people choose confessors or directors by reason of human considerations, by sympathies or likings which are not founded in virtue. It is necessary then to take care to choose not those who flatter us or spare us, but those who boldly lead us to God, although it is necessary to choose them willingly and by an entirely free choice and not by force. Besides that, it is necessary to take heed that, when a soul has for a long time been under the direction of a spiritual father, and when it comes to meet some other better one, and when it even has light to see that the one it finds later on is more beneficial to it, it must resolve to leave the first, not saying: How is it possible that I am leaving this father to whom I have so many obligations? That is impossible to be without ingratitude. And although it turns out that this good director himself finds it very odd that someone wants to leave him, not seeing that there is anything better than what he knows, the soul however that has this insight and enlightenment must, without human respect, go freely where it finds its best director, going there where God inspires it to go, and giving this new encounter every benefit. [*The Spiritual Guide*]

Jean Joseph Surin, French Jesuit, 1600–1665

Although it is best usually to confide in only one director, there is no need to be so completely attached to him. One should be sufficiently indifferent in him in order to be able to do without him; to be free to consult another, or even to change him altogether if need be. [*Teaching on Mystical Theology*]

Père Yves Ernest Masson, Dutch Dominican priest and scholar, 1883–1971

Directorship in its experimental period should be undertaken for a three-month period and then perhaps on a yearly basis. Our recommitment time might also be the time when we consider whether or not we want to continue the relationship for another year. It is always possible, however, to terminate it at any time should there be something fundamentally wrong with it, such as a lack of openness. This should be done only after considerable prayer. [*Call to Commitment*]

> *Elizabeth O'Connor, Protestant author and member of the*
> *Church of the Savior in Washington, D.C., b. 1921*

We conclude the chapter with two letters: one concerns the choice of director and the other leaving a director.

A letter from Saint Francis de Sales:

Sales, 14 October 1604

LIVE JESUS!

Dear Madam,

May God grant me as much power as I have desire to make myself well understood in this letter. I feel confident that you will be helped by at least some of my responses to your difficulties, especially in your doubts, which are insinuated to you by the devil, about your choice of me as your director. I will try to explain briefly what I consider appropriate for your needs in this matter.

First of all, your choice shows every sign of a good and proper election. I beg you to have no further doubt. You were motivated and almost forced to it by a strong and calming force. I thought carefully before agreeing to it; neither you nor I rested on our own opinion in his matter but applied the judgment of your confessor, a good, learned, and prudent man. We gave your first enthusiasm time to quiet down to see if your conscience had been mistaken. We prayed, not for one or two days but for several months. All things considered, they are beyond all doubt infallible signs that we acted according to God's will. [*Spiritual Letters*]

> *Saint Francis de Sales, French bishop and theoretician*
> *of spiritual direction, 1567–1622*

Now permit me to speak of the welfare of your soul. Tell me, Celeste, why have you left Msgr. Falcoia, who is so saintly and so intelligent, as you yourself have often told me? You know that God himself has given him to you as your director. He has guided you so wonderfully for many years, that, kneeling on the ground, you ought ceaselessly to give thanks to God and to him. What flaw have you now perceived in him? Has he perhaps cast you into a low mood? Have you turned on him because he disturbed you by humbling and denying you? But, my dear Sister, do you not see that this course is absolutely necessary to conquer your proud heart, and to prevent you from becoming attached to your personal judgment? . . . It is a fault, of which St. Philip Neri has said that there can be nothing more dangerous in the spiritual life; and St. John Chrysostom tells us that there is more danger for a saint in pursuing such a path than for any other person. Another saint tells us that he who confides in himself has no need for devils to tempt him. . . .

Let us grant a reasonable doubt which you have concerning the vision, and which you ought to have, if you wish to walk confidently. In whose judgment should you place more confidence than in that of your spiritual director, unless you really wish to ignore that beautiful order of obedience which Jesus Christ has left in his Church to make known to us his holy will? You reveal the vision to your director; he tells you it is an illusion, and you do the contrary! Answer me, would St. Teresa have acted in that manner? You also do a serious injustice to Father Falcoia, who was at one time so dear to you, if you say that this saintly man, through favoritism counseled you to act contrary to the will of God, and thus betrayed his own conscience. When it is not clear and evident that our spiritual guide speaks through sinfulness, we must obey him. [*Letter #7*]

Saint Alphonsus de Liguori, founder of the Redemptorists
in Italy, 1696–1787

Chapter Four

SECRETS OF THE HEART

"Blessed are the poor in spirit, for theirs is the kingdom of heaven. . . .

"Blessed are those who hunger and thirst for righteousness, for they shall be satisfied." [*Matthew 5:3, 6*]

Woe to you, when all men speak well of you. [*Luke 6:26*]

Therefore, putting away falsehood, let every one speak the truth with his neighbor, for we are members one of another. Be angry but do not sin; do not let the sun go down on your anger, and give no opportunity to the devil.

Therefore be imitators of God, as beloved children. And walk in love, as Christ loved us and gave himself up for us, a fragrant offering and sacrifice to God. [*Ephesians 4: 25–27; 5:1–2*]

The openness and the honest seeking of the directee are of primary importance to both individuals in a spiritual-direction relationship. It is also the search and openness of the directee that calls forth and creates the power and gifts of the director. The selection by Henri Nouwen in chapter three referred to the effect of the search of the directee on the director. He wrote "Many would, in fact, become wise and holy for our sake if we would invite them to assist us in our search for the prayer of the heart." As the first selection in this chapter says, the searching "disciple" activates the inner disciple in the guide enabling him or her to teach and guide out of their own discipleship.

Writing about the directee, one author suggests in a selection below that the greatest danger for the directee is to not be known by his or her director because it then becomes difficult or impossible for the director to aid in the directee's growth in self-knowledge and in the discernment of the directee's path to know God. In addition, the openness of the directee in speaking of his or her spiritual life is likened to being open to God.

The first group of selections in this chapter speaks of the nature of the direction relationship itself. Their emphasis on the reciprocal interaction between the two people provides a context for looking at the suggestions about the open disposition of the directee, the appropriate content for spiritual direction, and the need for confession.

The following paragraph by Sister Donald Corcoran describes one aspect of true mutuality in a spiritual-direction relationship. The other selections in this first section are examples of this mutuality or reexpress her sentiment.

The master-disciple relationship is truly mutual. The master does not do all the giving. In Jungian terminology, the master-disciple relationship is a manifestation of a two-part archetype that should not be split; it should not be divided between two persons (one superior, the other inferior). For "master-disciple" are parts of the nature of *each* person in the relationship. The element of "master" (teacher, guide) in the spiritual guide activates the potential and growing inner master in the disciple, just as the strong and eager "disciple" in the student activates the inner "disciple" in the guide. There is a type of chiasmal relationship as far as the psychological dynamics of the relationship is concerned. In an authentic master-disciple relationship there is no abuse of power. There is also a deep humility and disposability in the master. The true healer is the wounded healer. So also the one who cares for souls teaches the most effectively when he/she is deeply a disciple.

> [Abba: Guides to Wholeness and Holiness East and West]
> Sister Donald Corcoran, American Benedictine sister
> and teacher, twentieth century

One has to look at what profit or strengthening results certain things have on the soul. I do not say this to you in order that by these or other signs you may judge for yourself what is happening to you, but that you keep in mind that the one whom you are advising can know and teach you the truth as well as you can give particular counsel to him (her). [Hear, O Daughter]

> Saint John of Ávila, Spanish diocesan priest, 1500–1569

I admit, it is indeed a difficult task to undertake the direction of individual persons, but one which also rewards with great comfort. It is similar to the toil of a farmer in time of harvest and vintage, who is never more pleased than when working hard and fully occupied. It is a labor of love which restores the hearts of those who do it through the great reward which flows from it.

> [Introduction to the Devout Life]
> Saint Francis de Sales, French bishop and theoretician
> of spiritual direction, 1567–1622

Two together invoke the Holy Spirit. The disciple receives the *charisma* of listening to the counsels of the father; the father exercises the *charisma* of interpreting the Holy Spirit.

> [Saint Seraphim of Sarov: An Icon of Orthodox Spirituality]
> Saint Seraphim of Sarov, Russian monk,
> hermit, and staretz, 1759–1833

The freedom which he [Père Lacordaire] exercised in his direction was a delight. He gave personal expression to his own soul as he spoke to those who inspired him with deep trust. He admitted to them his own weaknesses and spiritual peace with a joyful simplicity, asking them to support him with their prayers, and also with their counsel. "The fall season is close at hand," he writes, "and you will soon be traveling at a distance. But there is no great divide between those who are united by the knowledge and the love of God. Since my own return I have experienced a deep inner peace. Your prayers and your affection without doubt are an important reason for that. Persons who understand one another, and work at their mutual perfection, possess a real influence over the heart of God. Jesus Christ said, 'If two or three of you agree on earth concerning anything you will ask in My Name, it shall be granted to them.' What a pledge. It seems to me that I am a better person since you have prayed for me. But be careful lest you fall into excessive optimism. Do nothing to injure your health, or needlessly stimulate your imagination. No one is really calm and simple except God Himself. Try to reflect God in this trait." [*The Inner and Religious Life*]

Père Henri-Dominic Lacordaire, French Dominican priest and preacher, 1802–61

The following selections encourage openness, honest seeking, and complete manifestation of the interior state of the soul to a spiritual director. This openness should not be forced or required, but allowed to develop naturally in a spiritual-direction relationship.

Every person who intends to make any worthwhile progress and to be in union in a way of life that corresponds with the commands of our Lord Jesus Christ should not hide deep within himself any movement of his soul. He should also not speak any thoughtless word, but he should reveal the secrets of his heart to those in the brotherhood whose office it is to show a compassionate and sympathetic care for the weak. In this manner, all that is praiseworthy will be accepted and that which is worthy of blame will receive the correction it deserves. By the practice of such mutual discipline, we shall gradually go forward to perfection of life. [*The Long Rule*]

Saint Basil of Caesarea, bishop of Caesarea and organizer of the monastic movement in Asia Minor, 329–79

The attitude of open seeking is found in the question disciples addressed to the abbas of the Egypian desert and to the Russian staretz, Saint Seraphim of Sarov.

Father, speak to me a word that I might live.

[*The Sayings of the Desert Fathers*]

My father, tell me what the Holy Spirit suggests to you as healing for my soul.

[*Saint Seraphim of Sarov: An Icon of Orthodox Spirituality*]
Saint Seraphim of Sarov, Russian monk, hermit,
and staretz, 1759–1833

Cassian spoke of "bringing to them [the fathers] every thought that rises in our heart." The reason he gives is that the "foul serpent from the dark underground cavern" must be released, otherwise it will rot.

An evil thought is made weak at the very second it is manifested to another person. Even before the counsel of discretion is given, the wicked serpent is by the very power of confessing dragged out from his secret dark cave. He is seen to be stupid and is dismissed in disgust. Evil thoughts can dominate us only as long as they are hidden in our hearts. [*Conference II*]

John Cassian, Eastern ascetic influential in the formation
of Western monasticism, 360–433

Abba Moses in Cassian's Conferences *well describes the necessity of the open disposition of the disciple when he advises that "it is as though we were always to be ploughing up the ground of the heart."*

All should constantly search about in the inner rooms of the heart to carefully trace the footsteps of all who enter there. If we do not a wild beast may enter secretly, like a lion or dragon, and leave the frightening marks of its tracks on our minds. This can lead to allowing others to find the inner sanctuary of our heart due to our own care-lessness of mind. Daily and hourly, then, we should turn over the ground of our heart with the plough of the Gospel, the constant remembrance of the cross of Christ. In this way we can crush out and free our hearts of the dens of wild beasts and the hiding places of poisonous snakes. [*Conference I*]

> *John Cassian, Eastern ascetic influential in the formation of Western monasticism, 360–433*

Were I capable of counseling souls whom God calls to contemplation, I would urge them to give a discreet and total account of their conscience to their spiritual guide. Openness destroys curiosity and makes the soul simple. It draws down upon it God's grace and unites the person to Him, a pure and simple Being who desires souls which resemble Him (in simplicity) so that He may reveal to them His holy communications which are enemies of the spirit of our lower nature. [*Personal Journal*]

> *Saint Marie of the Incarnation, French Ursuline nun and missionary in Canada, 1599–1672*

In a letter to his spiritual daughter, Jean-Jacques Olier encourages her to "open everything to him."

My dearest Daughter,

It is a relief for me to know that you are strengthened in spirit to carry your cross. I praise God for it with all my heart. I find myself at peace after seeing you determined to follow your call. I still ask you to use the grace of writing to me always, in the simplicity and the trust of a child, which are truly the dispositions of your heart. I grant this to you with all the power that Our Lord gives me for your spiritual well-being.

You know quite clearly, in matters of this kind, how seriously we need to be attentive to God and to the voice of the Divine Bride in our heart. It is my duty to discern the voice of the personal love and charity of Jesus Christ in you. That is why you should not hesitate to expose your confusion to me, your difficulties and inclinations. Without these you could be mistaken, and thus not get the counsel and advice that you should observe in your life, either the things to do, or the time you should do them. Be faithful to your spiritual father, my dear girl, and hide nothing from him. Open everything to him, and reveal everything to him with honesty. My dear daughter, send me your clearest feelings in this matter, and the most personal and deepest tendencies of your heart. I would weep if I disregarded any of your thoughts, inclinations, and feelings. . . .

Tell me especially if you have any idea of being able to get along where you are, and if there is anything that will someday be of service for Our Lord. Tell me what you really think and do not omit anything before God, and to recommend everything to Him. Help me to save your soul and to do the will of God on your behalf. . . .

[*Spiritual Letters*]
*Jean-Jacques Olier, French priest and founder of the
Society of Saint Sulpice, 1608–57*

The absolute importance of manifesting our entire conscience and interior state of soul to our spiritual director is clearly established from all we have already written. By this exercise we defeat the devil, who, when he sees his wicked plans made public, is disheartened and flies, hoping to bring them to their real end only as long as they remain secret. Our spiritual guides, if they have an intimate knowledge of our inner life, will fashion their advice and counsels appropriately for our state and personal need. He who does not open his heart to his spiritual guide closes it to God also. Since spiritual fathers watch over us in God's place, it is proper they should be able to see all the hidden chambers of our heart, as God penetrates the innermost secrets of the heart. Then, if we happen to leave the path of salvation, they may recall us to the right way, and we may again more easily persevere in the way of holiness we began, and make further progress. For that reason the holy Fathers, especially monks, placed such high value on this self-manifestation, that they made it the main help of spiritual progress. Now the following are to be revealed to the spiritual Father; all matters good and bad; the former, that they may be safe and increase, the latter that they may be taken away; also the roots and sources of the good, such as inspirations, spiritual lights, good resolutions conceived by God's grace; likewise the fruits of the good,

like prayers, penances and holy practices. The roots and fruits of the bad should be manifested in the same way. The former are unruly appetites, bad habits, evil inclinations and temptations. The latter are sins, which are to be mentioned in so far as is necessary to explain our weakness and personal need. [*A Treatise of Spiritual Life*]
John Cardinal Bona, Italian Cistercian abbot, 1609–74

Never hide anything from your director, for any reason whatsoever, even if it should be thoughts and false suspicions we may have had against him. The more the director is doing the work of God, the more the soul is tempted in reference to him, through the instigation of the devil. He will attempt in every way to withdraw the confidence of the soul from the director. But we must resist his temptations, and make a rule for ourselves to tell everything, and always to begin with that matter we would rather be silent about.
[Manual for Interior Souls]
Jean Grou, Jesuit classics scholar
and spiritual director, 1731–1803

It is so rare in our profession to find oneself treated with real confidence, especially by young persons, that when such a thing does happen, one feels quite refreshed by it: for my sake, therefore, as well as your own, let me beg of you to address me and tell me things without scruple, as long as I can be of any use to you, or to any one for whom you are interested. I do not wonder at the feeling you express to me of dread as to what may happen by and by, when your situation is a more dangerous one, nor at your almost seeming as if you were a hypocrite in your correspondence with me. We are, almost all of us, such double-minded persons, our best moments so miserably unlike our worst, that it is but natural we should sometimes feel so, and then our enemy will endeavour to make us think it is all over with us, at least for the present, and that we may just as well be consistent, at least for a time, in pursuit of present enjoyment; but let me beg of you not to listen to him, but rather to the good angels who would make you consistent the other way.
[Letters of Spiritual Counsel]
John Keble, Anglican priest and founder of the
Oxford Movement, 1792–1866

The person who desires to live without manifesting his thoughts suffers much. Many and varied empty thoughts and passions are born in him. As a vine left abandoned produces many new shoots, so too, a novice, if he does not reveal his thoughts and actions to the staretz to cut them off, grows, develops, and gives life to a multitude of thoughts and passions. The devil, knowing full well how deadly is the habit of concealing everything in oneself, encourages and in-spires the ascetic person to live without manifesting his thoughts. The person who accepts such an evil inspiration is tricked, thinking that he lives well and without sin in his relation to the staretz, while he is not honest by hiding his thoughts. He does not feel any peace and consolation in his soul. Because he lives with his staretz without faith and love he is possessed by murmuring, pride, condemnation of others, dissatisfaction, and desolation. These spiritual illnesses, made strong by being secret, make the life with the staretz unbear-able. They finally force this man to leave his Father and the broth-erhood. Overcome by his own self-will and his own wisdom, such a man abandons the right road approved by the Holy Fathers.

[*Sayings of Father Zosima*]
Father Zosima Verkhovsky, Russian staretz of Optino, 1767–1833

Manifestation of conscience which is the essential condition of the discipline of self-revelation is a powerful means of progress, terrible to the enemy of our salvation. The unrevealed thought vexes and depresses the soul. When revealed, it falls away and does no spiritual harm. [*Counsel of Father Leonid*]
Leonid Nagolkin, Russian, staretz of Optino, 1768–1841

An honest openness of soul demands an unusually great simplicity. "Have a heart clear as crystal," says a spiritual writer; "fear one thing only, that of not being adequately understood by your director." "How I desire," shouts Père Lallemant, "to hold my inner life in my hands so that I could reveal it to you as it is." St. Jane de Chantal required from her daughters a simple and childlike trust; "this trust fills Par-adise with religious souls," she said. St. Francis de Sales also asked the Sisters of the Visitation to open their souls simply and fully, revealing all its deepest secrets with the same honesty and frankness that a child shows to its mother with its scratches, or sores, or the stings of a bee. [*The Christian Life and the Spiritual Life*]

Père Yves Ernest Masson, Dutch Dominican
priest and scholar, 1883–1971

These three letters were chosen because they have the quality of openness and honest seeking just described.

In this letter Robert Bellarmine writes to his spiritual director, the Reverend John Baptist Carminata, concerning his new life as a cardinal.

Dearest Father in Christ,

It is quite unusual that you have not received any of the five letters I wrote to you with my own hand. I will try to make up for their loss by the length of this one. Personally, I am doing my best to bear the burden of the purple cardinal's robe which has been imposed on me with as little harm to my soul as possible. But I must admit to you that I am very frightened and in much danger, for I now possess a magnificent and attractive apartment and have servants who are at my beck and call to do my least bidding with speed and care.

In addition to this, my position carries with it quite a few creature comforts, and though I try not to give my heart to them, still, here they are. I am fearful that it may be said to me, you have received your reward. Having no counselor and not knowing personally what to do, I commend myself entirely to God's close friends that they may take me with them, who am unworthy of their company, to the "everlasting dwelling-places" which by my own efforts I could never attain. I have a good will and firm intention not to offend God, not to enrich or make my relatives wealthy, not to shoot for higher honors but rather to fly from their approach with all my power, not to give scandal in anything, and to say Mass every day as I have always done. But I know clearly that this is not enough. . . .

My reason for putting these matters before you, dear Father, is that you, as the guide and master of my soul, may admonish me if in anything I am wrong, and that by your advice, I may be turned to wiser pursuits. I will now give you some exact details. There are ten gentlemen in my employ, to perform various higher duties. Most of the ten men have two servants each, but some have only one. Besides these, I have fourteen servants for ordinary house and stable work, so the sum total of my domestic help does not exceed thirty. I told each of them privately when I hired them that, according to the law of my house, swearing, impurity, or any other serious sin meant instant dismissal. Each week I call them together and admonish them as earnestly as I can to lead good lives and to perform their religious duties. I continue to say the Divine Office at the canonical times as of old, and have not given up the practice of fasting on Wednesdays and Fridays which I adopted in the past.

I try never to send away a poor man sad or empty-handed, but, as I am poor myself, I can only give little amounts at a time. If ever I become rich, then I shall be lavish with my gifts, according to the counsel of Tobias. . . . As for austerities, I am afraid I am not given to hair shirts, sleeping on the ground, a bread and water diet, etc., for as I am now fast approaching my sixtieth year and my health is not good at all, I doubt whether I could sustain such hardships for long. Still, if ever a spiritual and prudent man would recommend them, I think, unless my self-love is playing a trick on me, I would be quite ready to accept this advice. . . .

I am writing thus to you that you may alleviate my doubts with your wise counsel, and tell me simply what I should do. You are my intimate friend and that is why I open my heart to you, but I would not like others to be told what I have said. The Pope wanted me to accept the bishopric of my native place, Montepulciano, but on condition that I would not leave Rome. I did not accept his terms, as I know how dangerous it is to be an absentee bishop. However, if he would allow me to live in the diocese I would not be so hesitant, because it seems to me that the episcopal office is more spiritual, more religious, more meritorious, and more secure than that of the cardinalate alone, which though sacred has still much that is secular about it. I am not forgetting the difficulties and dangers involved in the care of souls, but when God calls, it is not for us to want safety first. Obedience is, without doubt, the safest state. As St. Francis says, in obedience there is profit and in honor peril. But our choice should fall rather on that way of life which is most pleasing to God and at the same time least dangerous for our souls. Forgive the length of my letter and pray for me, Father. I shall eagerly expect your good advice, and I beg you with all my heart to pull me with you to Heaven, somehow, even though I resist it. God bless you.

> [*Life and Work of Saint Robert Bellarmine*]
> *Saint Robert Bellarmine, Jesuit priest, cardinal*
> *and theologian, 1542–1621*

In this letter Brother Lawrence seeks confirmation, if it can be given, of his experience in prayer.

Dear Reverend Father: Since I do find my way of life in spiritual books, even though I am at peace with it, yet for greater self-confidence, I would be grateful to know your thoughts about it. . . .

What is going on inside me at present I am unable to express. I have no pain nor any doubt about my condition, because I have no will but that of God, which I really try to carry out in everything, and to which I am so obedient that I would not pick up a straw against His will, or from any other motive than purely that of love for God.

I have stopped doing all forms of devotion and rote prayers but those to which my vows oblige me. My only business is to persevere in His holy Presence, wherein I keep myself by a simple attending to and an absorbing loving regard for God. This I call an actual Presence of God; or, to say it more accurately, a silent and secret conversation of the soul with God. . . .

When my thoughts occasionally wander from it by necessity or weakness, I am soon recalled by inward emotions so peaceful and joyful that I am hesitant to mention them. I beg you to reflect rather upon my great sinfulness, which you know quite well, rather than upon the great blessings God gives me, as unworthy and lacking in gratitude as I am.

My regular hours of prayer are only a continuation of the same exercise. Sometimes I consider myself there as a stone before a carver, of which he is to make a statue. Giving myself thus before God, I desire Him to mold His perfect image in my soul, and make me over totally like Himself.

At other times, when I give myself to prayer, I feel all my spirit and all my soul lift itself up without any great difficulty or energy on my part, and it remains as it were in elevation, fixed steadfastly on God as in its center and its dwelling place.

I am aware that some persons condemn this state as passive delusion and empty self-love. I admit that it is a holy inactivity, and it would be a happy self-love if the soul in that state were capable of it. While the soul is in this state of repose, it cannot be bothered by such acts as it was usually accustomed to, and which were then its strength, but which would now harm rather than help the soul. . . .

But I cannot allow this to be called delusion, because the soul which enjoys God desires nothing but Him. If this is delusion in me, God must remedy it. May He do with me what He pleases. I desire only Him, and to be totally given to Him. You will greatly please me if you send me your opinion, to which I always give great credence, for I have a special respect for your Reverence. . . .

> [*The Practice of the Presence of God*]
> *Brother Lawrence, Discalced Carmelite brother*
> *and cook, 1611–91*

Charles de Foucauld wrote to his spiritual director Abbé Huvelin on September 22, 1893.

Is there any way of forming a little religious group to lead that kind of life, living by the labor of its own hands only as did our Lord, who supported himself neither by gifts nor offerings? Would it be impossible to find a few persons prepared to follow our Lord in this, to follow him by following all his precepts, completely giving up all property, common as well as individual, and thus setting aside what our Lord himself discarded, all legal matters, conflicts, and troubles? Making almsgiving an essential of life, when they have two coats, they give one away; when they have food, they give to those who have none, keeping nothing back for the morrow. They follow all the examples set by his hidden life and all the commands spoken by his lips.

With great earnestness I desire to see such small "nests" of men living an intense and hardworking life, reliving our Lord's own life, established under his protection and under the patronage of Mary and Joseph. Being close to all the mission stations of the East, now so isolated, they could offer a haven to the souls of the people of these countries called by God to serve him and love him alone.

Is it a dream, my dear Abbé, or a diabolical illusion? Or is it an idea, or an invitation, sent from God? If I knew that it came from God, I would take the first steps necessary to travel that path today, not waiting until tomorrow. When I reflect on it, I find it a wonderful idea; to follow the model and counsels of our Lord could not help but be an excellent thing. Moreover, it is exactly what I have always been looking for. It was exactly this that led me to seek him at La Trappe. It is not a new calling. If such a group of persons had been in existence a few years ago I should, as you know, have gone directly to it. Since there is no such group, or anything like it, or anything to replace it, should not an effort be made to form it? And to form it in the hope that one would see it grow especially in lands without the faith, Moslem and others?

I shall, as you know, be guided by your response and your advice, for a father never stops being a father, especially you to me! You see how much I depend on you still.

Bless me, my dear Abbé, and also those I love so much, praying that this letter may also be a blessing to them.

Your dearest son in our Lord Jesus Christ.

Brother Marie-Alberic
[*Spiritual Autobiography*]
Charles de Foucauld, French priest and hermit, 1858–1916

A person entering spiritual direction and desiring to be open with his or her director may wonder what it is most important to speak about. The selections that follow give specific suggestions about the appropriate content and manner of self-disclosure. The viewpoints offered reflect somewhat distinct views of spiritual direction.

The manner in which we should open our heart, and declare all the secrets of our conscience to our spiritual director, is well explained by these words of the Prophet Jeremiah: "Pour out your heart like water in the presence of the Lord." Other liquids do not pour out so entirely, that they do not leave something in the receptacles where they were before. You pour out, for example, a pitcher of oil; there always remains a little of it in the bottom of the vessel. If you pour out a jug of wine, the wine drops down, but the scent remains; it is the same with other fluids. But with water, it is poured out entirely and nothing remains in the container where it was, neither liquid, nor scent, nor taste, nor any other indication that could reveal that it was there. It is thus that you should pour out your heart before the person who directs you and who for you represents Our Lord Himself: "Pour out as water your heart in the sight of the Lord"; that is to say, retain nothing, of however little importance it may be. Tell everything to your director. . . .

You should appear so clear and so transparent to the eyes of your director, that there is nothing in your soul that he doesn't see and perceive distinctly. By this means, all that there is of good in you will be strengthened. What would not be good will be reformed, and thus, little by little, in uprooting the bad and strengthening the good, you will arrive at the perfection of your life. . . .

Explain all these things, present and past, in a manner that is clear, simple, unsophisticated, and without any embarrassment. The fear of letting the director see too clearly certain things which cause us more confusion, makes us sometimes seek ambiguous words, obscure speech, and equivocal terms. We employ circumlocutions or involved discourse. We mix with our account a thousand superfluous things, and many useless circumstances, so that the mind of the director, divided among several objects, pays less attention to the evil whose root we don't want him to discover. Such language can come only from a mind filled with guile and deceit. But simple and very open people speak always with guilelessness, simplicity, and candor. There is not in their conscience any fold, not any little corner that they do not uncover. They know that it is in these folds and these cavities that the filth and dirt usually accumulate. This is why they are unwilling to leave any of it in their conscience. They explain and expose, as much as they can, all that goes on in their soul, in order that it appear to the director in the condition in which St. Paul depicts the Church: "Not having spot or wrinkle, or anything of the kind, but that it be holy and immaculate" [Eph. 5:27].

For this result, we must avoid with care several detours which self-love cleverly uses to cover itself. The first is merely to hint at things, leaving it to the director to guess the rest. He is not a prophet, and we are only fooling ourselves, wishing that he know us without our exposing ourselves completely to him. The second is to speak with caution, using ambiguous and equivocal speech, and all ways of speaking which keep us from being well understood. The third is to pass lightly over what is most important, and causes you the most trouble. When one has something humiliating to say, one says it, but in two words. One passes over lightly, as over hot bricks or burning coals. For fear that the idea linger with the director, that he pay too much attention to it, that he go all the way to the bottom of the ulcer, one immediately enlarges upon other matters. One talks at length, one fills the mind of the director with useless things, to cause what was most important to escape from his memory. You really understand what I mean, and this is what you must avoid with care in rendering an account of your conscience to your director, in order to speak to him as the saints advise you: "As to an angel, who knows the secrets of the heart." [*Obedience to One's Director*]

> *Louis Tronson, French priest and third superior general*
> *of the Sulpicians, 1622–1700*

For the avoidance of errors, have someone to advise you—a spiritual father or confessor, a brother of like mind: and make known to him all that happens to you in the work of prayer. For yourself, act always in great humility and with the utmost simplicity, not ascribing any success to yourself. Know that true success is achieved within, unconsciously, and happens as imperceptibly as the growth of the human body. Therefore when you hear an inner voice saying "Ah! Here it is!" you should realize that this is the voice of the enemy, showing you a mirage rather than the reality. This is the beginning of self-deception. Stifle this voice immediately, otherwise it will resound in you like a trumpet, inflating your self-esteem. [*The Art of Prayer*]

> *Theophane the Recluse, Russian bishop and abbot, 1815–94*

In order that a soul should not only begin well, but also advance in the way of perfection, there are certain essential points which directors should keep in mind. The first is the need of establishing the soul in a true peace. To this end not only is a general confession advisable, but also a full and frank account of one's life, circumstances, difficulties, graces received, etc. A soul cannot be directed, as I have said, unless it is known, and many go on making routine confessions for years without ever knowing themselves or making themselves known in such a way that any adequate direction can be given.

> [*The Art of Mental Prayer*]
> *Bede Frost, Anglican Benedictine monk, 1877–1961*

We are going to say what takes place in the dialogue of direction, and what points it must touch upon if it is to bring the help that is to be expected from it. These points, as we shall see, are simple. They are the very ones which give the Christian life its adult character: respect for freedom, the life of the Spirit, the sense of individual vocation, personal relationships, the variety of the grace of God. *Direction can be defined as the help that one man gives to another to enable him to become himself in his faith.*

[*The Direction of Conscience*]
Jean LaPlace, French Jesuit, twentieth century

It is an open relationship where your fears, feelings of rebellion, critical attitudes, misgivings, etc., are confessed. These matters should always be confined to a Spiritual Director lest they contaminate the fellowship. Your Spiritual Director is one to whom you want to reveal your hidden self. . . .

The responsibility of a Spiritual Director is to help another grow in Christ. Special attention is given to a program of study, prayer, service, the disciplines of the church, and to growth in personal and group relations. [*Call to Commitment*]

Elizabeth O'Connor, Protestant author and member of the Church of the Savior in Washington, D.C., b. 1921

There is need above all for a reappraisal of the nature and tasks of spiritual direction. It is both a "humanist" and a "spiritual" process. . . .

Hitherto, as a rule, the theological and "spiritual" element was perhaps unduly stressed. Very often, too little attention was paid to the fact that spiritual growth is only possible, as a deliberate personal commitment, within a framework laid down by nature and personal history. It is true that spiritual direction must be concerned with spiritual initiatives, with disposing for the incalculable encounter with the mystery of God and his word, whose impact is never quite the same in any two cases. It is essentially concerned with the discernment of spirits and the finding of the will of God in a concrete situation. Nonetheless, all these things must be integrated into a man's life as a whole, and the spiritual cannot be treated as a sort of superstructure on top of the human element. Spiritual direction cannot be confined to the religious realm, as though this existed in isolation, but must deal with the whole man and his actual problems. The main tasks of spiritual direction may therefore be outlined as follows: a) to help the individual to self-knowledge; b) to help him to self-acceptance; c) to help him to detachment from his own ego; d) to help him to find the actual will of God.

[*Spiritual Direction in* Sacramentum Mundi
Friedrich Wulf, German theologian and priest, twentieth century

Counseling a person in the spiritual life requires a context of prayer. In fact, it is very difficult to give spiritual direction to someone who is not seriously trying to pray. Moreover, it is helpful to know the subject of his prayer. One of the advantages of a retreat is that, because you know what material the retreatant is considering, you can give him counsel in full awareness of the context of his prayer. It follows, I think, that outside the time of retreat a director ought to inquire about his client's spiritual reading, habitual methods of prayer, and about any movements and changes that may be occurring in his personal relations with God.[*Spiritual Freedom*]

John J. English, Canadian Jesuit, twentieth century

Spiritual direction is not concerned only about the spiritual dimension of the person. It is concerned with the whole person, body, soul or psyche and spirit combined. This wholeness, the "whole heart" in Biblical terminology, which makes the person be most profoundly who he or she is, must be taken into account in spiritual direction. The human has its place too. The laws of human development and unfolding, of necessity and limitation must be respected and trusted as initially good and given by God. Spiritual direction that ignores the structures of human emergence and its implied limitations as well as its possibilities will not be helpful to real human beings who are called to respond to God's initiative in a truly human and whole manner. [*Guidelines for Spiritual Direction*]

Carolyn Gratton, American teacher of psychology
and spirituality, twentieth century

The open manifestation of the state of the soul to a spiritual di-
rector involves a confessional element, as some of the authors just

quoted have stated. If the director is a priest, the confession may be a sacramental confession. If the director is not a priest, a person may turn to a priest for sacramental confession according to the teaching of his or her tradition. However, in this situation or where the priest/spiritual director and confessor are different people, it is important that the absence of a formal confessional relationship with the director not preclude the director knowing well the person seeking direction.

The following selections speak to the importance of confession and absolution for the growth of the soul. They include a quotation discussing the tradition of confession of lesser sins to a lay person.

We have often expressed a condemnation of our evil ways: that is, we have often made a confession of sin. Reflect on what sacred Scripture teaches us; that sin is not to be hidden deep within us. Perhaps there are some who have an amount of food in the stomach needing to be digested, or an excess amount of body fluids or liquids remaining in the stomach where they rest heavily and with discomfort. If they vomit it out, they experience relief. The same thing happens to those who have sinned. If they hide their sin and keep it hidden inside, they will suffer an internal pressure, and may come close to being stifled by the fluid or liquid of evil. When a person in this situation becomes his own accuser, as soon as he accuses himself and confesses, he vomits out his fault and makes right again what was the principal reason for his illness.

Seek diligently for the one to whom you ought to confess your sin. First approve the physician to whom you should make known the cause of your sickness, one who knows how to be weak with the weak, to weep with one who weeps, who has learned the art of caring and compassion. More concisely, when he gives good counsel and proves himself a learned and merciful physician and when he shall give any spiritual counsel, you will act upon it and follow it. When he is convinced and foresees that your sickness is such that it should be made known in the assembly of the whole church, from which other people may also be cured, this will have to be planned with great care and on the advice of a very skilled physician.

[*Homily on Psalm 37*]
Origen, Alexandrian priest, exegete, and theologian
of the early Church, 185–254

This is the Lord's command. Every sin must be made known to the superior, either by the sinner himself or by those who know of his fault, if they themselves are not able to bring about a cure; for secret evil is a decaying wound in the soul. We would not consider a person a benefactor who would shut up deadly poisons in our body, but rather the person who frees them by a painful incision, so that either the poisonous matter is dispelled by vomiting or, in any case, that the proper remedy may be readily indicated because the real illness is made clear. In the same way, it is surely clear that hiding one's sin contributed to the death of the sick person, "for the sting of death is sin," says the Scripture, and also: "Open rebukes are better than hidden love." [*The Long Rule, #46*]

Saint Basil of Caesarea, bishop of Caesarea and organizer of the monastic movement in Asia Minor, 329–79

. . . If the sick are in sins, and shall confess them to the presbyters of the Church, and shall with complete sincerity do all that is necessary to stop sinning and make amends for the same, they shall be forgiven them. For sins cannot be forgiven without confession of amendment. So it is rightly added: "Confess therefore your sins to one another, etc." Now in this phrase such discretion should be had as to confess daily any lesser sins to one another among your equals, and to believe by their daily prayer they are forgiven. But the uncleanness of more serious leprosy let us lay bare, in accordance with the law, to the priest and be subject to his judgment. Let us be cured of it in the manner and for the period he shall enjoin on us.

[Homily on St. James' Epistle]
Venerable Bede, monk and historian of the Christianization of the British Isles, 673–735

There is also another kind of confession in which one takes another person aside and tells him what bothers one, so that a person may hear a word of consolation from him. . . .

I will allow no person to take private confession away from me, and I would not give it up for all the treasures in the world, since I know what consolation and strength it has given me. No one knows what it can do for him except the person who has struggled long and hard with the Devil. The Devil would have killed me long ago, if the confession had not supported me. There are many confusing matters which a person cannot resolve or find the answer to by himself, and so he takes his brother aside and tells him his trouble. What harm is there if he humbles himself a little before his neighbor, embarrasses himself, looks for a word of consolation from him, accepts it, and believes it, as if he were hearing it from God himself, as we read, "If two of you agree about anything they ask, it will be done for them.". . .

If any person is wrestling with his sins and wants to get rid of them and desires a secure piece of advice on the subject, let him go and confess to another in secret, and accept what he says to him as if God himself had communicated it through the mouth of this person. However, one who has a strong, secure faith that his sins are forgiven may omit this confession and confess to God alone. But how many have such a secure faith? Therefore, as I have said, I will not let this private confession be stolen from me. I will also not have anybody forced to it, but left to each one's free will. [*Sermon 8 at Wittenberg*]

Martin Luther, theologian and Protestant reformer, 1483–1546

Bear the sufferings of the operation so that you may be restored to health—I speak of confession. I mean that at confession you must declare all your shameful deeds to your confessor, without conceal-ment, though it may well be painful, shameful, ignominious and humiliating. Otherwise the wound will remain unhealed, will con-tinue to pain you, will undermine your spiritual health, and remain as a leaven for other spiritual weaknesses, or sinful habits or vices.

[*Spiritual Counsels of Father John of Kronstadt*]
*Father John Sergieff, married parish priest
in Kronstadt, Russia, 1829–1908*

Quite apart from the internal logic of human relationship as it moves toward more complete meeting and union, I have need to make confession to one other human being in order to keep my grip on my own identity. I need a human confessor, one who may represent to me the rest of humanity, against whom in my own "otherness" I am required to win my individuation, my identity, my integrity. One's identity, as Emily Dickinson reminded us, is a hound that all too easily slips its leash. Regular confession to one other human being provides another leash that serves to restrain this willful hound.

This person need not be a priest or professional confessor, of course. The Confession may be quite informal. It may take place by correspondence with a trusted friend at some distance, and at irregular intervals. The one requirement is that the confessor should have demonstrated in some way that he is capable of seeing me as I see myself, particularly at the point of that elusive edge where I reach forward toward a cherished self-image with the infinite pathos that characterizes us all in this crucial, hidden drama. The ideal confessor I am commending here is not the traditional priest, the impassive, detached, holy man of God, who projects a general love for all mankind. This confessor must have a very particular love for this particular man or woman who risks rejection for deeper acceptance in his quest for sustained identity. We demand nothing less than that this confessor love the same me that I love most. Happy the man whose wife is also his friend and confessor! . . .

As all the authentic saints have known, no man is so good that he has no need of a confessor, self-chosen from among his fellow men. Apart from this discipline, it is too easy to be self-deceived, to engage in rationalizing about the inner enemy until it amasses at last enough strength one day to assault the real identity. All men, without exception, need confessors. Woe unto that man who in his illusion of the grandeur of independence neglects to bind himself to another as he climbs the steep ascent! [*Rediscovering Prayer*]

> *John R. Yungblut, American Quaker retreat leader,*
> *former director of Pendle Hill, twentieth century*

Some men who have been spiritual directors and who were also priests and confessors have written about their understanding of the relationship between the two roles.

Saint Francis de Sales teaches that the confessor should normally be the director also.

Be not too quick to change your confessor, but stay with the same one. Visit him regularly and confess your sins quite candidly and sincerely. Every month or so make known your hidden tendencies, independent of any sin. Examples may be that you were bothered with sadness, felt joyful or greedy and so on.

[Introduction to the Devout Life]
Saint Francis de Sales, French bishop and theoretician
of spiritual direction, 1567–1622

A distinction between the director and the confessor should not be made any more than we draw a distinction between the physician who cures an illness and the one who prescribes a remedy for preserving health. The confessor hears the admission of our sins, and absolves us from the guilt of them. He tells us what we are to do, that we may avoid sin for the future. He also gives us good advice, that we may advance in virtue. The tribunal of reconciliation, then, includes confession and direction, and it is as essential for it to preserve us from failings as it is to absolve us for them. Nevertheless, by fault of the penitents as well as that of the confessors, there have always been very few confessors who are good directors at the same time. [*Manual for Interior Souls*]

Jean Grou, Jesuit classics scholar
and spiritual director, 1731–1803

Let me clearly state what a confessor is, what a spiritual director is, and what difference there is between them. The confessor imparts absolution; he concerns himself with the sins which are confessed to him; he assesses and weighs them; he says what is right and wrong according to the laws of God, what is permitted and what is not. He appraises the penitent's attitude, and, when he determines it good, he proclaims the prayer of absolution . . . considering nothing but the divine precept in these serious words, "Sins shall be forgiven to those to whom they should be forgiven them." One would deduce from that, that direction is not at all as necessary as confession. But to receive absolution for sins, is that the only need of the soul, the only aid that priestly ministry can provide? Do you not see that so often the confession of sins involves more than admission of guilt? It expands the circle of confidence and in the same way, the action of the confessor comes to include not only that of judge but also of physician and counselor. Direction is necessarily bound up with confession. Every confessor, if he has zeal, becomes to some extent a director also. [*Essay on Confession*]

Félix Antoine Dupanloup, politician, preacher,
and bishop of Orleans, France, 1802–78

Usually spiritual direction cannot be separated from confession as long as the soul, clinging to attachment to sin, remains mostly in the purgative way. When the soul has seriously begun to advance towards holiness of life, it becomes easier to give direction distinct from confession. Some priests, in order to make certain that the two will not be confused, will only give direction after the absolution, and usually give spiritual direction only once a month to those who confess weekly. [*Soul of the Apostolate*]

Dom John Baptist Chautard, French Cistercian abbot, 1858–1935

As confessor the priest's relationship to his penitent is that of spiritual physician and, so far as counsel is concerned, his business is to deal with the matter of the confession and prescribe remedies. As director, he has an even graver responsibility, for he has to take cognisance not only of the matter of a confession, or even several confessions, but of the whole spiritual life of the soul, and show it the way in which it should go in prayer, mortification, the practice of virtue— indeed, in every department of its life.

[*The Elements of the Spiritual Life*]
Frederic P. Harton, English Anglican priest, 1889–1964

Chapter Five

DIRECTORS' ADVICE
TO THEIR COLLEAGUES

If you love to listen you will gain knowledge, and if you incline your ear you will become wise. [*Ecclesiasticus 6:33*]

Brethren, if a man is overtaken in any trespass, you who are spiritual should restore him in a spirit of gentleness. Look to yourself, lest you too be tempted. Bear one another's burdens, and so fulfil the law of Christ. [*Galatians 6:1–2*]

I charge you in the presence of God and of Christ Jesus who is to judge the living and the dead, and by his appearing and his kingdom: preach the word, be urgent in season and out of season, convince, rebuke, and exhort, be unfailing in patience and teaching.

[*2 Timothy 4:1–2*]

We turn now to consider the response and task of the director. We have divided this material into several categories: listening; the prayer of the director; respect for the uniqueness of individuals seeking direction; thoughts on the direction appropriate to the stages of spiritual maturity; emotional dimensions of the spiritual-direction relationship; discernment; and the director's teaching, encouragement, comforting, and admonishment of the directee.

The first task of a spiritual director is to listen, writes Edward Carter in a selection to follow. Listening is not simply focused concentration on the words spoken but openness and attention to the entire person as loved by God and called by God beyond our preconceived images and expectations.

Spiritual direction is the ministry of the listening heart given by a companion and guide on the journey with us to the Father, helping us to be more aware of the action of the Spirit in our lives and supporting us in our response to His call. [*Anonymous*]

To "listen" another's soul into a condition of disclosure and discovery may be almost the greatest service that any human being ever performs for another. But in this scrutiny of the business of listening, is that all that has emerged? Is it possible to set forth the perfect listener without a flash of realization that we have been engaged in something more? Is it blasphemous to suggest that over the shoulder of the human listener we have been looking at, there is never absent the silent presence of the Eternal Listener, the living God? For in penetrating to what is involved in listening do we not disclose the thinness of the filament that separates men listening openly to one another, and that of God intently listening to each soul? . . .

The more we come to realize the extent of the penetrating influence which our own hidden life and the hidden life of our friend exert upon each other, the more acutely do we come to appreciate how inadequately prepared we are to listen, no matter how mature we may be. The deeper this sense of humbling inadequacy soaks into our minds, the more open we are to realize the wisdom of seasoned spiritual guides like Francis de Sales or George Fox who both insisted that the task of all spiritual guidance is to take men to Christ, to bring them to the living Listener, and to leave them there. . . .

The more conscious a listener becomes of the influence of the living Listener in searching both speaker and listener and in drawing out both to confirm in the other what is high and to reject in the other what is low, the more certain he is that only the cleansing radiations of an utterly loving and charitable one will do. Human listening then becomes what it is: a preciously thin point in the membrane where the human and divine action can be felt to mingle with the least opaque cloud of concealment. The human action can begin at any point, the conversation can start where it will, but if it goes on, the living Listener's presence may almost imperceptibly rise into awareness and with that awareness the total situation is altered.

[*On Listening to Another*]
Douglas V. Steere, philosophy professor
and Quaker retreat leader, b. 1901

The first service that one owes to others in the fellowship consists in listening to them. Just as love to God begins with listening to His Word, so the beginning of love for the brethren is learning to listen to them. It is God's love for us that He not only gives us His Word but also lends us His ear. So it is His work that we do for our brother when we learn to listen to him. Christians, especially ministers, so often think they must always contribute something when they are in the company of others, that this is the one service they have to render. They forget that listening can be a greater service than speaking.

Many people are looking for an ear that will listen. They do not find it among Christians, because these Christians are talking where they should be listening. But he who can no longer listen to his brother will soon be no longer listening to God either; he will be doing nothing but prattle in the presence of God too. This is the beginning of the death of the spiritual life, and in the end there is nothing left but spiritual chatter and clerical condescension arrayed in pious words. . . .

It is little wonder that we are no longer capable of the greatest service of listening that God has committed to us, that of hearing our brother's confession, if we refuse to give ear to our brother on lesser subjects. Secular education today is aware that often a person can be helped merely by having someone who will listen to him seriously, and upon this insight it has constructed its own soul therapy, which has attracted greater numbers of people, including Christians. But Christians have forgotten that the ministry of listening has been committed to them by Him who is Himself the great listener and whose work they should share. We should listen with the ears of God that we may speak the Word of God. [*Life Together*]

Dietrich Bonhoeffer, German Lutheran pastor
executed by Nazis, 1906–45

What does the spiritual guide do? His first task is to listen. This is the manner in which he comes to know the one he is to help. One writer, in addressing himself to spiritual directors, puts it this way: "A lot of people expect us to question them. It is important to accustom them not to count on our questions, but to talk of their own accord. It is only after we have listened to them for a long time like this that we shall be able to ask the essential question." [*The Spirit is Present*]

Edward Carter, American Jesuit priest, b. 1915

Listening is at the service of knowing. "To care for someone, I must know many things. I must know, for example, who the other is, what his powers and limitations are, what his needs are, and what is conducive to his growth; I must know how to respond to his needs, and what my own powers and limitations are." The director knows what the spiritual life is, but in direction, he must know what the spiritual life of this individual is. The knowledge he will attain of him will be explicit, for it will be able to be verbalized, and implicit, for he will know more about him than what he can verbalize. Again, he may come to know something is so without being able to deal with it, just as he can know the person directly as existing in his own right, or he can simply have information about the person.

In all these cases, listening skills need to be developed. An exercise that might prove helpful to the beginning director is the writing of a verbatim. This is a word by word account of the interview, with the felt reactions of the participants. By recalling a particular session with a directee, and by writing it down in this way, the director will be able to see whether or not he had actually listened and heard what was being said or had missed the point completely. Better yet, change the names and circumstances and have a colleague or a professional counselor read it and make his observations. In this way we express our own accountability to our directees. [*The Spiritual Director*]

Damien Isabel, Franciscan theologian teaching in Chicago, twentieth century

The following selections describe the director's need for prayer.

Since Gertrude was often asked advice on all subjects, not only by those who had the good fortune of living under her direct guidance, but also by hundreds who came from a distance, pulled to her by the fame of her sanctity, it occurred often that she was seized with a holy fear that her words and her advice could hinder rather than profit those who came to her. As she prayed for light on this important subject, our Lord replied: "Fear nothing from now on; be comforted, take courage, and be at peace. I am the Lord your God; I am your Loved One, who has created you by the pure force of My love. I have chosen you to make you My dwelling place by My grace, and to take My delight in you. Be sure that I will reply truly by you to those who seek Me through you with sincerity and humility. I promise you also, that I will never permit any one whom I consider unworthy of receiving My Body and Blood to ask your counsel about that serious concern. So send forward the scrupulous and fearful in the greatest security, because, for your sake, I will never refuse them My fatherly love, but I will hold them in my tender love, and not hesitate to give them My tender kiss of peace."

[*The Life and Revelations of Saint Gertrude*]
Saint Gertrude the Great, German nun, 1256–1302

This art of direction is a science not of memory, but of spirit; not of study, but of prayer; not of theory, but of practice; not of personal competition, but of humility; not of human pondering but of love, love of Jesus who delivered himself up and gave himself up, forgot himself and expended himself for the salvation of souls. This science is part of the science of the saints, as Scripture speaks of it. It is a science which belongs to the saints, which the saints do and which directs saints in the ways of heaven. . . .

The direction of souls . . . is a ministry of internal and exceptional grace of which it is necessary to avail oneself by contemplation and by interior and personal holiness. Do we not know that it is by love and contemplation that the divine essence is in the Holy Trinity? . . . It is also in the same contemplation and in the love of heavenly and divine things that we should try to form the Son of God and his spirit in souls. [*Memorial of Direction to Superiors*]

> *Pierre Cardinal de Bérulle, French diocesan priest, cardinal,*
> *and founder of the Oratory in France, 1575–1629*

Without personal prayer, our ministry will be empty, our words meaningless, our direction totally fruitless. Without prayer we shall never be able to support souls in their weaknesses. They have given themselves to us as those upon whom they may trust, but without prayer we would be the cause of their falls, since they will not find in us the strength and light they need. We being dark and weak ourselves, it is only by the means of prayer that we can be enlightened and made strong in Christ Jesus. All the failures which arise in the direction of souls come from the fact that directors do not apply themselves to the holy exercise of prayer. [*Life of M. Olier*]

> *Jean-Jacques Olier, French priest and founder of the Society*
> *of Saint Sulpice, 1608–57*

Finally, he whom God calls to direct souls must be prepared to experience in himself, not only many temptations, but in particular the severe trial of aridity in prayer and the suffering caused by the necessary exercise of pure faith unaided by consolation and that feeling of certitude which so buoys one up in the face of external difficulties. The apparent abandonment of the soul by God, at times accompanied by physical suffering, is one of the marked characteristics of the lives of the great directors of souls. They, more than others, dwell in the wilderness in silence, obscurity and suffering.

> [*The Art of Mental Prayer*]
> *Dom Bede Frost, Anglican Benedictine Monk, 1877–1961*

It is also essential for directors to pray for the people they are guiding.

It is important that you have great concern for all those who are under you, in imitation of the care that the Only Son of God had of his disciples and apostles, keeping watch and praying while they were sleeping, and interrupting this prayer in the Garden of Olives in order to visit them in their need and weakness. Speak to him often in order to ask him to keep in the way of perfection these souls who belong to him. I humbly pray to him to lead us all in his ways.

[*Letter #880*]
Pierre Cardinal de Bérulle, French diocesan priest, cardinal, and founder of the Oratory in France, 1575–1629

Finally, one should pray much for one's spiritual children. Nothing is more beautiful in the letters of that great spiritual director, Abbot Marmion, than the way in which he says over and over again "Je prie beaucoup pour vous." Those words may well be the motto of the guide of souls, whatever form his guidance may take, for it is by prayer, even more than by counsel, that he can bring and keep them close to the Heart of God. [*The Elements of the Spiritual Life*]
Frederick P. Harton, English Anglican priest, 1889–1964

The Spiritual Director has the responsibility of intercessory prayer, of staying in God's presence on behalf of the person in order that there may be divine light in his directing. [*Call to Commitment*]
Elizabeth O'Connor, Protestant author and member of the Church of the Savior in Washington, D.C., b. 1921

The following selections remind the director of the remarkable uniqueness among individuals in their manner of knowing God and following Christ, and, as a consequence, of the importance of the director not having a preconceived plan to apply to all souls. Directors must accept and listen for this uniqueness and guard against assuming a person will be like themselves.

Just as the same medicine and the same food are not administered to everyone's body, but an allowance is made according to their degree of health or sickness, so also are persons treated with a variety of instruction and guidance. This treatment is acknowledged by those who have experienced it. Some are led by doctrine, others are guided by example. Some need the spur, others need restraint. Some are lazy and hard to rouse to the good, and must be provoked by the sting of the word. Others are unusually excessive in their mood with tendencies difficult to restrain, like thoroughbred colts, who run wild outside the marked course, and to help them grow, the word must have a restraining power and a checking obedience. [*Ascetic Discourse*]

> *Saint Gregory Nazianzen, theologian, poet*
> *and Cappadocian bishop, 330–90*

A brother asked an old man this question, "What virtuous action should I do so that I may have life?" The old man said, "God knows what is good. It has been told to me that one of the Fathers asked Abba Nistheros the Great, the friend of Abba Anthony, and said to him, 'What virtuous action is there that I could do?' He said to him, 'Are not all actions of equal value? Scripture says that Abraham was hospitable and God was with him. David was humble, and God was with him. Elias loved inner peace and God was with him. Do what you know your soul desires in accord with God's will and keep watch over your heart.' " [*The Sayings of the Desert Fathers*]

> *Abba Nistheros the Great, Egyptian desert father,*
> *friend of Saint Anthony*

It is necessary to recognize that in the inner life one must never take his own experiences or their lack as the model for everyone else. The person who labors a long time in coming to contemplation and then rarely enjoys the perfection of this endeavor may easily be misled if he speaks, thinks, or judges other people with the rule of his personal experience. Similarly, the person who frequently experiences the joy of contemplation almost at his own volition will be just as deceived if he measures others by himself. Do not squander precious time with these useless comparisons. [*The Cloud of Unknowing*]

> *Anonymous, England, fourteenth century*

All that we know of God, of his only Son, of the economy of His grace, of His ways over souls, of souls even, and of the art of governing them in grace and for grace, is so little in comparison to what we do not know. In comparison to what it is necessary to know about it, in order to correspond to truth, we are obliged to make much more a profession of ignorance than of knowledge. We must try to act only by reason of a power guided by obedience and charity. Even then we must behave as having real personal need and feeling a great need of light and guidance by the Holy Spirit in order to make up for our powerlessness and blindness.

Creature can be useful to creature only by the grace of the Son of God and in the command of his providence. Outside of that, other creatures can be only very injurious, taking interest in and sometimes even mutually ruining one another by their self-love and lack of good judgment.

It is necessary . . . to minister to souls with the cross and through the cross. [*Spiritual Letter*]

> *Pierre Cardinal de Bérulle, French diocesan priest,*
> *cardinal, and founder of the Oratory in France, 1575–1629*

There are directors who get an idea and a plan into their heads, which they think much of, and apply to all the souls who come to them, thinking that they will accomplish something great if they bring them into line with it. They have no other object that that of carrying out what they have decided another should look like, as wishing all should wear the same clothes. [*Foundations of the Spiritual Life*]

> *Jean Joseph Surin, French Jesuit, 1600–65*

These spiritual directors should consider seriously that they themselves are not the chief agent, guide, and mover of souls in this matter, but that the principal guide is the Holy Spirit, who never overlooks persons. Directors must remember that they are instruments for directing souls to perfection through faith and the law of God, according to the spirit God gives each one. Consequently, the director's total care should be not to force people to accept his own method and condition, but he should observe the road along which God is leading them, and if he does not completely comprehend it, he should let them alone and not disturb them. In accord with the path and spirit along which God leads them, the spiritual director should strive to conduct them into greater solitude, peace, and freedom of spirit. He should give them room so that when God introduces them into this solitude they do not fasten their corporal or spiritual faculties to some particular object, interior or exterior, and do not become apprehensive or afflicted with the thought that nothing is being accomplished. Although the soul is not doing anything itself, God is doing something in it. Directors should try to free the soul up and bring it into solitude and idleness so that it may not be enslaved to any particular knowledge, earthly or heavenly, or to any insidious desire for personal gratification or pleasure, or to other anxieties that it may be empty, through the pure disregard of every creature, and placed in spiritual simplicity. [*Living Flame of Love*]

Saint John of the Cross, Spanish cofounder (with Saint Teresa of Ávila) of the Discalced Carmelites, poet, 1542–91

Every person in particular, of whatever condition he may be, has some characteristics which are quite unique to him. You know by experience, Theophane, that it is important to give this person guidance which is not less particular. Just as there is no universal remedy which is prescribed for all particular diseases, so also there is no general guidance so perfect that each one in particular, according to his different needs, can be beneficially helped by it. . . .

Do we not also see that God Himself adapts Himself to our personal dispositions in order to arrive at His purposes in the work of our sanctification? He regulates His graces to us, so they are either secret or obvious, gentle or strong, delayed or prompt, according to the character of our dispositions. He waits for the right moment, when our temperament is better disposed. Then he can in a more natural manner make His entrance and His move. He adjusts Himself and accommodates Himself to us until He witnesses in us some tendency in these directions, daring to do nothing which does even the smallest harm to our unique dispositions.

After saying this, is it not necessary to say that on this point the director is obliged to imitate God? It is, therefore, his duty, in order to fulfill it well, to consider very attentively the temperament of the persons he is directing in order to adapt in himself the gentleness of the spirit of God. . . . Since God adjusts His manner of guidance according to the order of our temperaments, so also the director must partly take the model of his direction from the temperament of the person. . . .

Not even a laborer refuses to adapt himself to the nature of the matter on which he is working, in order to give it the form of which it is capable and which he means to accomplish. Reason alone and common sense teach us to make good use of raw material. If that is the case, is the director not more obliged in every sense of the word, to adapt himself in such a free manner in order to allow grace to realize in a person all the divine forms possible? . . .

Finally, is it not necessary to say that one of his greatest duties is to have respect and reverence for the work of God when He is operative in a soul and to regard it only as God's work? . . .

He must humbly acknowledge that this is a truly great honor for him to simply help in the continuance of this divine operation by the removal of all obstacles, without wanting to interfere by adding his own directing to that of God. [*Manual for the Direction of Souls*]

Francis Quilloré, French Jesuit, 1615–84

I consider it an important emphasis in spiritual direction to discover the dispositions whereby a soul is motivated, . . . to discern how far you can urge it, to allow grace full power, to distinguish true from false attractions, and prevent souls from getting lost or running to excesses. . . . The spiritual director having once learned God's action in a soul, has nothing else to do but to guide it that it may obey the inspiration of grace. . . . He must never attempt to inspire a soul with his personal tastes and individual preferences, nor lead it after his own way of acting, or his own personal point of view. A director that would act in this way, would often turn souls from God's own guidance and oppose the action of divine grace in them. . . . God alone guides the soul and the director simply sees to it that the soul follows the guidance of God. . . .

In the direction of a soul it is necessary to begin, and this is essential, with an understanding of its interior, supernatural state, the state of grace and the action of grace in that soul, seeing how well the soul is responding to its grace, to what degree the life of our Lord, Divine grace, is dominant in the soul and all its activities. This first consideration is of the highest importance. If you know the state of a soul well, the action of God and the action of grace within it, you have gained a very clear knowledge of the designs of God for it. But that is not all. The obstacles which grace finds there must also be seen, the action of the soul and its character, the vices and faults which exist. . . . Finally, to cause a soul to grow it must be brought back to the principle of sanctity within it, to Divine grace, that it may become docile to it and be allowed to experience victory only by its power. [*Spiritual Letters*]

If we want to rightly direct people, we must learn how to be flexible and adjust ourselves to them. We have to be in touch with their individual psychological makeup, respect them at all times, and respond in a manner best suited to their personal characteristics. That is what St. Paul means when he says "Be all things to all people."

Be patient with sinfulness for a long time, and if there are occasions when you think you cannot stand it another minute, accept it again. In the end you will recognize that you did a good thing.

[*Spiritual Letters*]
Venerable Francis Libermann, French superior general
of the Society of the Holy Ghost, 1803–52

Rabat, April 19, 1932

Your letter of December 12th reached me when I could hardly write. I wondered then if the Good Lord might not impose on me the terrible sacrifice of abandoning my work.

I needn't tell you that if sickness prevents me from writing, it doesn't make me forget you nor keep me from praying. You have often been in my thoughts and prayers. What else does a sick father think of but his children? Yet I have been eager to write you at least a few words.

Not that I mind, once in a while, leaving to their own devices those I am directing, as I don't want them to lean on me too much. And I always avoid making detailed rules for their spiritual life. I am convinced that Christ leads souls by most diversified roads, and so I don't mind leaving for a while those who have entrusted themselves to me, even if they feel temporarily at a loss.

When the human director is not there, the true one, the great Director who is Christ Himself, is less easily forgotten. Each person must look for her own "way," and even though the human director can help in her search, she alone can find it. Christ reveals it to her only and not to others, and it is He who sets her on her way. . . .

[*Voice from the Desert*]

El Kbab, December 9, 1933

To apologize for my long delay would be superfluous, wouldn't it? I repeat the offense over and over again, and because I believe it is good for you to be left as much as possible alone with God.

It is God Himself who shows me that this method of spiritual direction is good for your soul. It is very clear that He has Himself taken charge of you. From the beginning I have simply watched Him at work in you, and my words were not so much inner as outer guidance. It is He who transformed these words from within, where He is light and warmth, into substance and life. So, if you agree, I shall continue to leave you largely to yourself. I mean leave you to the Master's action. He is the great Spiritual Director, as I have told you from the beginning, so when no letters come from me, He will suffice. [*Voice from the Desert*]

Albert Peyriguère, French priest, disciple of Charles de Foucauld, hermit in the desert, 1883–1959

Spiritual direction, which is non-directive, as it is known in psychological language today, is more beneficial to the directee. This technique calls for the director to listen and to refuse directly to intervene in an authoritarian and outright manner, so that the person in direction may more easily discover for himself, by prayer and reflection enlightened by the Word of God, what the will of the Holy Spirit is for him. Christian spiritual direction does not seek to impose itself on a person and thus makes itself in the end expendable. [*Confession*]

Max Thurian, monk of Taizé, 1899–

Direction is a mode of assistance, not of domination. The director gently assists the person in his free responsiveness to the Spirit. If the response to grace would not flow freely from the inmost being of the directee himself it would not lead to a true spiritual life; a forced expression of love would be worthless in the eyes of the Divine

Beloved. Assistance implies that the director avoids dogmatic suggestions as to the life direction the directee should take. Rather he
facilitates the directee's own awareness of what the Holy Spirit is
asking of him and helps him to work through the illusions, poor
judgments and self-centered motivations that diminish his ability to
hear this sacred invitation. [*The Dynamics of Spiritual Self-Direction*]
Adrian Van Kaam, American priest of the
Society of the Holy Ghost, b. 1920

To determine the components of a genuinely helpful spiritual direction, let us begin by looking at direction as help toward growth in
response to the Spirit. Concretely this help will include the willing
ear, may include advice, and may well result in relief from anxiety
and more respectful observance of law. But its primary goal is growth,
the development of lived dialogue with the Lord. Understanding spiritual direction in this way, I will suggest that there is an approach
to "direction" that concentrates primarily on a person's strengths and
another that concentrates primarily on his weaknesses, and that the
choice between these approaches is a crucial one. . . .

The choice between emphasis on strength and emphasis on weakness is one of the elements of spiritual direction in which the director's
view of his role is of crucial importance. If he sees himself primarily
as a defender of law and order, he will focus on violations of law and
so distract the person he is directing from the development of
strength. If he is fascinated by problems, he will allow and even
encourage an emphasis on them. If he likes to tell people what to do,
weakness will be an opportunity for him. The director has to remain
aware that because helping a person to grow offers few quick rewards
to either the director or the person seeking help, he will often be
tempted to try the short cut of problem-solving, telling the directee
what to do, or invoking the law. If he develops and maintains the role
of helping persons to grow, he will do so, with the help of much self-
criticism, because he sees the enduring value of this kind of help.
[*Contemporary Spiritual Direction*]
William J. Connolly, American Jesuit priest, twentieth century

How did Jesus provide guidance for others?
Our problem in reading the Gospels whole is that they contain a

patchwork of different situations (most of which we know too little about for certain interpretation), and in each situation Jesus responds uniquely to the person and situation, with mind- and heart-opening questions and comments, and with symbolic and healing acts.

Here he sets a pattern for the best of Christian awareness concerning human guidance: each of us needs a special "saving" word or act at this moment in our lives. What I need may be contradictory to what another needs. And yet this is not simply subjective individualism; it is within the framework of a shared covenant, i.e., an affirmation of the trustworthiness of the Intimate, reigning Unknown/Known Force of Life, and the guidelines of the covenant community's tested, evolving experience for living in the reconciling intent of this trustworthiness. [*Spiritual Friend*]

Tilden Edwards, Episcopal priest and director
of spiritual-formation program, b. 1935

Not only do souls differ in temperament and disposition but also in the maturity of the soul. Classically, the spiritual journey has been divided into three ways: purgative, illuminative, and unitive or perfective. These three ways are very broad designations, and some authors, such as Saint John of the Cross and Saint Teresa of Ávila, have further refined the three stages in helpful ways. However, we will use these three broad designations to serve to give general indications concerning the direction appropriate to each. These three ways are often conceived as being sequential although the spiritual journey often begins with an illuminative experience and an advanced soul continually experiences purgation and illumination. In this section, after some general observations on direction in relation to the stages of the spiritual life we include descriptions of the direction appropriate to each of the three ways.

It is not a novel attempt to classify Christian persons according to the degree of perfection, which they have reached. The ancient author of the works which bear the name of Dionysius the Areopagite had already clearly stated the principle that we must distinguish three successive phases in the process of the formation of a soul by grace, namely, the stages of purgation, illumination, and perfection. . . .

Moreover, if it is not a novel idea to classify the stages through which persons progress in their search for perfection, it is by no means an empty or a superfluous endeavor. If this were true, the Fathers, theologians, and mystical writers would not have insisted as much on this point as they did. Furthermore, the accounting of the successive phases of the ascetical life forms a whole spiritual psychology, which is as instructive as it is interesting to study. Is it not clearly certain that beginners and advanced persons should be guided according to quite different principles? In order to direct souls wisely, it is necessary to keep in mind the degree of perfection which they have reached. [*The Degrees of the Spiritual Life*]

Abbé Auguste Saudreau, French diocesan priest and
spiritual writer, 1859–1946

The terms *virtue* and *perfection* are used in order to point out clearly the unity and diversity of direction. This reflects that there are three classes of pilgrims on the road: those whom spiritual writers class as beginners, those who are progressing, and the perfect. All need to be guided; but it is quite clear that the guidance of a person struggling in the painful work of fleeing from and repenting of sin, is different from the guidance of another person who has already progressed somewhat and is trying to reach the higher levels of the perfect life. In regard to the first, it is adequate direction to apply carefully the normal rules of psychology and morality, to lead the soul to the ful- fillment of the ordinary duties of the Christian life, and to turn its personal efforts prudently toward a better life. The second person is a different matter. Here we are in the presence of a person called to a state of high perfection, sometimes overwhelmed by God with un- usual graces, and requiring an appropriate spiritual direction which demands of him who gives it, great gifts of knowledge and of prudence and a high degree of holiness.

[*The Christian Life and the Spiritual Life*]
Père Yves Ernest Masson, Dutch Dominican priest
and scholar, 1883–1971

Another important criterion is the state of mental prayer. We have seen . . . how each of the three ways has its own form of mental prayer. Meditation is the proper prayer of the beginners (purgative way); affective prayer is proper to the proficient (illuminative way); acquired contemplation is the prayer of perfect souls (unitive way).

Any form of passive, infused contemplation is a sign of the mystic state and mystic union.

Evidently those in the unitive way and the beginners in the purgative way should not receive the same direction, just as the food of the adult cannot be the same as the food of an infant. Nor can the mystics be guided according to the same rules as others in every respect. Once the spiritual director has learned the duties and the difficulties of the various stages of the spiritual life and also the personal difficulties and graces of the individual soul seeking his guidance, it should not be difficult to direct it. The golden rule of direction is: Firmness with kindness, or *fortiter in re, suaviter in modo.* [*The Ascetical Life*]

Pascal P. Parente, Italian-American diocesan priest
and teacher of ascetical theology, 1890–1971

Spiritual direction should be progressive and accommodated to the soul's degree of virtue, temperament, age, and circumstances of life. If the direction given is far above the needs and capacities of the soul, the soul will become disheartened and discouraged because more will be demanded of it than it is capable of doing. If, on the other hand, the soul has advanced beyond the type of direction that is given, the wings of the soul will be tied so that it cannot soar to God.

The director must, therefore, discern what are the needs of the soul at a given time, and then take care that the direction given will satisfy those needs. When he wishes to intensify the spiritual life of the soul, he may propose things by way of a trial or test, in order to see how the soul reacts. He need not and should not tell the soul that this is his method, but he should take every precaution not to hold the soul back when God wishes to lead it to a higher stage, and not force the soul to a higher stage when it is not yet ready to make the step. Growth in the spiritual life, like any other kind of growth, must be gradual and continuous.

Consequently, the spiritual director should know the various steps that mark the phases of growth from the beginning of the ascetical life to the transforming union, and in dealing with particular individuals he should expect that they will not remain static in any given phase, but that they will progress in gradual stages from one phase of the spiritual life to another. And although it is true that God could take a soul in his arms, so to speak, and carry it from one stage of life to a much higher stage, this is not to be presumed in any given case, because it is not the ordinary working of God's grace.

[Spiritual Theology]
Jordan Aumann, American Dominican priest
and spiritual writer, twentieth century

As a result of a religious awakening, a soul has often seen its self-centered, distorted, and sinful life in the light of a new vision of reality. In the period of purgation, the soul longs to reorder its disordered life and reorder its disordered loves, to establish a correspondence with the divine life. Purgation, often occurring over a period of years, is particularly concerned with the cleansing of pride and learning of humility.

The formal object of direction varies according to the circumstances. In the beginning of the spiritual life it is much more detailed and exhaustive since the young person is inexperienced, insufficiently instructed, and is liable to suffer from many illusions. The imagination can become easily disturbed and the devil can suggest with great cunning false ideas of perfection. A person can, for example, confuse sentimentality with love, be mistaken about his true duties, and not understand what is the right proportion to maintain in the practice of certain virtues. A person can improperly choose his reading and establish bad relationships. A person can falsely discern temptations and not know how to overcome them. A person can also be confused about the best means to take to uproot his faults in order to acquire virtue. It is necessary to be instructed on all these points.

[The Degrees of the Spiritual Life]
Abbé Auguste Saudreau, French diocesan priest and
spiritual writer, 1859–1946

The director can and should endeavor to explain the fundamental principles of the spiritual life and to suggest certain readings and more especially to impart knowledge about meditation methods and to check progress in meditation at regular intervals. The predominant passion must be isolated and instructions given on how to subdue its force. The director ought to prescribe a daily examination of conscience, and over and over again, recall to the beginner's mind the real object of the spiritual life. To lose sight of the object is fatal. . . .

The director must strive to inspire his charge with the idea that it is better to correct the least vice than to acquire all the wealth in this world. He must strive too, to make those striving for perfection surrender their false ideas of the value of human things and to implant the true ones that they may procure that peace without which no one can arrive at union with God. The director should, then, counsel and advise those in any of the three ways, but especially those in the purgative way: (1) to avoid interesting themselves in the affairs of others, unless obliged to do so by justice or charity; (2) to calm all the impulses which arise in the soul with any vehemence, ruling or quenching them promptly by prayer—for instance, St. James says: "Is any one sad among you, let him pray"; (3) to take care not to harbor unprofitable thoughts in the mind, but rather to stifle them at the outset; (4) to avoid the occasions that might lead to disturbances and especially those objects which excite the appetites most violently; (5) skillfully to avoid an accumulation of affairs, which induces eagerness and stimulates over-activity.

[*Guidance In Spiritual Direction*]
Charles Hugo Doyle, Canadian Catholic priest, theologian,
and spiritual writer in the United States, b. 1904

Saint Teresa herself suggests that obedience is particularly appropriate to the purgative period (the "3rd mansion" can be considered part of the purgative period).

Persons who are by God's mercy carried this distance [to the 3rd mansion characterized by a life of high virtue, still susceptible to lapses], which as I said, is no minor grace, for they are probably going to ascend still higher. These persons will greatly benefit from practicing prompt obedience. Even if they are not in some religious order, it would be good for them, just like some other people, to get a spiritual director, so as never to follow their own will, which is the cause of most of our ills. They should not choose a director with their same mentality, as the saying goes, who is excessively prudent in his actions, but should select a person completely detached from worldly things. It is very helpful to consult a person who has personally learnt and can teach this. It is encouraging to know that trials which seemed to us impossible to bear are possible to others, and that they bear them patiently. Their flight makes us try to fly also, like nestlings taught by the parent birds, who, though they cannot fly far at first, little by little imitate their parents. I personally know the immense profit of this. No matter how resolved such persons may be not to offend our Lord, they must never subject themselves to temptation. They are still near the first mansions, to which they might easily return. Their strength is not yet established on a solid basis, like that of persons experienced in suffering, who know how little cause there is to fear the storms of this life and do not care for its pleasures. Beginners might fail before any harsh trial. Some great harassment which only the devil knows how to stir up to injure us, might make beginners lose heart. While they sincerely try to withdraw others from sin they might be defeated by the attacks made upon themselves.

[*Interior Castle*]

Saint Teresa of Ávila, Spanish founder of the reformed order
of Discalced Carmelites, 1515–82

What kind of help does the pilgrim in earnest about the journey need? At the outset he will probably need advice about prayer. It is true that we learn about prayer by praying and there is no substitute for this mode of gaining experience. Almost certainly a person who seriously decides to aim at a closer walk with God will have done a good deal of praying before ever he comes to this decision. But his prayer may be based on what he learnt as a child and may not be suitable for him any longer. There are rules and methods founded on the experience of thousands down the centuries which can prevent a person from falling into some of the pitfalls which the untaught may stumble into. The elementary grammar of prayer may be learnt from books of which there is an abundance today. But not everyone can learn from books, nor is it easy always to select from a book what is appropriate to one's own state and leave what is inappropriate. People are of very different types, and a method of prayer suitable to an extravert, who has no difficulty at all in relating to people and affairs around him but experiences the greatest difficulty in looking within, will be unsuitable to an introvert, whose problems and difficulties are precisely the opposite, and vice versa. To someone who is beginning to take the enterprise of prayer seriously it can obviously be of value to talk it over with one who is well versed in the practice and literature of prayer. A simple procedure for someone so consulted would be to invite the person to state what he actually does in prayer, how much time he gives to it, what difficulties he finds, etc. The adviser can then make suggestions about the difficulties, point out ways of strengthening the prayer, perhaps suggesting a new approach to praying. There may be need of some elementary instruction on such matters as stillness, or realising God's presence, or about how to get spiritual food from reading and reflecting on the Bible, about meditation and contemplation, about the different parts of prayer—adoration and praise, confession, thanksgiving, petition and intercession. Some things are more easily caught than taught, and the spiritual guide may be able to help a person more by five or ten minutes' prayer with him at the end of an interview than by any advice given during the course of it. During this initial stage of learning to pray it is generally a help to see one's adviser regularly, perhaps every three months, to report progress or failure to progress, to mention unforeseen difficulties, to gain the encouragement which comes from the understanding and sympathy of one who is behind you in your endeavours. [*The Heart in Pilgrimage*]

Christopher Bryant, English Anglican monk of the Society of Saint John the Evangelist, twentieth century

A person emerges from the period of purgation into the illuminative period able to apprehend another order of reality in contemplation. There is no longer joy in discursive thought and meditation but a desire to be quiet with God. In Saint John of the Cross' schema, the attachment of the senses has been purified in the dark night of the senses so the attention may be focused inwardly on God. In the illuminative period joy and trials alternate so that at times a person experiences contemplation and at times returns to meditation.

The author of The Cloud of Unknowing *warns against a premature desire to enter into contemplation.*

A new novice in the school of the Lord, who has just recently left the world, thinks that since he has given himself to prayer and penance for a short time under the guidance of his spiritual father, that he is now ready to begin contemplation. He has merely heard others speak about it or has probably only read about it. A person like this will hear it read or said that "a person shall draw all his senses into himself" or that "he shall climb up beyond himself." He no sooner has heard this than when through personal ignorance of the interior life, or sensuality and curiosity, he totally mistakes the meaning. He feels deep within himself a natural curiosity about the secret and only imagines that grace is calling him to contemplation. He becomes so blindly attached to this belief that although his spiritual father disagrees with him, he becomes indignant. He starts thinking and saying to others, as ignorant as himself, that no one understands him. So he changes his life and, motivated by boldness and pride, he stops humble prayer and spiritual discipline too soon and falsely begins the work of contemplation. If he continues to persist in this, his work is neither human nor divine but, to put it crassly, something unnatural, artificial, and guided by Satan. It is a straight path to the death of body and soul, because it is a perversion which leads to insanity. But he does not recognize this and, foolishly thinking that he can grasp God with his intellect alone, forces his mind to focus on God alone.

[*The Cloud of Unknowing*]
Anonymous, England, fourteenth century

After describing the beginner's stage, Saint John of the Cross discusses the transition from purgation to illumination through the night of the senses.

For a clear understanding of the state of beginners, it should be known that the practice of beginners is to meditate and make acts and discursive meditation with the imagination. A person in this state should be given material for his meditation and discursive reflection, and he should by himself make inner acts and benefit from spiritual things by the pleasure and satisfaction of his senses. By being fed with the delight of spiritual things, the appetite is torn away from sensual things and finds the things of the world less attractive.

When the appetite has been partially fed, and has become in some manner accustomed to spiritual things, and has acquired some courage and stability, God begins to wean the soul, as they say, and establish it in the state of contemplation. This occurs in some persons after a very short time, especially with religious, for in denying the things of the world more quickly, they accustom their senses and appetites to God and, in their activity, pass on to the spirit which God manifests in them. This happens when the soul's discursive acts and meditations stop along with its initial sensible satisfaction and enthusiasm, and it is unable to practice discursive meditation as before, or find adequate sustenance for the senses. The feeling part is more totally arid because its riches are transferred to the spirit, which has no relation to the senses.

Since a person cannot function naturally except by means of the senses, in this state it is God who is the agent, and the soul is the recipient. The soul conducts its life only as the receiver and as one in whom something is being done. God is the giver and the one Who works in it by giving spiritual goods in contemplation, i.e.: knowledge and love together, that is, loving knowledge, without the soul's usual acts and discursive reflections, for it can no longer engage in these acts as it did earlier. [*Living Flame of Love*]

A person in this stage (when the soul is led to contemplation) should be guided in a manner completely different from the former. If, before this, directors suggested content for meditation, and he meditated, now they should instead withdraw all content, and he should not meditate. He is unable to meditate even if he may want to, and should he try he would be distracted instead of recollected. If earlier he had sought satisfaction, love, and devotion, and found it, now he should neither desire nor seek it. Not only will he fail to find it by his personal efforts, but, on the contrary, he will find dryness. By the activity he desires to carry on with the senses, he distracts himself from the peaceful and quiet good secretly being given to his soul. In losing one good, he does not find the other, because these goods are no longer granted through the senses as earlier. Therefore directors should not demand meditation of persons in this state, nor should they command them to make acts or seek for satisfaction and enthusiasm. Such activity would place an obstruction in the path of the main actor Who, as I have already said, is God, Who secretly and quietly gives the person loving wisdom and knowledge, without individual acts. At times He does make specific ones in the soul for a certain length of time. Consequently, the person also should live only with a loving attention to God, without making specific acts. He should live his life passively, as we have said, without individual efforts of his own, but with simple, loving awareness, like a person who opens his eyes with wonder and love. [*Living Flame of Love*]

How frequently God may be anointing a contemplative with some very exquisite ointment of loving knowledge, serene, peaceful, secluded, and far withdrawn from all the senses and all that is imaginable. Because of this a person cannot meditate, nor reflect on anything, nor enjoy anything heavenly or earthly, since God has placed him in that lonely passivity and given him the deep desire for solitude, when a spiritual director will come along like a blacksmith, who knows nothing but how to meditate. He will demand, "Come, now, give up these rest periods, which are the same as laziness and a waste of time. Be active and meditate and make interior acts, for it is necessary that you do your part. What you are now doing is the way of deception and is characteristic of foolish persons."

[*Living Flame of Love*]
Saint John of the cross, Spanish cofounder (with Saint Teresa of Ávila) of the Discalced Carmelites, poet, 1542–91

The director must teach with Blosius that a soul cannot arrive at intimate union with God unless it has become entirely pure and simple and thus has a likeness to God. In order then that it may deserve to be united to God it must preserve itself from all sin, from all pleasure indulged in for its own sake, and become free in heart and mind from everything created. By true and deep humility the soul must always acknowledge itself to be the most vile and unworthy, must always subject itself absolutely to the Will of God and keep itself raised up to Him.

The director, too, must prepare himself for disillusionments resulting from sin in those who would appear to have made great spiritual progress. Negligence, surprise, exposure in a rash moment and under specious pretexts to some dangerous occasion of sin, is often sufficient to cause the most lamentable falls. According to St. Francis de Sales, a fall even into mortal sin does not impede the progress of a soul in the way of perfection, provided only that it does not remain in that state for any length of time. Sin is the most powerful humiliation of all for destroying self-love; in everything else there is room for pride. In such cases, the confessor-director may console the penitent by pointing out the truth of St. Paul's words: "All things work together unto good, to such as . . . are called to be saints." "All things," St. Augustine adds, "even sin."

[*Guidance in Spiritual Direction*]
Charles Hugo Doyle, Canadian Catholic priest, theologian,
and spiritual writer in the United States, b. 1904

Something must now be said about how to advise those who are on the threshhold of contemplation or are actually embarked upon it. Should a person who is able to let his mind work passively, resting in the presence of God, be encouraged to do so and abandon what we have called expressive prayer—acts of penitence and petition, of thanksgiving, adoration and praise? The old guides assumed that contemplation was normally the climax of years of prayer and self-discipline, as a result of which a person found himself drawn increasingly to a simpler, more intuitive kind of prayer, that is to contemplation, which consists in looking and loving. Such a prayer as it develops leads to a kind of blankness in the active reasoning mind which allows or is caused by a deep Godward aspiration of the heart. Such masters of contemplation as St. John of the Cross and the author of *The Cloud of Unknowing* teach that those drawn in this way should not resist the emptiness of mind but accept it as a condition of the approach to God by the way of unknowing, of loving knowledge. But there are dangers in this contemplative attitude, for passivity not only opens a person to heavenly aspirations but also to very unheavenly emotions and impulses. The old guides assumed that only those of firm faith and disciplined character could safely embark on the waters of contemplation; for only they would have the strength to cope with the powerful energies of the unconscious. . . .

Much the surest test as to whether a person is on the right lines in his prayer is the effect of his prayer in his daily life. Loving attention to God in prayer will issue in a loving concern for others and a growing indifference to a person's own wishes and interests. If there are no signs of this there must be some doubt as to the genuiness of the prayer. What advice can be given to one who is in doubt about the reality of his contemplation? It may be that I can perceive signs of a growing love and humility which the person himself cannot, and

I can be reassuring. But suppose I do not see these signs and suspect that the person's doubts are justified, what advice can I offer? I can only offer tentative suggestions, for people vary greatly. I should encourage the individual to seek ways of actively thinking about God, Christ and spiritual truths and of the world in the light of these invisible realities. One way of doing this would be by reading and reflecting on the gospels and the psalms. A method I recommend is to read a short passage from a gospel, write out a prayer based on it and then pray the prayer over a number of times. I would further recommend such a person to reduce the time he gives to interior prayer to no more than twenty minutes in one session. I would further recommend him to vary the mantras he uses, having two or three for a twenty-minute period of prayer. But perhaps the greatest help one can give is to enable him to see more clearly the nature of his problem.

[*The Heart In Pilgrimage*]
Christopher Bryant, English Anglican monk of the Society of Saint John the Evangelist, twentieth century

The unitive or perfective stage is also called the spiritual marriage. In Saint Teresa of Ávila's use of the image of watering the garden for degrees of prayer, it is the period of drenching rain. We include two selections from both Saint Teresa of Ávila and Saint John of the Cross to give some suggestions about this unusual stage.

Personal experience and a spiritual director are necessary once the person has reached these boundaries. Many things happen now about which it is important to have someone to talk to. After seeking such a person, and no one is found, the Lord will not fail the person. He has not allowed me to falter in spite of what I am. I believe that there are only a few who have arrived at the experience of these many things. If no one is found with experience, this is no good at all, because without experience, a master will only disturb and trouble a person. But the Lord will also make up for this. For this reason it is important, particularly for women, to discuss this with her confessor, and that he be a competent person. All of this has been said before, I think, but I repeat it now because it is very important. There are many more women than men to whom the Lord gives these graces. I heard this from the holy Friar Peter of Alcantara—and I have observed it myself. He said that women make much more progress along this path than men do. He gave excellent reasons for this, all in favor of women. Now there is no need to enumerate them here.

[*The Life of Teresa of Ávila*]

Saint Teresa advises the following for her sisters in the "6th mansion," a period of growing intimacy with God.

Sisters, the major emphasis I make is that you should be perfectly frank and straightforward with your confessor. I do not mean in confessing your sins, since that is clear enough, but in describing to him your prayer. Unless you do this, I cannot promise you any security nor that you are being led by God. Our Lord desires that we should be as truthful and open with those who stand in His place as we would be with Him. We should allow our confessors to know not only our thoughts but especially all those underlying actions, no matter how small. Then you do not need to feel any fear or anxiety because even if your vision is not from God, it could not harm you if you are humble and have a clear conscience, for His Majesty knows how to harvest good from evil. What Satan intended would injure you will benefit you instead. Truly believing God has given you such unusual graces, you will try to please Him more and will preserve His image before your memory always. [*Interior Castle*]

Saint Teresa of Ávila, Spanish founder of the reformed order of Discalced Carmelites, 1515–82

In the next two selections, Saint John of the Cross describes the night of the spirit, a period of aridity preceeding or at the beginning of the state of union or perfection. In this state an individual needs comfort and encouragement from his/her director.

Due to the solitude and desolation this night of the spirit causes, there is also the fact that a person in this state finds neither consolation nor support in any teaching of the spiritual director. Although his spiritual director may point out many reasons for being consoled because of the blessings included in the hardships, he cannot believe this. Because he is almost drowning and immersed in that sensation of evil by which he so clearly sees his own agony, he believes his directors say these things simply because they do not understand him and do not see what he sees and feels. Instead of consolation he experiences greater sorrow, thinking that the director's teaching is no real remedy for his evil. Truly, it is not a remedy, because until the Lord finishes purging him in the way He desires, no remedy is a help to him in his sorrow. His helplessness is even more painful because of the little he can do himself in this situation. He resembles one who is imprisoned in a dark prison, bound hands and feet, and able neither to move, nor see, nor feel any goodness from heaven or earth. He stays in this state until his soul is humbled, softened, and purified, until it becomes so delicate, simple, and refined that it can be one with the Spirit of God, exactly to the degree of union of love that God, in His mercy, wants to give. The purgation is of greater or lesser force and endures for a longer or shorter time in exact conformity to the degree of God's will. [*Dark Night of the Soul*]

When an individual is being led by God along a sublime path of dark contemplation and aridity, in which he feels abandoned, it can happen that he will meet in the midst of the height of his darknesses, trials, conflicts, and temptations someone who, in the style of Job's comforters (Job 4:8–11), will proclaim that all of this is due to some mental illness, or depression, or temperament, or to some hidden personal evil, and that as a result God has abandoned him. The normal verdict is that, since such trials afflict this person, he must have lived an evil life.

Others will tell him that he is regressing, since he experiences no pleasure or consolation as he previously did in the things of God. Such talk only doubles the trial of the poor soul, because its greatest suffering is caused by the knowledge of its personal miseries. That it is filled with evil and sin is as clear as day, and even clearer, for, as we shall say presently, God is the creator of this enlightenment in the night of contemplation. When the soul finds someone who agrees with what it feels, that these troubles are all its own fault, its suffering and distress grow without any limit. This pain usually becomes worse than death. An incompetent confessor is not satisfied with this but, in judging these trials to be the result of sin, he urges souls who experience them to review their past life and make many general confessions, which is another crucifixion. The director does not understand that now perhaps is not the time for such an exercise.

Rather, it is a time for leaving these persons alone in the purgation God is allowing them, a time to give comfort and encouragement that they may desire to endure this suffering as long as God wills, for until then, no remedy, no matter what the person does, or the confessor says, is going to change things. [*Ascent of Mt. Carmel*]

> *Saint John of the Cross, Spanish cofounder (with Saint Teresa of Ávila) of the Discalced Carmelites, poet, 1542–91*

Some writers in the Christian tradition, though surprisingly few, have addressed themselves to the emotional complexities of the intimate personal relationship involved in spiritual direction.

An unfaithful spiritual director is like a bad hunting dog. Instead of bringing the rabbit to its Master, it devours the rabbit itself.

> [*Attributed to John Tauler*]
> *John Tauler, German Dominican preacher and mystical writer, 1300–1361*

Directors who rivet themselves on to souls are ordinarily the cause of far greater evil than they think. They deprive God of that which He would have received by His Son in those souls if they had been perfectly established in grace. Finding them attached to creatures, our Lord does not communicate Himself to them so abundantly. This is the reason why we see so little progress in them, so few graces and strong virtues, so little union with God, but, on the contrary, so much inconstancy, superficiality, and self-love. Directors who encourage such attachments, instead of being "men of God" are in reality "men of the Devil," since in place of destroying the enemies of Jesus Christ in hearts that He may reign there, they diminish His kingdom and increase that of His enemy, whose power over souls is always strengthened by these kind of attachments. . . . Spiritual directors have been chosen by Our Lord to go forth to conquer kingdoms, that is to say, the hearts of people, which belong to Him, which He has bought by the shedding of His Blood, and in which He wants to establish His reign. What ingratitude! What fraud! What outrage! What a betrayal! If instead of offering these persons to Him as to their lawful king, they establish themselves their lords and masters. . . .

Spiritual directors who seek for themselves the heart of their penitents are like a person recruited by a king to conquer a kingdom for him, and who, after receiving all the assistance necessary for this undertaking, would by a shameful betrayal steal this kingdom. They use for selfish purpose the word of God and the talents given to them by Our Lord for the explicit purpose of gaining hearts for Christ. What an ingratitude, what an infidelity, what a serious evil. This is equal to taking God's rightful place in a person. [*Complete Works*]

Jean-Jacques Olier, French priest and founder of the Society of Saint Sulpice, 1608–57

The wisdom, the restraint, the beauty of von Hügel as a spiritual director can be seen in his utmost respect for the uniqueness of the other person. Where so many other spiritual directors fail, he was a master; he let his students come into their own and to be separate from him. The Baron is very explicit about this.

Although it is difficult for a spiritual father to let his child grow up and become an equal, von Hügel realized well that without this pain and death there would be no spiritual growth. He writes to his niece: "To try and help on the life of another soul means, Dear, a specially large double death to self on the part of the life-bringing soul. For it means death to self before and in the communication."

[Letters from Baron Friedrich von Hügel to a Niece]
Baron Friedrich von Hügel, lay Catholic theologian and writer, 1852–1925

As regards himself, the director should aim at a very real and fundamental detachment from all things and people in themselves. Instances are common, far too common, of priests who, often with the best possible intentions, attach souls to themselves rather than to God, with disastrous consequences when the inevitable break comes. The relationship between confessor and penitent or director and directed is so intimate, being concerned with the deepest things of the spirit, that it creates a real bond between them, and when that bond is truly spiritual and in God, it is right and good; the difficulty is that it is apt to become, on the penitent's side at least, something merely emotional. This can be counteracted by real detachment on the part of the priest, who should also train his child in this fundamental austerity. [*The Elements of the Spiritual Life*]

Frederic P. Harton, English Anglican priest, 1889–1964

It is not surprising that so subtle a relation involves certain pitfalls and demands certain precautions; nor indeed that it is so frequently misunderstood. . . . The serious, sincere, and creative guidance of one Christian soul by another often gives rise to emotional aspects which are by no means unnatural or unhealthy. In fact some sense of trust, respect, and even affection, may add much to the strength and progress of both parties. On the other hand, here as in any other human relation, things occasionally go wrong. . . .

In the first place, I do not think the Church is very well served by a small group of priests and writers who insist that this relation is "impersonal"; it is untrue, it denies a great deal of tradition, and logically, of course, an impersonal relation between persons is a contradiction in terms. What is really meant by this evasion is that it is a special kind of relation; which is perfectly true if equally ambiguous.

A little progress is made by those who are bold enough to bring in the word Love, but, abused as this glorious word is, it still seems curious that the very first-fruits of the Christian religion should need so much apology. Christian love we are reminded is firstly the love of Christ for men, thence secondly, the love of men and women for one another in Christ; and it is something that demands will before emotion and service before feeling. That again is quite true, but it is more true than the evasive school cares to admit, for this familiar Christian teaching is concerned with priorities not alternatives; emotion, feeling, trust, and attraction are of minor importance, but they cannot be left out altogether. The crux of the matter seems to be that Christianity also teaches the solidarity of human personality wherein all experience contains elements of all our characteristics: mind, body, spirit, senses, emotion, feeling, will, and of course, sex.

Our pastoral relations go wrong because we do not try to understand and face up to them. The evil is not that a close pastoral relation of love is wrong, but that the scruples of the devil (and the newspapers) make us think that it might be. We become inhibited through ignorance and frustrated by un-Christian convention.

No one will quibble if I say that all pastoral relations are qualified by a "love of souls" but a "soul" is an embodied person not a disembodied "spirit" and the dangers of this common misinterpretation are twofold. First, an exaggerated fear of "attachment"—which St. Teresa bluntly calls scrupulous—gives rise to that unattractive clerical crust which laymen not unreasonably find hard to penetrate. Secondly, if some sort of relation is achieved it invariably hardens into a pompous authoritarianism wholly opposed to the warm domestic tone inherent in the English pastoral tradition. "By this shall all men know that ye are my disciples, if you have love one to another" suggests a perfectly obvious manifestation of love rather than a cold impersonal secret. Now we are incorporated into the glorified humanity of Christ by Baptism; we are made members of him and of one another. His humanity is full, perfect, and complete; all the relations and inter-relations are of God freely flowing to the whole world and to all persons. That is the universal aspect, but what of the personal and pastoral? What example does Christ give to us? . . . What then were his feelings, emotions, and reactions, when the beloved disciple rested his head on his breast at supper? and when Magdalene wept over his feet and caressed them with her hair? when he shed tears for Lazarus and embraced children? To call this "impersonal" is not only Puritan, not only Apollinarian, but blasphemous. [*Christian Proficiency*]
Martin Thornton, Anglican priest and theology professor, b. 1915

Friendship is perhaps the best model of the affective element of the master-disciple bond. In my own discussions with zen practitioners about their relationship with their roshi I have found that even in the apparently austere and formal interaction of roshi and student there is a deep affective bond. The love of a genuine master for his disciple is a love that frees, creates, and enables another. It does not bind another in emotional dependency. The master and disciple's affective energy is really focused on the divine, the numinous, the Absolute—the goal of the spiritual process, so there is a freeing factor at the heart of the relationship. Furthermore, since the master is a channel of God's love, there is a particular quality of depth, beauty and tenderness manifest in the affective quality pervading the lives of genuine masters. The human emotional bond acts as a kind of sacrament of divine love. There must be a deep joy in the master when he/she sees the spark of life grow in a new generation. "And now I call you friends, for I have given you everything I received from my father."

[*Abba: Guides to Wholeness and Holiness East and West*]
Sister Donald Corcoran, American Benedictine sister
and teacher, twentieth century

Chapter Six

DISCERNMENT

There came a woman of Samaria to draw water. Jesus said to her, "Give me a drink. . . ."

Jesus said to her, "Go, call your husband, and come here." The woman answered him, "I have no husband." Jesus said to her, "You are right in saying, 'I have no husband'; for you have had five husbands, and he whom you now have is not your husband; this you said truly." The woman said to him, "Sir, I perceive that you are a prophet. . . ." [*John 4:7, 16–19*]

Now there are varieties of gifts, but the same Spirit; . . . to another the working of miracle, to another prophecy, to another the ability to distinguish spirits, to another various kinds of tongues, to another the interpretation of tongues. [*1 Corinthians 12:4,10*]

But the fruit of the Spirit is love, joy, peace, patience, kindness, goodness, faithfulness, gentleness, self-control; against such there is no law. [*Galatians 5:22–23*]

Beloved, do not believe every spirit, but test the spirits to see whether they are of God; for many false prophets have gone out into the world.
[*1 John 4:1*]

Discernment is a key word in direction and no one becomes himself in faith until he develops this capacity. Just to allay the fears of the uninitiated—discernment is not simply a Jesuit technique. Discernment is as old as Scripture; it was practiced by the Fathers of the desert and all the spiritual masters throughout the centuries. It is to the credit of the Jesuit Order that they have preserved, developed and refined the patristic teaching and made it available in modern dress.

Discernment, in the Christian interpretation, is "the process by which we examine in the light of faith and in the connaturality of love, the nature of the spiritual states we experience in ourselves and in others. The purpose of such examination is to decide, as far as possible, which of the movements we experience lead to the Lord, and to a more perfect service of him and our brothers, and which deflect us from this goal." (E. Malatesta, ed., *Discernment of Spirits,*) This definition by Malatesta explains precisely what a director is trying to do.

He is involved in a process which requires time, knowledge, judgment, patience, and continuity. In the process, his spiritual life and that of the directee touch each other and slowly a new spirit is born within which both will see more clearly what God wants.

> [*The Spiritual Director*]
> *Damien Isabel, Franciscan theologian*
> *teaching in Chicago, twentieth century*

The necessity of discernment occurs when the external demands of a situation and moral and ethical norms do not make a choice clear. It is based on the assumption that reason alone is not adequate for discernment, since God also guides individuals through subjective experience. Consequently, it is important for people to become attuned to their psychic and spiritual states as they are instruments of discernment. The first group of selections in this chapter discusses the importance of self-awareness and self-knowledge as a foundation for discernment and the means by which the self-awareness grows in a person.

A spiritual director must aid another person in both a growth in self-awareness and in the actual process of discernment. The discerning capacity of a director has had two distinct emphases in the Christian tradition: one is the discernment of spirits (from the Greek

diakrisis pneumaton), *a special divine gift granting to certain in-*
dividuals unusual intuitive capacities; and the other is a learned,
rational capacity, (from the Latin discretio spirituum). *The latter*
has been considered a virtue, moderating other virtues, important
for confessors and directors in the Western church, while the gift of
discernment of spirits was honored in the early church, in Russian
Orthodoxy, and in numerous groups and individuals, including char-
ismatic groups today. In this tradition, the spiritual director's gift
is a charism. Both of these emphases are discussed in this chapter.
A couple of examples show a blending of intuitive capacities with
long experience and continuity with a person.

The chapter concludes with criteria for judging spirits. These cri-
teria are based on the effect the spirit has on the soul and personality
and on the fruits or lack thereof in a life. Since the criteria based on
the effect on the soul and personality depend on subjective experience,
the necessity of attunement to subjective states of the psyche and
spirit becomes clear.

One of the reasons people writing about spiritual direction have
insisted on the importance of the directee's openness to the director
in disclosing experiences and inner thoughts and feelings (see chapter
four) is the resulting awareness of subjective states and the increase
in self-knowledge. The first three selections speak of this process. The
remaining selections in this section describe the importance of self-
knowledge and self-awareness as a foundation for discernment and
spiritual growth.

Whatever is acquired by any supernatural means should immediately
be revealed clearly, totally, and simply to one's spiritual director. It
may seem that there is no serious reason to manifest this to one's
spiritual director, or that doing so would be a waste of time, since as
we stated earlier a soul is secure in not wanting these communications and in rejecting and not attending to them, especially in the
matter of visions, revelations, or other supernatural communications,
since it would not really make much difference if they were not clear.
Still, it is always important to reveal the entire communication,
though there is no clear reason for so doing. This requirement is
founded on three reasons:

First, the effect, clarity, validity, and security of many divine communications are not firmly established in a person, as pointed out

earlier, until the person discusses them with one whom God has established to be spiritual judge over him, one who has power to bind, loose, approve, and reprove. This principle is established by daily experience. We see humble recipients of these experiences get new contentment, strength, light, and security after freely discussing them with the proper person. This is so true that to many persons it seems that these communications are not theirs nor do they feel comfortable with them until they thoroughly discuss them. Only then do the communications seem again to be given by God.

Second, a person ordinarily needs instruction related to his experiences in order to be guided through the dark night to spiritual detachment and poverty. Without this instruction a person would unknowingly become hardened in the way of the spirit and accustomed to that of the senses, the way these communications are largely received by the person.

Third, for purposes of humility, obedience, and mortification, a person should give a complete account to his director, even when he disfavors or considers these communications worthless. Because these communications seem to be of little value, or because of concern about the director's possible reaction, some persons may be afraid to tell their director about them. This indicates a lack of humility, and for that very reason one should pursue this task fully. Others are hesitant to manifest these special graces because they do not want to appear to be saints due to these experiences, and because of other problems they experience in speaking about them. They think that because they themselves do not heed these experiences, a manifestation of them to their director is unnecessary. Because of this very difficulty they should mortify themselves and manifest it all to their director, and thereby become humble, simple, meek, and prompt in relating these communications. From this time on they will always do so with ease. [*Ascent of Mt. Carmel*]

> *Saint John of the Cross, Spanish cofounder (with Saint Teresa*
> *of Ávila) of the Discalced Carmelites, poet, 1542–91*

The spiritual father's gift of insight is exercised primarily through the practice known as "disclosure of thoughts" (logismoi). In early Eastern monasticism the young monk used to go daily to his father and lay before him all the thoughts which had come to him during

the day. This disclosure of thoughts includes far more than a confession of sins, since the novice also speaks of those ideas and impulses which may seem innocent to him, but in which the spiritual father may discern secret dangers or significant signs. Confession is retrospective, dealing with sins that have already occurred; the disclosure of thoughts, on the other hand, is prophylactic, for it lays bare our logismoi before they have led to sin and so deprives them of their power to harm. The purpose of the disclosure is not juridical, to secure absolution from guilt, but self-knowledge, that each may see himself as he truly is. [*The Spiritual Father in Orthodox Christianity*]
Kallistos Ware, member of the Greek Orthodox Church,
English priest-monk, twentieth century

Here is an even greater mystery: no one comes to know himself through introspection, or in the solitude of his personal diary. Rather it is in dialogue, in his meeting with other persons. It is only by expressing his convictions to others that he becomes really conscious of them. He who would see himself clearly must open up to a confidant freely chosen and worthy of such trust. It may be a friend just as easily as a doctor; it may also be one's marital partner.
[*To Understand Each Other*]
Paul Tournier, Swiss physician, twentieth century

Watchfulness, self-knowledge and discernment are the real guides of our souls. [*The Sayings of the Desert Fathers*]
Abba Poeman, Egyptian hermit

For Richard of Saint-Victor, Joseph in the Old Testament serves as a model of a person with discretion (see next section of this chapter). By Joseph we learn to know ourselves first before knowing God.

This Joseph continually instructs the person and at times leads him to full knowledge of himself, just as by his twin brother Benjamin he is at times lifted up to the contemplation of God. For just as the grace of discretion is implied by Joseph, so also grace of contemplation is implied by Benjamin. Both are born from this same mother because knowledge of God and of oneself are leaned from reason. Benjamin is born much later than Joseph because the person that has not been trained for a long period of time and not fully tutored in knowledge of self is not elevated to knowledge of God. He raises the eye of the heart in vain to see God when he is not fully prepared to see himself. Let a person first learn to know his own concealed reality before he considers himself capable of grasping invisible divine things. You must know the invisible things of your own spirit before you can be capable of knowing the invisible things of God. If you are not able to know yourself, how do you dare the audacity of grasping for those things which are beyond you? [*Benjamin Minor*]

Richard of Saint-Victor, theologian and prior of the abbey
of Saint-Victor in Paris, d. 1173

With clearest certitude I saw that it is quicker and easier for us to come to the knowledge of God than it is to know our own soul. Our soul is so deeply rooted in God and with unlimited value that we cannot come to knowledge of it until we first have knowledge of God, who is the Creator to whom it is joined. Nevertheless I did see that we need to desire wisely and truly from the fullness of our nature to know our own soul, through which we are taught to seek it where it is, and that is in God. By this leading through grace by the Holy Spirit we shall know them both in one; whether we are moved to know God or our soul, either movement is good and true. God is nearer to us than our own soul, for he is the foundation on which our soul rests, and he is the balance which keeps the substance and the feelings together, so that they will never come apart. For our soul relaxes in God in true rest, and our soul stands in God in true might, and our soul is naturally rooted in God in eternal love. Therefore if we want to have knowledge of our soul, and communion and converse with it, we must seek this in our Lord God in whom it dwells.

[*Revelations of Divine Love*]
Juliana of Norwich, anchoress in Norwich, England,
1342–1416 or 1423

This matter of self-knowledge must never be ignored. No soul on this road is such a super soul that it does not often need to become a nursing infant again. This should never be forgotten; I may repeat it again and again, for it is of great urgency. There is no state of prayer, no matter how high, in which it is not necessary often to go back to the beginning. And self-knowledge of our own sinfulness is the bread which must be eaten with food of every kind, no matter how delicious it is, on this road of prayer. Without this bread we could not eat our food at all. But bread must be taken in modest shares. When a soul finds itself totally worn out and clearly sees that it has no goodness of its own, when it feels ashamed in the presence of so great a King and sees how little it is paying for all that it owes Him, what purpose does it serve for it to waste its time on learning to know itself? It will be wiser to go on to other matters which the Lord brings to its attention, and we are not doing right if we neglect such things, for His Majesty knows better than we what kind of food is right for us. [*The Life of Teresa of Ávila*]

The example I gave seems to me a very good one for helping you to understand how glad Our Lord is when we get to know ourselves and always continue to realize our poverty and sinfulness, and to reflect that we possess nothing that we have not been given. Therefore, my sisters, courage is necessary for this and for many other things that happen to a person which the Lord has brought to this state [6th mansion]. To my mind, if the soul is humble, more courage is necessary for this last state than for any other. May the Lord grant us humility by his gracious goodness. [*Interior Castle*]

Saint Teresa of Ávila, Spanish founder of the reformed order of Discalced Carmelites, 1515–82

Accordingly, discernment of the presence and will of God is always complex and difficult, especially in a post-Enlightenment age which is at once critical not only of authority (as the first Enlightenment was) but also of the capacity of reason itself (as the second Enlightenment was). There is more to knowing, in other words, than reasoning alone. We are moved not only by external events but also by the dark and utterly mysterious world of the unconscious. To what extent do our emotions, our imagination, and the other affective faculties of human consciousness determine the judgments we make about the will of God for us, for others, for the world, and for history itself? To transcend the limitations of one's own vision and to begin to see reality against a wider horizon ("as God sees reality") is to experience conversion. [*Catholicism*]

Richard P. McBrien, American Catholic diocesan priest
and theologian, twentieth century

Granting that all the proper preliminary steps to discernment have been taken (basic commitment to Christianity, knowledge of objective norms relevant to a situation, etc.), how exactly does discernment take place? What is the formal nature of the process? To explain that it is necessary to reach to the very depths of religous anthropology, to come to a fundamental understanding of man before God. Drawing from the best of current religious anthropology (Rahner, Lonergan, etc.) we can note that there are two basic levels or rhythms to human existence. One of these levels or rhythms is the level of the particular concrete experiences which man has from day to day. The other level is the level of man's deepest subjectivity, of man's deepest self aware- ness before God. No particular human experiences would be possible for man were it not for this level of deepest self-awareness. It is a concomitant, often only implicit, in all human experiences. Now ob- viously, if a person is going to discern spirits, to understand how God is operating in various human motions, it is critically important that such a person become more conscious of his deepest self-awareness before God. Thus all discernment must be based upon an opening of man's consciousness to God, on man's grasping the very foundation of his personality as this personality is given to him by God.

[*Discernment of Spirits: A Theological Reflection*]
Philip S. Keane, American Sulpician priest, teacher,
and theologian, twentieth century

In this section on discernment in the director, there are descrip-
tions and examples of both the discernment of spirits and of
discretion.

Very important in the asceticism of Anthony was possessing the gift of discerning spirits. As I wrote earlier, he recognized their move- ments and he knew for which end each one of them had a desire and appetite. He not only did not suffer any derision from them, but he offered encouragement to those who were confused in their thinking and he taught them how they might destroy the plans of the devils by explaining the weaknesses and the deceits of the ones who perpetrated them. Each visitor, after being anointed for the battle by Anthony, came away acting boldly against the deceits of the devil and his demons. Many young women who had men considering marriage with them, when only seeing Anthony at a distance, would remain virgins for Christ. People also came to him from foreign lands, and having received his help like all the other people, they returned home as if they were sent on their way by a father. And now that he has died, they all feel the loss of a father and comfort one another just by the memory of him, holding on to his counsel and his admonitions of caution. [*Life of St. Anthony by St. Athanasius*]

> *Saint Anthony of Egypt, Egyptian hermit*
> *and spiritual master, c. 251–356*

Some brothers found Abba Anthony and told him about the visions they were having, in order to find out from him if they were true or if they were given by the demons. They had an ass which died on the way. When they reached the place where the old man was, he spoke to them before they could ask him anything, "How was it that the ass died on your journey to me?" They said, "How do you know about that, Father?" And he told them, "The demons showed me this." So they said, "That was why we journeyed here to ask you because we were afraid that we were being deceived, for we have visions which often happen to be true." Thus the old man convinced them by the example of the ass that their visions were from the demons alone. [*The Sayings of the Desert Fathers*]

> *Abba Anthony, Egyptian hermit, c. 251–356*

Anselm was inwardly more certainly enlightened with the light of wisdom and guided by his power of discernment, and he comprehended the characters of people of whatever sex or age so well that you may easily have seen him revealing to each person the secrets of his heart and exposing them to the light of day. Besides this he revealed the fountains and the very seeds and roots and process of growth of all virtues and sins. He made it clearer than light how virtue could be acquired and sin avoided or weakened. And you may have seen such power in every form of good counsel shine forth in him, so that it left no doubt that the spirit of counsel ruled in his heart. It is superfluous to say how ready and how industrious he was in holy discourse, for it is said that he wore out almost all his listeners, while he himself was tireless. [*Life of St. Anselm*]

Saint Anselm, Benedictine monk and
archbishop of Canterbury, 1033–1109

From a vision, Blessed Angela of Foligno gained a capacity for true judgment.

Concerning the fourth comforting appearance and vision, in which she saw God, as the Highest Wisdom and learnt from it how everything should be judged.

Having been requested by some one to pray to God on an occasion for certain things, which he wished to know, I doubted whether I should do so, because it seemed to me pride and foolishness to pray God for such things. As I was standing there thinking of this, suddenly my mind was lifted up, and at the first lifting up, it was placed by a table without beginning and without end, yet I was not seated there to look on the table itself, but on what was on the table. There I saw a certain unspeakable fullness of God, about which I can tell nothing, nor say anything at all, except that I saw the plenitude of the Wisdom of God and all Good.

Then I saw this plenitude of the Wisdom of God, and in it I saw that it was not permissible to ask about or to wish to know what the Wisdom of God will do, for this is to try to anticipate it, and dishonour it. Therefore, when I see persons asking about this, it appears to me, and I understand that they are in error. From that time on, and by what I saw on that table, namely, the Divine Wisdom, there has stayed with me the power of understanding and judging all spiritual persons and other spiritual things, when I hear them spoken of or discussed. I do not judge with that judgment with which I used to judge, and at the same time to be in error and sin; but with another and true judgment by which I understand from where I have come or can have the consciousness of sinning when I do it.

[*Book of Visions and Instructions*]
Blessed Angela of Foligno, married woman
and Franciscan tertiary, 1248–1309

Archimandrite Kallistos Ware of the Greek Orthodox Church writes that discernment is one of the gifts that particularly distinguish the spiritual father. Saint Seraphim of Sarov was a Russian monk, hermit, and starets who lived from 1759 to 1833.

The first is insight and discernment (diakrisis), the ability to perceive intuitively the secrets of another's heart, to understand the hidden depths of which the other is unawar. The spiritual father penetrates beneath the conventional gestures and attitudes whereby we conceal our true personality from others and from ourselves; and, beyond all these trivialities, he comes to grips with the unique person made in the imaghe and likeness of God. This power is spiritual rather than psychic,; it is not simply a kind of extra-sensory perception or a sanctified clairvoyance but the fruit of grace, presupposing concentrated prayer and an unremitting ascetic struggle. . . .

Endowed with discernment, the spiritual father does not merely wait for a person to reveal himself, but shows to the other thoughts hidden from him. When people came to St. Seraphim of Sarov, he often answered their difficulties before they had time to put their thoughts before him. On many occasions the answer at first seemed quite irrelevant, and even absurd and irresponsible; for what St. Seraphim answered was not the question his visitor had consciously in mind, but the one he ought to have been asking. In all this St. Seraphim relied on the inward light of the Holy Spirit. He found it important, he explained, not to work out in advance what he was going to say; in that case, his words would represent merely his own human judgment, which might well be in error, and not the judgment of God. [*The Spiritual Father in Orthodox Christianity*]

Kallistos Ware, member of the Greek Orthodox Church,
English priest-monk, twentieth century

A description of Thomas Merton.

Still, he had a secret prayer and this is what gave the inner life to all he said and wrote. His secret was his secret to himself to a great extent, but he was a skillful reader of the secret of the souls that sought his help. It was because of this that although we laughed at him, and with him, as we would a younger Brother, still we respected him as the spiritual father of our souls. [*Thomas Merton, Monk*]

> *Patrick Hart, Trappist monk, Thomas Merton's secretary*

When spiritual direction is conducted in an atmosphere of faith and prayer, silence will characterize the director. The silent guide is one who has not internalized the pressures of our society and who is not unconsciously seeking success, efficiency, control or competition with other directors. The director is the servant of God and he will be effective when he can say, "Here I am, Lord. I come to do your will." In the last analysis, he will not be able to discern the presence of God in the life of his directee unless God Himself open his heart and his mind. [*The Spiritual Director*]

> *Damien Isabel, Franciscan theologian*
> *teaching in Chicago, twentieth century*

The following selections describe discretion.

In Cassian's Conferences, *Abba Moses discusses discretion. The* Conferences *were derived from conferences or talks Cassian had heard years earlier in Egypt from the Egyptian masters and written to guide the newly developing monasticism in France.*

Abba Moses said true discretion is only made certain by true humility. The first proof of this humility is given by placing everything, not only what you do but also what you think, before the judgment of the elders, so as not to trust in your own judgment at all but to rest in their decisions in all points, and to acknowledge what ought to be considered good or bad by their customs. And this habit will not only teach a young man to walk in the right path through the true way of discretion, but will also keep him unharmed by all the crafty wiles and deceits of the enemy. For a person cannot possibly be deceived, who lives not by his own judgment but according to the example of the elders, nor will our devious enemy be able to misuse the ignorance of one who does not have the bad habit of false modesty, by concealing all the thoughts which rise in his heart. Rather he either leaves them or allows them to remain, according to the mature judgment of the elders. [*Conferences*]

John Cassian, Eastern ascetic influential in the formation of Western monasticism, 360–433

Prayerfully consider your zeal, your mercy, and also your discretion, which serves to moderate all these virtues. Prayerfully consider your way of forgiving and of righting wrongs, and in each incident watch how carefully you take into account means, place, and time. These three dimensions must certainly be considered in the exercise of these virtues, for without them, they will no longer be virtues. Indeed, it is not nature but exercise which brings to fruition virtues of this kind. These qualities are known to be essentially different. You can make them into sin by misusing or confusing them or turn them into virtues by using them properly and well. When the eye of discretion is blinded, it is normal for zeal and mercy each to seize a place for itself and possess it. Discretion is blinded by two realities, anger and excessive tenderness. The latter weakens decisions of judgment, the former forces them overboard. How can a balanced mercy or righteous zeal fail to be placed in jeopardy by either of these? An eye raging in anger sees nothing with compassion and one that is filled with a flood of weakness cannot see anything rightly. You will not be blameless if you punish a person who perhaps should have been spared, or if you spare a person who should have been castigated.

[*Five Books of Considerations*]
Saint Bernard of Clairvaux, Cistercian abbot, preacher, 1091–1153

For Richard of Saint-Victor, Joseph in the Old Testament serves as a model of a person with discretion. Richard of Saint-Victor taught that true discretion leads to contemplation.

Who does not know that the true good of the person can be neither developed nor retained without discretion? Thus that virtue is rightly and greatly loved without which nothing is searched after, nothing completed, nothing retained. . . .

Sharpness of reason is finely honed by discretion, from which it arises. The whole brotherly unity of virtues has limits determined by discretion. Any virtues that are not contented with his counsel or do not subject themselves to discretion himself quickly forfeit the name of virtue. It is he who does not disregard the things overlooked by his brothers. Discretion is the one who condemns their extremes.

Finally, it belongs to Joseph to consider with anticipation, to foresee cautiously, to grasp skillfully, to reveal quickly, and to condemn sharply not only this vice but any concealed and hidden evil. To the custody of Joseph belongs the care and keeping of all his brothers. To it belongs the discipline of each one. To it, the order of things to be done, to it, the anticipation of future things. It belongs to his custody to pay attention carefully and to discuss frequently how much progress the soul makes daily, or perhaps how much it fails to make; also by which thoughts it is assaulted more, by what affections it is more frequently drawn. Joseph himself ought to know perfectly not only the evils of the heart but also the weaknesses of the body, so that he requires that everyone seek health-preserving remedies and apply what is learned. He must know not only his evil ways but also the gifts of grace and the merits of virtues. He must distinguish diligently and reflect with inner skill on realities which are goods of nature and those realities which are gifts of grace. He ought to know like his hand what temptations the evil spirit fights him with and what consolations of spiritual joys he is filled with. How frequently the divine spirit visits him should be known, and although the spirit is one, he is neverthless not always affected in a uniform and identical way, but he is filled now with the spirit of wisdom, now with the spirit of understanding, now with the spirit of counsel, or any other of its manifestations. In order that I may briefly conclude, this Joseph of ours ought to know fully, insofar as this is possible, the full condition and quality of the inner and outer person and to search skillfully and to explore with care not only what kind of person he is but also even what kind of person he may be able to become.

[*Benjamin Minor*]
Richard of Saint-Victor, theologian and prior of the abbey
of Saint-Victor in Paris, d. 1173

The gift of discerning spirits is so necessary to a spiritual guide, that except thereby he be able to fit a soul with a sort and degree of prayer

suitable to her natural disposition, not tying all souls to begin according to any general methods (for none such can be prescribed but
will be prejudicial to some), and unless he teach how she may become
illuminated without him, by God alone, by the means of prayer and
abstraction of life (wherewith the mists of images and passions being
dispelled, a light will spring forth in the soul far more clear and
certain than any that can come from human instructions), not all the
instructions of men and angels, joined with all mortifications imaginable, will be able to bring a soul to contemplation. For seldom or
never doth God work contrary to our natural complexions; and till
souls come to exercises in spirit and prayer, infused by God alone,
they are far from contemplation.

Now at the first it is very hard for any director to know exactly the
secret inclinations of imperfect souls, which are so infinitely various;
and therefore, for the most part, their instructions about prayer and
attendance to divine inspirations must be general, the which the
disciples themselves must make a particular use of by observing their
own abilities and inclinations, and by marking what more particular
forms of prayer, etc., suit best with them and do them most good.
And this if they be not able in a reasonable manner to do, or if they
have not the courage to abide in a way in which they are put, it will
be in vain for them to proceed in those secret internal ways.

[*Holy Wisdom*]
Dom Augustine Baker, English Benedictine monk, 1575–1641

Judgment based upon a light given from heaven is a quality of only
a few people. . . . Therefore, we must seek another manner of discerning spirits, one which is both more common and available. It is
certainly a method which operates after the manner of an art and of
sound teaching. One examines the principles and effects of spiritual
movements, weighing carefully at the same time the rules prescribed
by the Holy Spirit in Sacred Scripture, and those principles which
have been handed down by the holy Fathers inspired by God, and
by other spiritual masters, who have learned from experience.

[*On Discernment of Spirits*]
John Cardinal Bona, Italian Cistercian abbot, 1609–74

The director should also be a prudent man—one who knows how to
apply the truths of the spiritual life in a concrete, practical way. He

is one who has the graced instinct of what is the really Christian thing to do in any given situation. He is one who can so act not only in his own life, but one who can assist the person directed to act likewise. He knows how to give prudent advice when necessary.

[The Spirit Is Present]
Edward Carter, American Jesuit priest, b. 1915

A number of authors have suggested criteria to aid in the process of beginning to learn what inner events and motions move us to choose loving actions within a Christian commitment and those that pull us astray.

The most important criteria have been considered to be the fruits. This section begins with statements to that effect. Then criteria for evaluating subjective influences of good and evil spirits follow. Today many people would not speak of evil spirits but of unconscious complexes and repressions negatively influencing our behavior, but the criteria are still helpful.

I am quite certain that no one will be fooled in this manner for a long time if he has a gift for the discernment of spirits and if the Lord has given him true humility. Such a person will discern these spirits by their fruits and their resolutions and their love, and the Lord will give him light to clearly see all of them. *[The Life of Teresa of Ávila]*

Saint Teresa of Ávila, Spanish founder of the reformed order of Discalced Carmelites, 1515–82

When charity is weak, spiritual vitality is weak also. It is a sign of spiritual malnutrition—some negligence in spiritual duties—or of the presence of venial sins and venial disorderly affections. From the degree of charity one may conclude the degree of perfection in general. *[The Ascetical Life]*

Pascal P. Parente, Italian-American diocesan priest and teacher of ascetical theology, 1890–1971

Direction frees us from the tyranny of feeling. Emotion plays a good, rightful, and important part in religious life, private prayer without any feeling at all would be unbearable for most of us, but emotion and feeling must be disciplined and understood. That is why all the great classics of the spiritual life contain large sections on "the discernment of spirits," to use the technical term. And in unique souls, each with his own characteristics and traits, feeling is the most capricious element of all. It would take volumes even to attempt a classification, but luckily we do not need volumes; we are served well enough for practical purposes by direction itself. The one vital point for us is simply this: it cannot be said too often that the only certain guide to spiritual progress is moral theology—we are making progress in prayer when we commit fewer sins. [*Christian Proficiency*]

Martin Thornton, Anglican priest
and theology professor, b. 1915

Discernment . . . is a gift given to the whole church, to both clergy and laity alike, and it is dependent on the collective wisdom of the whole church for its testing and verification. If we are to respond seriously to the unique gifts given to the church for its ministry, we are talking about discernment. For it is through the gift of discernment that we are able to identify gifts in ourselves and in others. If we are to respond seriously to the movements within the church calling us to a more disciplined spiritual life, we are again talking about the gift of discernment. For growth in the Spirit involves both our ability to see where the Spirit is leading us and our capacity to identify the presence of evil that stands in the way. Discernment is the gift of prophetic vision that moves Christian spirituality from sentiment to reality. [*Ministry and Solitude*]

James C. Fenhagen, American, Dean of General Theological
Seminary, former parish priest, b. 1929

The selections that follow give specific criteria for discernment.

With the help of God it is possible easily to distinguish the presence of the good and the bad. A genuine vision of the holy ones does not perturb. "He shall not protest and cry out; none will hear his voice." It happens so quietly and gently that joy and gladness and confidence are given birth immediately in the soul, for the Lord who is our joy, and the power of God the Father, is with his holy ones. The thoughts of the soul keep untroubled and calm, so that, enlightened within itself, it contemplates those who appear. A desire for the heavenly things to come takes possession of it, and it now wants to be completely united to them if it could leave with them. When some people, being human, are overcome with fear at the vision of good angels, the visitors immediately do away with fear by their love, as Gabriel did for Zachary, and the angel who appeared to the women at the holy sepulchre, and the angel that said to the shepherds in the Gospel, "Fear not." Their fear does not come out of littleness of spirit, but from the full knowledge of the presence of heavenly beings. This is what the vision of holy ones is like. [*Life of St. Anthony*]

Saint Anthony of Egypt, Egyptian hermit
and spiritual master, c. 251–356

Selections from Saint Ignatius of Loyola's rules for discernment. These rules are for a more exact manner of distinguishing between different spiritual influences:

The usual effect produced by God and His angels in their spiritual actions is a genuine lightness of heart and spiritual joy, abolishing every disquieting sadness produced by the enemy, while his usual activity is to prevent such joy of heart and spiritual comfort, assigning false causes, subtle suggestions, and limitless falsehoods.

Spiritual peace with no prior occasion causing it comes from our Lord God alone. It is the Creator's privilege to come into and leave the soul, to move it with inspirations of love for His Divine Majesty. "With no prior occasion" means without any previous awareness or knowledge of anything which might cause such peace in the soul, by means of its own acts of intellect and will. . . .

We should pay much attention to the whole line of thought. If beginning, middle, and end are altogether healthy, tending to what is completely innocent, this is a sign of the good angel. The line of thought suggested sometimes leads to something that is bad, or at least confusing, or less good than what the person had previously wanted to do. Occasionally it erodes our strength of mind or disturbs us by destroying our peace and tranquillity of mind and the undisturbed state already present in us. These are clear signs that the thoughts come from the evil spirit, the enemy of our growth and our eternal life. . . .

When persons are advancing from good to better, the touch of the good angel is soft, light, and gentle, like a drop of water being absorbed by a sponge. The touch of the evil angel is rough, accompanied by noise and disturbance, like a drop of water hitting a rock. But their action is the opposite with those who are going from bad to worse. The reason is that the state of soul is either in contrast or exactly alike these angels. When it is contrary they make their way in with noticeable noise and feeling. When it is like theirs they come in quietly, like a person entering his own home when the door is open.

[*The Spiritual Exercises*]
Ignatius of Loyola, Spanish founder of the
Society of Jesus, 1495–1556

Among the things that you need to notice, which are happening in the soul, the principal one is whether they leave the soul more humble than before. Because humility, as a teacher says, has such weight among the spiritual coins it is easily distinguished from the false and light coins. According to St. Gregory, an obvious sign of the chosen ones is humility, and of the reprobate it is pride. Note well, then, what special impression remains on your soul of the vision, or the consolation, or the spiritual experience. Do you see yourself staying more humble and contrite because of your faults, and with greater reverence and fear of the infinite wonder of God? Do you overcome imprudent desires to communicate to other persons that which has happened to you, and do not occupy yourself by reflecting a lot on it or paying attention to it, but rather try to put it out of your mind as something that might bring esteem to you? . . .

In anything that may happen to you, however good it may seem, whether it be tears, or consolation, or knowledge of the things of God, and even if you may be taken up to the third heaven, if your soul does not remain in profound humility, do not put faith in it nor hold on to it. The higher a thing is, the more dangerous it is; and your fall will be the greater. Ask this grace of God, for you to know yourself and to humble yourself, and above all, that He give you that which may be for His service. Indeed, lacking this, everything else however precious it may seem is not gold but tinsel, not the bread which supports you, but the ashes of frivolity. This evil is pride, which despoils the soul of the true grace of God, and if it leaves you some good, they are false goods, for they do not please God and may be the occasion, for the one who has them, of having a greater fall. We read about our Redeemer, when He appeared to his disciples on the day of His Ascension, that first He reprimanded them for the unbelief and hardness of heart, and afterwards He ordered them to go and preach, giving them power to perform many and great miracles. He also gives them to understand that the one whom He lifts up to great things, He first brings down, making him recognize his own weaknesses, so that even though he may fly to the heavens, he may remain aware of his own lowliness without power to attribute to himself anything except his own unworthiness. . . .

Let the substance of all this, then, be that you keep in mind the effects of those things working in you, not to be your own judge of them, but to inform the one who is to give you counsel and then to take his advice. [*Hear, O Daughter*]

Saint John of Ávila, Spanish diocesan priest, 1500–1569

In the next two selections, Saint John of the Cross describes the difference between visions and locutions caused by the devil and those caused by God.

There is a great difference between those visions which come from the devil and those that are of God. For the effects produced in the soul by the Devil's vision are not the same as those produced by good visions. The visions of the Devil produce dryness of soul as to communion with God and a tendency to regard self too highly, and to receive and believe in these and in no way do they bring about the gentleness of humility and love of God. The forms of these visions do not stay impressed upon the soul with the peace and light of the others. They do not remain, but are quickly erased from the soul, except when the soul greatly regards them, so that this excessive regard for self causes it to recall them naturally, but with much dryness of soul, and without giving the effect of love and humility which is produced by good visions when the soul brings them to memory. [*Ascent of Mt. Carmel*]

Locutions caused by the Devil can sometimes be difficult to discern and recognize. Usually, they leave the will in dryness in regard to the love of God, and the intellect inclined toward pride and self-esteem or even smugness. Nevertheless, they can produce a false humility and a false fervor of the will rooted in self-love. A person, as a result of this, will have to be very spiritual to discern this. The Devil causes these false apparent virtues so that he may be more deceiving. So that he may establish in people the attachments he desires them to have, he is a master at causing false tears from the feelings he introduces. He always tries to prod the will toward a regard for these inner communications so that it might dedicate and hold itself bound with things that instead of increasing real virtues cause the loss of spiritual progress already experienced. [*Ascent of Mt. Carmel*]

> *Saint John of the Cross, Spanish cofounder (with Saint Teresa of Ávila) of the Discalced Carmelites, poet, 1542–91*

The three best and most certain characteristics of lawful inspirations are perseverance, against instability and frivolity. Inner peace and gentleness of heart, against nervousness and anxiety and humble obedience, against hardness of heart and dissipation are the other two. [*Treatise on the Love of God*]

> *Saint Francis de Sales, French bishop and theoretician of spiritual direction, 1567–1622*

Jonathan Edwards prepared a remarkable list and description of the distinguishing signs of truly gracious and holy affections from which we quote in part. By gracious and holy affections he refers to those affections that arise from "those influences and operations on the heart which are spiritual, supernatural and divine."

The primary impartial basis for gracious affections, is the surpassingly excellent and amiable nature of divine favors, as they are in themselves, and not any imaginative relation they may bear to self or to self-interest. . . .

Truly gracious affections are accompanied by a conviction of the reality and certainty of divine things, as they are in themselves; and not any conceived relation they bear to self, or self-interest.

Gracious affections are accompanied by evangelical humility. Some, who think themselves quite free of self, confident that they are as low as the dust, are full as they can be with the glory of their own humility, and lifted up to heaven with a high opinion of their abasement. . . . The deceitfulness of the heart of a person appears in no one thing so much, as that of spiritual pride and self-righteousness. . . .

Such is the nature of grace, and of true spiritual light, that they naturally dispose the saints in the present state, to look only a little upon their grace and goodness, and a great while on their deformity. . . .

Another thing, wherein gracious affections are distinguished from others, is, that they are accompanied by a change of nature.

Other power may make a great change in people's present condition and feelings, but it is the power of a Creator only that can change the nature. No discoveries or illuminations, but those that are divine and supernatural, will have this supernatural effect. This is the effect all those discoveries have, which are truly divine. The soul is deeply affected by these discoveries; so affected as to be transformed.

Therefore, if there is no great and remarkable lasting change in persons, who think they have experienced a work of conversion, vain are all their imagination and pretenses, however they may have been affected. . . .

Truly gracious affections differ from those that are false and delusive, in that they naturally beget and promote such a spirit of love, meekness, quietness, forgiveness, and mercy, as appeared in Christ. . . .

Another great and very distinguishing difference is, that the higher gracious affections are raised, the more is a spiritual appetite and longing of soul after spiritual attainments increased. On the contrary, false affections rest satisfied in themselves. . . .

Gracious and holy affections have their exercise and fruit in Christian practice. . . .

Christian practice is a distinguishing and secure evidence of grace to persons' own consciences.

> [*A Treatise Concerning Religious Affections*]
> *Jonathan Edwards, American theologian and*
> *Calvinist preacher and pastor, 1703–58*

Rufus Jones describes the effects of mystical experience.

It is a notable fact that their experiences, and their stabilized faith through what they believe to be their contacts with God, in many cases, in fact usually, result in a unification of personality, in a great increase of dynamic quality—a power to stand the universe—and in a recovery of health and normality. While it must be admitted that this pathological factor, which cannot be ignored, presents an element of liability in the mystic's testimony, there nevertheless seems to me on the whole to be an overwhelming balance of asset in favor of the significance of the mystic's life and message. Hysteria does not unify and construct life as mystical experience indubitably does do.

[*The Flowering of Mysticism*]
Rufus M. Jones, Quaker teacher and a founder of the American Friends Service Committee, 1863–1948

Reference to the experience of God and of Jesus leads us to a final criterion which Christian tradition has seen as one of the paramount tests by which people are able to decide whether it is God who is leading them in a particular situation. It can be summarized with the question, "Is it like God?" or "Is it like what Jesus would do?" We can readily find that the point of these questions gets blunted by hermeneutical consideration or by adherence to a purely external model. However, if the questions are used appropriately they can be of crucial help in determining what is of God. An example of appropriate use of these questions is found in *The Life of Saint Martin*, a fourth century work of hagiography. Martin has a vision and has to decide whether the vision is really from the Lord. He decides that it is not because the figure of Jesus in the vision is dressed in the raiment of a Roman imperator. Martin's conclusion is, "I will believe that Christ has come only when I see him wearing the garments of the Passion." [*The Practice of Spiritual Direction*]

William A. Barry and William J. Connolly, members of the Society of Jesus, teachers of spiritual directors, twentieth century.

Chapter Seven

PERSONAL TEACHINGS

And Jesus looking upon him loved him, and said to him, "You lack one thing; go, sell what you have, and give to the poor, and you will have treasure in heaven; come, follow me." At that saying his countenance fell, and he went away sorrowful; for he had great possessions. [*Mark 10:21–22*]

But as for you, continue in what you have learned and have firmly believed, knowing from whom you learned it and how from childhood you have been acquainted with the sacred writings which are able to instruct you for salvation through faith in Christ Jesus.

[*2 Timothy 3:14–15*]

An important role of the spiritual director is one-to-one trans-mission of the tradition as it applies to the personal situation and need of the directee. It is in letters and other writings to particular individuals that we see this personal teaching and evocation of truth and new life. We have chosen mostly letters because they illustrate personal teaching with particular clarity. The selections were chosen to illustrate the director's role as teacher, comforter, and encourager, and occasional admonisher.

A brother asked Abba Joseph, saying, "What ought I do, since I do not have the strength to undergo evil, nor to work for alms?" The old man said to him, "If you cannot do any of these things, do keep watch over your conscience against all evil in regard to your neighbour and you will save your soul." [*The Sayings of the Desert Fathers*]
> *Abba Joseph in Panepho, a hermit with a few disciples*
> *in Panephysis, fourth century*

One of the spiritual fathers speaking about the Cells, said there was once an industrious old man there who was clothed with a mat. He went to find Abba Ammonas, who, when he saw him wearing the mat, said to him, "This mat will not help you!" But the old man questioned him in the following way, "Three thoughts demand my attention, either, should I go about in the deserts, or should I travel to a far-off land where no one knows me, or should I close myself off in a cell without opening the door to anyone, eating only every other day." Abba Ammonas told him, "It is not proper for you to act on any of these three things. You should sit in your cell and eat a little every day, keeping the word of the publican always in your heart, and you will save your soul." [*The Sayings of the Desert Fathers*]
> *Abba Ammonas, a disciple of Anthony at Nitria*
> *who later became a bishop, c. 350*

To his literary spiritual child, Theotimus, Francis de Sales gives this counsel:

The choice of one's vocation, the plan of some business undertaking of great consequence, of some work demanding much time, of some very large expenditure, the change of home, the choice of associations, and the like, deserve to be seriously reflected on, in order to see what is most pleasing to the will of God. But in little daily matters, in which even a mistake is not of serious consequence nor irreparable, what need is there to make a business of them, to scrutinize them, or to pester someone for counsel about them? For what purpose should I put myself on the rack to learn whether God would rather that I should say the Rosary or Our Lady's Office, since there is no difference between them, that a big testing should be held. Or should I go to visit the sick in the hospital or to Vespers, or should I go to a sermon or to a church where there is an Indulgence? Really there is no importance in the one more than the other that it is worthwhile to take any great deliberation. We must walk in good faith and without minuscule deliberations in such matters, and, as St. Basil says, freely choose what we like, so as not to tear down our spirit, lose time, or put ourselves in danger of losing our peace or becoming scrupulous and superstitious. But I mean always where there is no great disproportion between two actions, and where there is nothing to deliberate over on one side more than on the other.

[*Treatise on the Love of God*]
Saint Francis de Sales, French bishop and theoretician
of spiritual direction, 1567–1622

Blessed Claude de la Colombière writes in a letter:

I am not amazed at those persons who fear confession because they do not want to give up their sins, as I am at those who fear it because they are fearful of revealing their sins. The proof that the latter is a temptation is that it is to be found in people who are not known to the confessor and in those whom he will never know. What does the priest know after the confession, except that there is a person who has committed sin? You give yourself no more danger than if you confessed to a statue. The more the confessor knows you the more he will reverence you. The greater difficulty you have, the more he will treasure the confidence you have in him and be touched that you have told him the one thing in the world you would naturally desire to keep secret. The worse the sin is, and the better the confessor knows you, the more your reward will be. If he is a reasonable person, the more he must revere you. He will admire you, if he has feelings at all like those of God and the angels, who see your humility with joy and wonder. What insanity it would be for a confessor to convict you in his heart when God absolves you and fills you with his grace. If he is un-Christian and a fool he will have such feelings, but if he is reasonable and a man of faith he will admire you and praise God while humbling himself. [*Spiritual Direction*]

> *Blessed Claude de la Colombière,*
> *Jesuit preacher, 1642–82*

You seem to apprehend that I believe religion to be inconsistent with cheerfulness and with a sociable, friendly temper. So far from it, that I am convinced, as true religion or holiness cannot be without cheerfulness, so steady or true religion. And I am equally convinced that true religion has nothing sour, austere, unsociable, unfriendly in it; but, on the contrary, implies the most winning sweetness, the most amiable softness and gentleness. Are you for having as much cheerfulness as you can? So am I. Do you endeavor to keep alive your taste for all the truly innocent pleasure of life? So do I likewise. Do you refuse no pleasure but what is an hindrance to some greater good or has a tendency to some evil? It is my very rule; and I know no other by which a sincere, reasonable Christian can be guided. In particular, I pursue this rule in eating, which I seldom do without much pleasure. And this I know is the will of God concerning me: that I should enjoy every pleasure that leads to my taking pleasure in Him, and in such a measure as most leads to it. [*Letters to Mrs. Chapman*]

> *John Wesley, founder of Methodism, 1703–91*

A letter answering a monk who suffered from the spirit of accidie:

I learn from your letter that you have been bothered by the spirit of depression. This is a terrible sorrow, against which Christians seeking salvation must struggle valiantly. Depression bothers persons who have bread and other things of necessity ready at hand. How much the more, then, does it attack those who live in solitude? I recommend the following things to you:

1. Urge yourself, force yourself, to prayer and all kinds of good works, no matter how contrary they may be to your mood. . . . Seeing your efforts and your labor, God will give you zeal and desire. Good

habits create this desire, and, it might be said, lead us toward prayer and good actions. Learn to develop this habit, and it will pull you to prayer and good actions.

2. Enthusiasm is also developed by a variety in our tasks, i.e., by turning from one task to another. This you must do as follows: pray, then do some manual work, then read a book, then prayerfully reflect on your spiritual situation, on eternal salvation, etc. Do these things by turns. If depression grasps you fiercely, leave your room, and walking up and down, prayerfully reflect on Christ. Elevate your mind to God and pray. Depression will then leave you.

3. The thought of death, which may perhaps cross your mind, the thought of Christ's judgment, of eternal punishment and of eternal joy do away with depression. Prayerfully reflect on these things.

4. Pray and groan, pleading with God Himself to grant you enthusiasm and desire. Without God we are good for no work at all.

If you follow these four admonitions, believe me, little by little you will receive enthusiasm and desire. God looks to us for labor and courageous actions. He has promised to be with those who labor.

[Letters of St. Tikhon]
Saint Tikhon of Zadonsk, Russian bishop, then monk
at the monastery of Zadonsk, 1724–83

Saint Madeleine Sophie Barat writes to one of her sisters in the Society of the Sacred Heart:

Paris, February 15, 1852
Dear Mother, make every effort to avoid a pitfall which often fools persons, who by their vocation and their profession, must observe and deal with a great amount of business. . . . If such a person looks at the excuses her occupations give her, she will get involved entirely with exterior works and her prayer life will easily be ignored. Little by little she will lose the spirit of prayer and her desire for it. Lack of purpose and distractions will take over the powers of her soul. Prayer will become a burden to her in place of being a satisfaction. Dryness will come, and it will be all the more difficult to accept because it will be the penalty imposed by an excessively active and busy life. If crosses and set-backs come she accepts them, of course, but bears them with difficulty and with great resistance because her

nature has not been sufficiently mortified, and because she has given too much attention to work and not enough to reflection and prayer which is an absolute necessity for a religious who must interact with other people.

Truthfully, dear Mother and daughter, by speaking about these problems to you I am far from implying that they are your own. My purpose is only to give you adequate warning against the illusion very common among persons who are involved in deeds of mercy, even religious. For it is certain that our calling to religion is, or should be, as contemplative as it is active.

[St. Madeleine Sophie: Her Life and Letters]
Saint Madeleine Sophie Barat, French founder of the Society of the Sacred Heart, 1779–1865

To a lady: [*Letter #79*]

You are acting like the silkworms who allow no stone to remain unturned in making themselves a prison and in smothering under the folds and layers of the little thread of their silk. Scrupulosity comes from too much attention given to everything one does, to all which one says, to all one thinks. It is a sickness of ceaselessly needing to judge oneself, and to judge the first judgment, then the second, then the third, and on and on. You give birth to that which has no end, like the silk thread of the silkworm. This is the distortion of good conscience, but it is certainly not a conscience. . . . In practice, my dear child, ride roughshod over these little ideas which have no basis in reality. Here is the cure. Since you know that you are scrupulous, treat yourself as scrupulous, and always give yourself the benefit of the doubt, when there is not complete certainty that you have freely chosen a bad action. [*Letters to his Spiritual Children*]
Msgr. Louis-Gaston de Ségur, blind Parisian priest, 1820–81

To a friend:

Yes, I do know about the hungry feeling that one wants something, impossible to say what; . . . and I think it is one of the deepest things in us. Isn't it (although we do not call it that at the time) the thirst for God, because we know so well that nothing less will satisfy us;

and the problem of the way to get what we want, and the knowledge that we can only partially reach it in this life, is the aching part of it.

But I am sure that it is meant to be thus, if anything could satisfy us down here we should be very small and tame indeed, and that profound discontent is the best thing about us, if we find out the right use of it. It is the thirst for the strong living God which makes contemplatives, and the fire which makes apostles, and it is only when we use it badly that it turns back on ourselves and makes us really unhappy.

I hope and believe that you will never be really unhappy. To be friends with God is the deepest spring of joy, and you have that, so I can only wish that you may have it more and more.

[*Life and Letters of Janet Erskine Stuart*]

September 1912

. . . I must write you a few lines to say a few things which I left unsaid for want of time when there was so much to say. It was this, and your letter brings it to my mind again, that when one gets into quite new circumstances and surroundings, among complete strangers, there is necessarily a moment—a period—of very great loneliness, before there is any new interest or stimulus on the human side or any new ties.

This is hard to go through, but precious supernaturally, it is the spiritual leisure which is more important for your soul's life. It is soul first, and everything that is not as you would wish or plan is to the good on that side; renunciation, disengagement from self, all the real "spiritual exercises" on which our life is strengthened. And in that solitude your friendship with God must ripen, and your soul grow strong.

So do not fret at the thousand and one things that will be contrary, but enter into them and learn through them, if not from them. . . . Pray quietly and constantly; now you know God better you must keep very close to Him, talk to Him of every trouble or joy or aspiration or knock-down and be very sweet to everyone.

[*Life and Letters of Janet Erskine Stuart*]
Janet Erskine Stuart, superior general of the Society
of the Sacred Heart, 1857–1914

Friedrich von Hügel wrote to his niece:

My most dear Gwen,   7 *April 1919.*

Your letter has set me thinking—rethinking your mind and soul, and how best quietly to feed and help them. I wanted to write an answer on Saturday, and then today. But my last four or five nights have been, upon the whole, so bad that I dare not yet write directly about your very important and delicate points, since, when I am in such "encompote" condition, such letter-writing means further bad nights. I will write as soon as I can. This is only a scribble, lest my silence were to end in making you fear indifference or offendedness on my part—neither of which would be at all the case.

I wonder whether you realize a deep, great fact? That souls—all human souls—are deeply interconnected? That, I mean, we can not only pray for each other, but suffer for each other? That these long, trying wakings, that I was able to offer them to God and to Christ for my Gwen-child—that He might ever strengthen, sweeten, steady her in her true, simple, humble love and dependence upon Him? Nothing is more real than this interconnection—this gracious power put by God Himself into the very heart of our infirmities. . . . And, my little Gwen, it is the Church (which, improperly understood, "dumbs" my little old, bewildered Child)—it is the Church which, at its best and deepest, is just that—that interdependence of all the broken and the meek, all the self-oblivion, all the reaching-out to God and souls.

[*Letters from Baron Friedrich von Hügel to a Niece*]

From letter of 17 February 1920.

My darling Child,   *Shrove Tuesday.*

I want this letter to reach you on Ash Wednesday, when we all start Lent, because there is one little practice I should like to dwell upon for a minute, in case you have not yet waked up to it, or that you require, perhaps, a little encouragement in it. I mean the practice of some little voluntary renunciation. I know well, of course, my Gwen, how much vague and airy wisdom oozes out of the comfortable and shallow modern mind about this. But then you see, we have the little (!) examples of the Baptist in the wilderness, with his wild honey and locusts meal; Our Lord's Fast of forty days; St. Paul's mastery of his body; and really, without a break, the asceticism of all the great saints. I say this not to suggest anything special in your food, sleep or dress; and as to the amount of church, half an hour a day will be enough, and it would be unwise to add to it, even in Lent. But I am thinking of something without thinking what—that would correspond, say, to my not buying any books for myself during Lent. Depend upon it, such little self-checks—checks on good propensions, and checks self-imposed—where they spring from love, really feed love. They are good things and still useful to your spiritual growth.

[*Letters from Baron Friedrich von Hügel to a Niece*]

Loving old,
Father-Uncle.

To a young girl on her Confirmation in the Church of England:
April 11, 1922

I know that you are to be confirmed tomorrow, and I feel an inward pressure to write you a little letter on this important step in your life. If you were engaged to be married, I would certainly write to you; so why should I not about an act, different indeed, but not necessarily less important?

Let me then go back in my mind to when I was your own age, and try to get on to paper one predominant desire which then came into my own inner life. You see, when I began to try to be good—to serve God—I already, alas, found myself involved in gravely bad habits and inclinations. But this, once I was, by God's grace, awakened to long to be straight and true—to go direct to God and Christ—had one great advantage. I saw young fellows all round me fretting to be free, to be their own sole, full masters. They fretted against this and that thing; against this and that person. They thought if only they could get away from these, they would be free. But I myself could not feel that to be nearly enough; I was too little happy in myself to fiddle-faddle at such little things! I wanted, I had to, get rid of—not those outside conditions, not those other people and their orders, etc.: but I had, somehow, to become free from self, from my poor, shabby, bad, all-spoiling self! There lay freedom, there lay happiness! And I see now at 70, more clearly again than at 17, that I was right there. That all external things, all persons, even if and when they may be not to our natural liking, that they none can really hurt us—indeed, that they all of them can readily help us, once we are awake, spiritually awake; and that our service of God really means for us the fighting of self. Of course God's service includes also our service of others— our relations, our friends. [*Spiritual Counsel and Letters*]

Baron Friedrich von Hügel, lay Catholic theologian and writer, 1852–1925

Letters on Prayer

Recalling your request and my promise to write you concerning prayer to God, whenever the time and opportunity given to me by the gift of Him to whom we pray, I should have paid my debt earlier and given my response to your loving desire in the charity of Christ. I have too few words to express my joy on receiving your request, which proved to me how much importance you give to this great duty. What activity is more proper for your widowhood than to persevere in prayer night and day, according to the counsel of St. Paul? As you know, he says: "But she that is a widow indeed and desolate, has trusted in the Lord and continues in prayers night and day." It might appear a bit unusual, since you are a noble woman in this world, as well as rich and the mother of such a large family, and not left desolate, although a widow, that the attraction of prayer should impress itself so deep in your spirit and compel you to pay attention to it, but you have a wise understanding of the fact that no person can be free of danger in this world and in this life. . . .

So, then, that you may continue in prayers night and day, until that consolation comes to you, remember that you are alone and desolate, no matter how well off you may be with worldly wealth. The Apostle did not say that this gift was to be given to just any widow, but he says: "She that is a widow indeed and desolate, has trusted in the Lord, and continues in prayers night and day." . . . The more fervent the desire, the more worthy the effect which follows. And that is why the Apostle says: "Desire without ceasing." Let us, then, always desire this gift from the Lord God and always pray for it. Since this desire grows a bit tepid by reason of our cares and daily absorption with other things, we bring our mind back to the duty of praying at fixed hours, and we give encouragement to ourselves in the words of our prayer to move forward to what we desire. If we do not do this, after our desire has begun to become tepid, it then becomes entirely cold and totally goes out unless it is frequently fired up again. . . .

Certainly, you will also remember to pray fervently for me, for I do not wish you, out of deference to the position which I occupy, to my own peril, to refuse me the help which I personally acknowledge as essential for me. [*Sermons*]

Saint Augustine, bishop of Hippo, 354–430

Dear Master Peter:

I shall explain to you as well as I know how what I myself do when I pray. May our Lord God help you and others to do it better. Amen.

First of all, when I feel that I have become cold and reluctant to pray because of my absorption with other thoughts and matters (for the flesh and the devil always stop and impede prayer) I take my little Psalter and go to my room. If it is during the day and there is the opportunity to join people in the church, I begin to repeat to myself the Ten Commandments, the Creed, and, if I have time, some teaching of Christ or verses from Paul and the Psalms. I do all this in a way like that of children. . . .

It is a good practice to make prayer the first order of the morning and the last at night. Carefully watch out for false and deceptive thoughts which say: "Wait awhile. I shall pray in an hour or so. I must first look after this important matter." Such thoughts will lead away from prayer and will entangle you in other matters which will so demand your attention that nothing will happen in your prayers that day. . . .

When your heart is made warm by prayerful reflection and you are fully present to yourself, kneel down or stand with folded hands, lift up your eyes to heaven, and speak or say quietly to yourself as simply as you can, "Dear God, Heavenly Father, I am a poor, unworthy sinner. I am not worthy to lift up my eyes or hands to you in prayer. But insofar as you have commanded us all to pray, you promised to hear us when we pray, and through your dear Son, our Lord Jesus Christ, have taught us both how and what to pray. At your command I come before you obediently, depending on your loving promise, and in the name of My Lord Jesus Christ pray with all your saints or

Christians on earth as he taught us, 'Our Father who art in heaven,' "
etc., going on word for word to the conclusion.

After this, repeat a part of this prayer, or as much as you want to.
For example, repeat the first petition, "Hallowed be your name," and
say: "Yes, Lord God, dear Father, you do hallow your name in us and
in all the world. Pull up and destroy the hatreds, self-worshiping. . . ."

My purpose is to rouse up and instruct your heart so that you may
know what thoughts to hold on to in the Lord's Prayer. When your
heart is properly warmed and in a mood for prayer, you may express
your inner thoughts with different words and perhaps with fewer
words or more. I do not bind myself to such words and phrases, but
use one form of words today and another tomorrow according to my
need and mood. However, I keep as closely as I can to the same
thoughts and meaning. It sometimes occurs to me that I get lost in
the rich thoughts of one part or petition and then I let the other six
wait. When such rich and good thoughts come, one should let the
other prayers rest, give place to these thoughts, listen quietly, and
in no way create a hindrance, for the Holy Spirit himself is preaching
here, and one word of his preaching is better than a thousand words
of our praying. In this manner I have often learned more in one
prayer than I have been able to glean from much reading and
reflection. . . .

Briefly, this is the way which I usually use the Lord's Prayer for
prayer. To this day I am still nursing myself on the Lord's Prayer like
a child and am still eating and drinking of it like an old man without
getting bored with it. I regard it as the best of prayers, superior even
to the Psalter, which I am very fond of. It was truly composed and
taught by the real Master. What a pity it is that such a prayer by such
a Master should be stammered and chattered so thoughtlessly
throughout the world. Many people probably repeat the Lord's Prayer
several thousand times a year, and if they pray like this for a thousand
years, they will not have savored or prayed a tiny speck of it. The
Lord's Prayer, along with God's name and the Word of God, is the
greatest victim on earth, for everybody abuses and punishes it while
few console and give joy to it by using it rightly.

When I have the time and the chance to move on beyond the Lord's
Prayer, I similarly reflect on the Ten Commandments, taking up one
part after another until I am as ready as possible for prayer. From

each Commandment I make a wreath of four braids. First of all, I take each Commandment as a teaching, which is what it really is, and reflect on what our Lord God truly expects of me from it. Secondly, I make a thanksgiving of it. Thirdly, a confession. Fourthly, a prayer. . . .

I shall not explain the Creed or the Scriptures here, for that would be endless. Anyone who is used to it can take the Ten Commandments one day and a psalm or chapter of the Bible the next day and with this fine producing stone he can bring fire to his soul.

[*Letters of Spiritual Counsel*]
Martin Luther, theologian and Protestant reformer, 1483–1546

To a lady who recently came under his direction:

. . . You tell me that you can do nothing in prayer. But what would you do different from the present except over and again to lay your nothingness and misery before God? Beggars usually think they can make no more touching claim to charitable persons than to show their sores and their afflictions. Sometimes, however, you do not even do this, you say, but you are as cold and paralyzed as a statue. Well, even that is something. In royal courts we often find statues which serve no purpose except that they please the prince's eye. Be satisfied to stand that way in God's Presence, and let Him bring the statue to life when He sees fit. Trees cannot bear fruit unless the sun's warmth nurtures them. Some bear fruit earlier than others, according to their nature. Let us consider ourselves happy if we but stand before God, and wait patiently to bear fruit sooner or later; every day, or on rare occasions according to His Holy Will, to which we must subject ourselves totally. [*Letters*]

Saint Francis de Sales, French bishop and theoretician
of spiritual direction, 1567–1622

A letter of spiritual counsel to widow Hemmings:

Friend, doubts and scruples may easily arise in the minds of persons concerning prayer, as they come to any depth or feeling of Truth from God's Holy Spirit. This is due to the fact that prayer was performed and practised so long from the fleshly mind and nature, and not in the guiding will and compass of the Holy Spirit and power of God. Those who doubt about this, cannot be satisfied, until the Lord opens their spirits, and makes the matter manifest to them. . . . Prayer is not in the time, will, or power of the creature. It is a gift of God, and the ability rests in his Spirit; it is not ours, but as given of his Spirit—which, therefore, is to be waited upon. When it will move and breathe in us, and so give us the ability of calling upon the Father, and the power of prevailing with the Father, in the name and through the life of the Son is to be waited upon. [*Letters*]

Isaac Penington, English Quaker, 1617–80

Portions of two letters to the Countess of Gramont from François Fénelon:

Madam, I counsel that you should now cultivate the habit of silence, so far as good manners concerning conversation will allow. Silence keeps us more easily in the presence of God, and keeps us from making stupid and superficial remarks, in short, prevents a lot of gossip or criticisms which may hurt our neighbors. Silence humbles the spirit and helps it withdraw little by little from the world. It makes a kind of solitude in our hearts, as you would like to have. It will supply all that you need in the trials you are experiencing. If you do not talk needlessly you will have plenty of free moments even in the midst of people whom you are forced to be with. . . . The one thing which I fear for you in this present stage of the spiritual life is distraction, but you can avoid this by silence.

If you are faithful in observing silence, when it is not necessary to speak, God will give you the grace to remain recollected, when you talk because there is a necessary need. When you are not free to save long periods of time, be careful to use brief ones. Fifteen minutes, used in a careful way and with faithfulness even in trial, will be worth as much to God as the whole hours you would give him if you had more free time. Single, separate moments used throughout the day, will add up to quite a large space of time. Perhaps this way will prove to be a benefit because you will turn to God more frequently than if you were only giving him some established period of time. . . .

[*Spiritual Letters*]

A letter to a soldier:

Paris, June 9, 1689

Nothing, dear sir, should prevent you from recollecting yourself in the presence of God, when you are on horseback and when you cannot read a book to choose a particular subject for meditation. But you must practice the following:

1. Never allow this recollection to replace your meditation, so that you can do away with it, when you can plan the time to make your meditation before or after your cavalry exercises.

2. To combine this presence of God with concrete acts and special reflections on the truths which you have already meditated, every time that these acts and these reflections will be likely to renew your feeling and make you more recollected.

3. Never wear yourself out in this recollection, and to relax your mind by little intervals of wholesome leisure and relaxation, whenever you feel the need of it.

I am certain that this presence of God will become unconsciously frequent and familiar to you. In regard to your way of meditating, it is good, and you, dear sir, should continue it as it is now.

[*Spiritual Letters*]
*François Fénelon, theologian, educator
and French archbishop, 1651–1715*

In a letter to a monk:

December 28, 1868

Having lost the prayer of the heart, you write me that now you are without any defenses. Earlier I wrote you that in all your temptations and in all the unusual happenings you experience, you must not stop praying. If you cannot pray in your heart, pray in your mind or with your lips. It makes no difference how you pray as long as you do not stop praying. During the ceremony of tonsure it is said to the person being tonsured that he should always have the name of the Lord Jesus in his mind, in his heart, in his thoughts, and on his lips. One must attend to God not only in the heart but also in the mind and thoughts and on the lips. In you, however, I sense an unacceptable demand of having things your own way. You demand to have prayer of the heart, and when you do not enjoy it, you are left completely without prayer. You write that, when you unsuccessfully tried to seek the place of the heart, the chiding of your neighbors began to defeat you. This shows that your prayer is still wrong, since the effect of true prayer is humility and love for your neighbor. You write that the Devil hints to you that you are better than everyone else. Send such trials back to him. Your own deeds show how virtuous you are living.

[Spiritual Letters of Direction]
Staretz Amvrosy (Alexander M. Grenkov),
Orthodox Russian ascetic and monk of Optima, 1812–91

Friedrich von Hügel writes to his niece:

To G. G.   *February 2, 1921*

I take it that God in His goodness has granted you the simple Prayer of Quiet—or, at least, that you get given touches, short dawns, of it, now and then. You know, dear, how much and often I insist with you on the visible, the historical, the social, the institutional. But this is done without even the temptation to doubt, or to treat lightly, moments of formless prayer. Such formless prayer, where genuine, is, on the contrary, a deep grace, a darling force, and still joy for the soul. May you have, and keep, and grow in this grace! What are the tests, the conditions of this genuineness? They are two. Such prayer may never become the soul's only form of prayer; formal, vocal or mental prayer—the reciting of e.g. the Our Father, the Glory be to the Father, Acts of Faith, Hope, Love, Contrition (as in the prayerbooks or made up by oneself)—prayers, all these, we can give an account of when we have done them: such prayers must never cease. And such formless prayer is the right sort if, in coming away from it, you find yourself humbler, sweeter, more patient, more ready to suffer, more loving (in effect even more than in affection) towards God and man; given the first (precaution) and this second (result) you cannot well have too much of this prayer. And I think God will lead you much along this path; and that you will get beyond the worldliness, and other faults, especially through it. For you will get to love it so; and it will grow or will intermit, in proportion as you are faithful in turning away from self. A homely heroism will feed this prayer of speechless love; and the speechless love will feed the homely heroism. [*Spiritual Counsel and Letters*]

Baron Friedrich von Hügel, lay Catholic theologian
and writer, 1852–1925

To a Sister: *El Kbab, June 16, 1936*
How often I ask the Lord to take from me and to place upon Himself the responsibility for your soul. Yes, that the Master, without the intermediary of my poor human voice, should speak to you directly. The human voice is vain, hollow and empty noise to our souls. Not so the silences of God in us, when suddenly all is quiet and nothing exists but Him and ourselves. We have reached Him; He has reached us. In a moment, like a flash of light, a wonderful gift of divine energy has filled us. In a single moment He gives us more than we could acquire in centuries, or, rather, than we could ever acquire except from Him.

How good it is, my child, that our whole spiritual life should consist of listening to God, waiting for God. He, the infinite Master, has always more of Himself to reveal. And so our role is to walk in the ways of God, in all the details of everyday life, not the ways that we have chosen, but those that He has chosen for us. And to keep on and on in these ways, satisfied in the knowledge that God wants us to follow them. . . . [*Voice from the Desert*]

Albert Peyriguère, French priest, disciple of Charles de Foucauld,
hermit in the desert, 1883–1959

3 July 1919
Consolation, Dear, is sooner or later followed by Desolation; and the latter is, when and where God sends it, and we have not ourselves brought it on ourselves by Laxness and dissipation, as true a way to God, and usually a safer one, than consolation. Day and night, sunshine and storm, union and aloneness—both are necessary, sooner or later, Sweet. But, of course, it is for God, for Him alone, to leave and to apportion these vicissitudes to each soul. And certain it is that it is of much help to have some older, more experienced soul handy also, who can and will, if and when we get into Desolation, cheer us on, by the reminder of the former consolation, and still more by the

great fact that only through such vicissitudes—through fidelity in them—can we grow strong and deep in God and for Him.

Loving old,
Uncle.
[Letters from Baron Friedrich von Hügel to a Niece]
Baron Friedrich von Hügel, lay Catholic theologian
and writer, 1852–1925

April 11, 1927.   *Downside Abbey, Stratton-on-the-Fosse,*
                                                          Nr. Bath.

My dear ———
As to advice, I can only tell you what I think.

I recommend you prayer, because it is good for everybody, and our Lord tells us to pray. As to method, do what you can do, and what suits you. It seems obvious that most spiritual reading and meditation fails to help you; and the simplest kind of prayer is the best. So use that.

But prayer, in the sense of union with God, is the most crucifying thing there is. One must do it for God's sake; but one will not get any satisfaction out of it, in the sense of feeling "I am good at prayer," "I have an infallible method." That would be disastrous, since what we want to learn is precisely our own weakness, powerlessness, unworthiness. Nor ought one to expect "a sense of the reality of the supernatural" of which you speak. And one should wish for no prayer, except precisely the prayer that God gives us—probably very distracted and unsatisfactory in every way!

On the other hand, the only way to pray is to pray; and the way to pray well is to pray much. If one has no time for this, then one must at least pray regularly. But the less one prays, the worse it goes. And if circumstances do not permit even regularity, then one must put up with the fact that when one does try to pray, one can't pray—and our prayer will probably consist of telling this to God.

As to beginning afresh, or where you left off, I don't think you have any choice! You simply have to begin wherever you find yourself. Make any acts you want to make and feel you ought to make; but do not force yourself into feelings of any kind.

You say very naturally that you do not know what to do if you have a quarter of an hour alone in Church. Yes, I suspect the only thing to do is to shut out the Church and everything else, and just give yourself to God and beg Him to have mercy on you, and offer Him all your distractions.

As to religious matters being "confused and overwhelming," I daresay they may remain so—in a sense—but if you get the right simple relation to God by prayer, you have got into the centre of the wheel, where the revolving does not matter. We can't get rid of the worries of this world, or of the questionings of the intellect; but we can laugh at and despise them so far as they are worries.

[*The Spiritual Letters of Dom John Chapman*]
Dom John Chapman, English Benedictine abbot,
biblical and patristic scholar, 1865–1933

Excerpts from two letters of Evelyn Underhill:

50 *Campden Hill Square, W.8.*
To S. P.   *April 12, 1939*
I shall be only too delighted if I can be of any help about your prayers. But I am rather frightened of giving detailed advice to anyone I do not know personally: as every one differs in temperament, capacity, etc., their prayer must differ too. So please take anything I say with a grain of salt.

I think an hour in the morning is enough at present and should not be added to; so the question is, how to use it best. Without being too rigid, or watching the clock, try dividing it roughly into 3 periods of about 20 minutes each.

(a) Will be given to a short N.T. reading and a meditation based on it, leading to

(b) Prayer, including adoration, intercession and a review in God's presence of the duties, etc., of the coming day, especially the contacts which may be difficult, or uncongenial jobs.

(c) Spiritual reading.

The point about this plan is that the meditation leads on naturally to prayer; and as soon as you perceive it has done this, you can drop it (because it has then done its work) and continue with that intercourse with God which it will have set going. And, on the other hand, if it is a "bad day," the meditation gives you something definite to do and a subject to attend to and think about which will help to control wandering thoughts.

As to subject, there are lots of books which provide set subjects, points, etc. But I think myself the best and simplest way is just to take some point from one's daily N.T. reading, either the appointed Church lesson or whatever it may be, and, asking God for His light, to brood on it in His presence till it leads you into acts of penitence, love, worship, as the case may be.

No fixed rules can safely be laid down, because some people are more imaginative and others more logical in their ways of meditating and each should follow their attrait and not try to force themselves into a particular method. Prayer should never be regarded as a science or reduced to a system—that ruins it, because it is essentially a living and personal relationship, which tends to become more personal and also more simple, as one goes on. . . .

If there is anything else you want to know, please do not hesitate to write again, or else come in one day for a talk when you return to London. [*The Letters of Evelyn Underhill*]

To M. R. September 26, 1908

. . . This, too, is where formal prayer comes in, for in (the best) formal prayers—the Psalms, and prayers of the Saints—we are making our own the best aspirations of the best minds. To say that you cannot pray for the things they prayed for—that your wants are not theirs— is merely to say that you are not really in the stream of Christian tradition. To use these prayers confirms one in this tradition. They are educative to the soul which wants to learn to pray, just as good literature is educative to the mind that wants to learn to write. Also is it not rather arrogant to refuse to avail oneself of the help of experts? They got to the place you want to get to, and their prayers presumably helped them to do it. By using these prayers you enter into their atmosphere. You ought to pray to the Saints too—ask them to help you. "The best way of knowing God is to frequent the company of His friends," said St. Teresa, and it is just as important to keep in touch with your brothers and sisters out of the body as in the body.

[*The Letters of Evelyn Underhill*]
Evelyn Underhill, Anglican married woman,
wrote on mysticism, 1875–1941

Letters of comfort and encouragement

Brother Andrew, dear to my soul, if you rightly knew the gift of God, if all the hairs of your head were mouths, you would still not be able to glorify or thank Him as He deserves. But I believe you are learning. And as God Himself knows, there is not a twinkling of an eye, or an hour, in which I do not keep you in mind and my prayer. If I so love you, God who formed you loves you much more. And I pray to Him that He guide you and direct you according to His will. And so He directs you for the good of your soul. And if He is long-suffering with you, He is multiplying many times the good of your spirit. Sit still then thanking Him for all things, demanding nothing of yourself in all things, believing in all that has been told you, that it shall be, in Christ Jesus our Lord. Amen. [*Letter to Andrew #113*]

> *Saint Barsanuphius, hermit in Gaza, spiritual father,*
> *c. sixth century*

Saint Catherine of Siena wrote to Pope Gregory XI:

This is what I wish to see in you. If up to now, we were not very resolute, I wish and pray in truth that the amount of time which remains be used as a real man would, following Christ, whose vicar you are, like a strong man. Fear not, reverend father, for anything that may result from these tumultuous winds which are now blowing against you, those rotting members of the Church who have rebelled against you. Fear not, for God's help is close to you. [*Letters*]

> *Saint Catherine of Siena, correspondent*
> *and advisor of popes, emperors, and kings, 1347–80*

Spiritual counsel to a man on the death of his son:

To Mr. De Richebourg   *Ratisbon, April 1541*

. . . I am in great sorrow that a most excellent and faithful friend has been snatched away from me, a friend with whom I was so familiar, that none could be more closely united than we were. It is a real cause of personal grief when I saw the young man, your son, taken away in the very flower of his youth, a man of excellent promise, whom I loved as a son, because he showed that loving respect and affection for me as he would to another father. . . . There is one sure sign of hope, a never-failing source of consolation, in which you, and men like you, ought to rest, because it flows from that inward feeling of piety which I know to excel in you. Therefore, take special care to call to mind those thoughts which are taught us by the excellent Master of all, and recommended for our understanding in the school of piety. It is not necessary at present that I should state these truths, which are all as familiar to you as to me. Nevertheless, because of your personal piety, and that goodwill which you express toward me, you will not, perhaps, be unwilling to recognize in my letter thoughts which have freely filled your own soul at some other time. The son whom the Lord had lent you for a season He has taken away. The Lord who had placed him here for a season, at this stage of his career has called him away. What the Lord has done, we must, at the same time, consider has not been done rashly, nor by chance, nor by some external forces, but by that predetermined counsel whereby He not only sees in advance, but also decides and executes nothing but what is just and upright in itself, but also nothing but what is good and wholesome for us. It is still painful, you will say, so to shake off or suppress the love of a father, as not to experience grief on the occasion of the loss of a son. Neither do I insist upon your giving up all grief. Nor, in the school of Christ, do we learn any such philosophy as requires us to give up that common humanity with which God has blessed us, that, being men, we should be turned into stones. These considerations reach only so far as this, that you set limits, and, as it were, temper even your most reasonable sadness. Having shed the tears which were due to nature and to fatherly love, you by no means give way to useless crying. By no means do I interfere because I am distrustful of your prudence, firmness, or high-mindedness; but only because otherwise I might here be wanting and come short in my duty to you. . . .

Adieu, most distinguished sir, and my esteemed in the Lord. May Christ the Lord keep you and your family, and guide you all with His own Spirit, until you may arrive where Louis has gone ahead of us.

[*Letters*]

*John Calvin, French theologian and Protestant Reformer
in Geneva, 1509–64*

A letter from John Woolman:

In this your later affliction I have found a deep fellow-feeling with you and had a secret hope throughout that it might please the Father of Mercies to raise you up and sanctify your troubles to you. That you, being more fully acquainted with that way which the world considers foolish, you may feel the clothing of divine fortitude and be strengthened to resist that spirit which leads from the simplicity of the everlasting Truth.

We may see ourselves crippled and halting and from a strong bias to things pleasant and easy find an impossibility to advance forward. But things impossible with men are possible with God, and our wills being made subject to his, all temptations are surmountable. . . .

And now on your part, after your sore affliction and doubts of recovery, you are again restored. Forget him not who has helped you, but in humble gratitude hold fast his instructions, thereby to shun those by-paths which lead from the firm foundation. I am sensible to that variety of company to which one in your business must be exposed. I have painfully felt the force of conversation proceeding from men deeply rooted in an earthly mind, and can sympathize with others in such conflicts, in that much weakness still attends me. . . .

There is a love which clothes my mind while I write, which is superior to all expressions, and I find my heart open to encourage to a holy emulation to advance forward in Christian firmness. Deep humility is a strong bulwark, and as we enter into it we find safety and true exaltation. The foolishness of God is wiser than man, and the weakness of God is stronger than man. Being unclothed of our own wisdom and knowing the abasement of the creature, therein we find that power to arise which gives health and vigor to us.

> [*The Journal and Major Essays of John Woolman*]
> *John Woolman, American Quaker, itinerant preacher,*
> *and witness against slavery, 1720–72*

It is true. There are some persons who are less open to suffering, as there are some on whom temptation has less impact. It is a matter of personality and of disposition. You make me smile, dear child, in worrying about the knowledge that you have not suffered much for Jesus Christ, and if you will still find his cross in your path. I will tell you my thought simply. The best of the least? It so happens that with your happy personality and the extremely pure and deep truth of your spiritual way that you are escaping a thousand crosses which are the plague of many other persons. [*Letters of Spiritual Direction*]

Msgr. Charles Gay, auxiliary bishop of Poitiers, 1815–92

A letter from Saint Thérèse of Lisieux:

Lisieux Carmel

Monsieur l'Abbé,   *26 December 1896*

I wanted to answer sooner, but the rule of Carmel does not allow me to write or receive letters during Advent. Our Venerable Mother did allow me, as an exception, to read your letter, because she knew that you had a special need to be supported by prayer.

Monsieur l'Abbé, I promise you that I am doing all I can to obtain the graces you need. Those graces will certainly be given, for Our Lord never asks us for a sacrifice beyond our strength. Of course, that divine Savior sometimes allows us to taste all the bitterness of the cup He is holding to our soul. When he asks the sacrifice of all that is dearest to us in this world, it is impossible, short of a most unusual favor, not to cry out as He did in the garden of His agony. "My Father, let this chalice pass from me. . . . Nevertheless not as I will, but as you will."

It is very consoling to remember that Jesus, the God of Might, knew our weaknesses, that He trembled at the sight of the bitter chalice, the chalice which He earlier had desired so longingly to drink. . . .

Your situation is very beautiful, Monsieur l'Abbé, for Our Lord chose it for Himself, because He first tasted the chalice He now offers you.

A saint has said: "The greatest honor God can give a soul is not to give much to it, but to ask much of it!" So Jesus is treating you as a privileged person. He wants you to begin your missionary work now and save persons by your suffering. Did He not redeem the world by suffering and dying? I know you desire the happiness of sacrificing your life for the Divine Master. But the martyrdom of the heart is not less fruitful than the shedding of blood, and that first martyrdom is yours already. I am right in saying that your situation is beautiful, is worthy of an apostle of Christ.

Monsieur L'Abbé, you seek support from one whom Jesus has given you as your sister, and you are entitled to. As our Reverend Mother permits me to write to you, I am very happy to accomplish

this pleasant task entrusted to me. But I feel that the most certain way to reach my goal is by prayer and suffering. . . . [*Spiritual Letters*]
Saint Thérèse of Lisieux, French Carmelite nun,
the "Little Flower of Jesus," 1873–97

Letters of admonishment

Letter of Barsanuphius to Brother Euthymius:
Brother, the divine Scripture says, "Do all things with counsel," and "Without counsel do nothing." When you were not acting with counsel, but from your own will, you were not laboring with your mind. For there is none who does not need a counselor, except only God, who created wisdom. But when you did seek according to God to cut off your own will and to come to humility, and to take me your very little brother for your counselor, you provoked to envy the demon who hates the good and always has envy towards all men. You see the crookedness of the Devil? Of myself I made no rule for you at all. And you asked me, and I counseled you as a brother. And hearing it you left it and made your own addition. And I spoke to you of the Pharisee. For he too was boasting when he said what he said. And you sought assurance, and that is nothing else but pride.

[*Barsanuphius and John, Letters*]
Saint Barsanuphius and John, master and disciple,
hermits in Gaza, Syria, c. sixth century

In Meister Eckhart's time there was a great priest, great not only in learning, but in life, who said to him: "Dear master and father, if you do not consider it bad of me, out of divine love, I would like to discuss a matter with you." In the friendliest manner he answered, "My dear sir, gladly; speak about anything you want to." The priest began by saying: "You know that I have listened to most of your sermons, and I have liked many of them, and I have not liked some of them."

Then Meister Eckhart said: "Dear sir, I ask you for God's sake to explain what you mean. Liking my sermons and disliking them are utterly contrary to each other."

Then the good priest said: "I will explain what I mean. What I have enjoyed hearing from you were the great, clever ideas, which by the grace of God I could understand. But thinking them over, I have also thought of the saying, 'Cast not your pearls before swine' and your sermons have disturbed me, and I thought; these high and mighty ideas should be discussed mainly in the universities. . . .

"Therefore, dear Meister Eckhart, to these three kinds of people, the beginners, those who are making progress, and those who are perfect, your sermons and teaching are not very helpful or useful. Although I am unworthy to give you advice, nevertheless I should like to advise you, out of divine love, and with God's help, to begin now and imitate the teaching of our Lord Jesus Christ and the method he used while he walked in this world of time. His instruction in the synagogues and the temple had this purpose in mind, that people should cease their evil and sinful deeds and learn to do good things. Learn how he drove out evil and ended it, until evil made way for virtue. This kind of instruction is as much needed today as it ever was, to focus the mind of Christ on the sinful, evil life of man, to preach and demonstrate to people how they may arrive at an orderly, virtuous Christian life. . . .

"Thus it is quite necessary to teach beginners and intermediate disciples and explain to them how they may begin to leave their evil lives and seek virtue. When, by the help of God, people have found out how to seek virtue, they, too, will be masters over wrong and from within, they will be instructed by the Holy Spirit. Then they will have no need of verbal teaching, and yet they will stay within the holy church."

When he had finished this explanation, the good priest said: "Dear Meister Eckhart, I have said too much and talked too long to you, forgive me. Now it is time for me to return home." Then Meister Eckhart turned toward him, gave him a kiss of peace, and said: "Dear sir, I tell you that for many years I have enjoyed hearing no conversation as much as this, which I have suddenly had to listen to from you. May God be your eternal reward. With divine love and Christian brotherliness, I plead with you and urge you for God's sake, as I may urge you, to tell me plainly about your own life, as God has given it you. By the grace of God, I plainly see that you have spoken to me from the heart of your own life." [*Fragments*]

*Meister Johann Eckhart, German Dominican priest
and theologian, 1260–1307*

*In giving spiritual direction to her own brother, Saint Catherine
of Siena writes:*

Dearest brother, I urge you to endure this in all patience. I would not allow it to escape your mind that you should repent of your own ingratitude, and your ignoring the duty you owe to your mother, to which you are bound by the commandment of God. I have seen your ingratitude increase so that you have not even paid her the obligation of help that you owe her. Certainly, I have an excuse for you in this, because you were unable. But if you had been able, I do not know that you would have done it, since you failed her even in your words. What ingratitude. Have you not considered the sorrow of her labor, nor the milk that she gave you from her breast, nor the many troubles that she has had, over you and all the others? . . . I urge you to correct this fault and others, and to forgive my own ignorance as well. Did I not love your soul, I would not tell you what I do. Recall your obligation, you and all your family. I will say no more to you. Remain in the holy and gracious favor of God. [*A Letter*]

   Saint Catherine of Siena, correspondent and advisor of popes,
emperors, and kings, 1347–80

Letter of admonishment to his friend concerning his dull preaching:

To Farel: *Geneva, 27 January 1552*

 There is something concerning which I wish to admonish you. It is my understanding that the length of your sermons has provided grounds for complaint to many. You have frequently confessed to us that you were aware of this failing, and that you were trying to remedy it. But if private complaining is ignored because it does not presently give trouble, it will one day break out into rebellious shouts. I beg and beseech you to try to restrain yourself, that you may not give Satan an opportunity, which we see he is so earnestly desiring. You know that while we are not called upon to pay too serious attention to the foolish, we are nevertheless bound to give them something to attract them. You are also smart enough to know that you have to deal with the morose and the choleric. In practice their antipathy to you comes simply from too much pride on their part. But, since the Lord commands us to ascend the pulpit, not for our own edification, but for that of the people, you should so temper the manner of your teaching, that the Word may not be brought into disdain by your monotony. It is better also for us to lengthen our prayers in private, than when we offer them in the name of the whole Church. You are mistaken if you expect from all a devotion like your own.

I have dictated this letter in bed. Adieu, most excellent and noble brother. Salute all friends. May the Lord preserve and guide you by His Spirit, and bless your work. [*Letters*]

> *John Calvin, French theologian and Protestant reformer*
> *in Geneva, 1509–64*

A letter from Saint Vincent de Paul to Louise de Marillac ends:

Mademoiselle, I have never seen a mother so completely a mother like you are. In no other way are you so much a woman. In God's name, Mademoiselle, give your son over to the care of his Father, who loves him more than you do. At least stop pestering him. Without appearing to be involved in this matter, I am going to send someone to the Holy Infant, were Michel is, to find out how things are going, and I will let you know. Good day, Mademoiselle. I am your servant.

[*Letters*]

A subsequent letter from Vincent reads:

Your son told Mademoiselle de la Salle that he was only entering religious life because you wanted him to, that he had longed for death because of it and that to please you he would take minor orders. Do you consider that a vocation? I believe he would rather die himself than desire your death. Be that as it may be, and whether it comes from nature or the Devil, his will is not free to determine a matter of such importance and you must not wish it. Some time ago a good boy from this town accepted the subdiaconate in just such a frame of mind and he was not able to go on to the other orders. Do you want to make your son liable to the same danger? Let God guide him. He is more his Father than you are his mother, and loves him more than you do. Leave him to the guidance of God. He is quite capable of calling him at another time if he wants to or to give him work suited to his well-being. I recall a priest, who used to be in this house, who took orders in this same troubled frame of mind. God alone knows what has become of him now.

Good day, Mademoiselle. Give yourself entirely to our Lord and be guided by His will. I am, in his love, your servant, Vincent de Paul.

[*Letters*]

> *Saint Vincent de Paul, French priest, founder of the Lazarists*
> *of the Confraternities of Charity, 1576–1660*

To an abbot whose power was a stumbling block, Macarius recommended his retirement:

Recall your intention and your sincerity when you entered the monastery, your vows, your concern, under the direction of the staretz, for the salvation of your own soul. All that was deserved, but where has it gone to? The time of emptiness came. But why? You say because of the honor of superior. This is true, without doubt. But it is not the honor of superior, strictly speaking, that is to blame, but your own spiritual cowardice and your unmastered passions, especially the love of glory, comfort and riches. . . .

When a person uses power not for his own sake, not for easy living, but for the salvation of his neighbors, then it is truly a means of sorrow and trouble. And if a person decides to wield power for honor, glory and pleasure, then he himself and all his subjects fall pitifully overwhelmed in a fury of sinful desires. "Woe to the city where the king is young." [*Letters to Monks*]

Macarius Ivanov, a spiritual father
in Central Russia, 1788–1861

To a certain disciple: March 1, 1969
You depicted in your last letter how a thought compelled you to pray that God would guide your mind into your heart. Not one of the Holy Fathers is ever seen to have prayed such a prayer. It is better to humbly pray in this manner: "O Lord! Have mercy upon me as You know best." We are commanded by the Lord to pray: Our Father. Thy will be done. In everything, even in prayer, it is apparent that you want absolutely everything to be according to your will or according to the suggestion of the Devil. May the Lord protect us from all evil and especially from the lies of the Devil. A clear sign of this is disorderly perplexity and the suggestion of self-conceit and, subsequent to this, tepid thoughts or worldly desires or a feeling of anger and an irascible spirit. [*Spiritual Letters of Direction*]

Staretz Amvrosy (Alexander M. Grenkov),
Orthodox Russian ascetic
and monk of Optima, 1812–91

Chapter Eight

OBEDIENCE

Therefore, my beloved, as you have always obeyed, not only as in my presence but much more in my absence, work out your salvation with fear and trembling; for God is at work in you, both to will and to work for his good pleasure. [*Philippians 2:12–13*]

Obey your leaders and submit to them; for they are keeping watch over your souls, as men who will have to give account. Let them do this joyfully, and not sadly, for that would be of no advantage to you.

[*Hebrews 13:17*]

We would not be true to the voice of the tradition of spiritual direction without including some of the innumerable passages found in the works about spiritual direction on obedience to the spiritual director. This is an unpopular and difficult subject in the twentieth century, with its emphasis on individual identity and freedom and on personal responsibility for discerning vocation and gifts. The word obedience calls up associations of childhood when we may have been required to unquestioningly do as we were told by our parents. It is especially difficult for women, who have become aware of the limited place they've been allowed in the male-dominated church.

To understand the nature of obedience in spiritual direction, we must remember that it is a freely chosen, voluntary association that has no canonical authority. A person may freely enter and leave spiritual direction. It is a pastoral relationship whose authority lies in the authority of the Spirit. Consequently, obedience to the authority of the Spirit as mediated and discerned by a spiritual director in a loving, caring relationship can be a source of freedom to enter into that Spirit, not enslaving and subjugating.

What is the meaning of the whole endeavor described in the foregoing chapters if those seeking direction do not enter the relationship with humility, knowing they need help, that they cannot pray, that they are blind and that they may find assistance in entering into God's truth through the relationship? It is this knowledge of our need and awareness that our willfullness and blindness betray us that makes us realize we may be required, for our own sakes, to follow and trust the insights, suggestions, and admonitions of another person who may discern for us what we cannot discern. It is important to realize that the question of obedience revolves around the same issues as described in chapter one concerning our need for spiritual direction. Without a realization of the place of obedience in spiritual direction, in the sense of a willingness to seek to enter a truth larger than we can consciously and willfully engineer, the relationship is reduced to a pleasant conversation, not a life-and-death matter of finding one's way.

Abbot Rufus said, "The person who continues under obedience to his spiritual father has a greater reward waiting for him than the person who runs off into the desert to be his own guide." He also tells this story of one of the fathers: "I saw four orders in heaven. In the first order was a sick man giving praise to God; in the second was one very carefully giving hospitality; in the third was a hermit, who never laid eyes on anyone; in the fourth was a man sitting at his spiritual father's feet, obediently subject to him for the sake of the Lord. The one endowed with this kind of obedience wore a gold collar with a bright medal and outshone the rest in glory. And," he went on, "I asked my guide, 'How is it that such a simple person rose to a state of glory above the rest?' He answered: 'the one giving hospitality did it of his own free will; and the one who fled to the desert did so because he wanted to; but the man who lived under obedience left his own will behind and depended on God and his spiritual father. This is why he obtained greater glory than the rest.' So then, my sons, obedience is good when it is embraced because of the Lord."

[The Sayings of the Fathers]
Abbot Rufus, early ascetic in the desert

She [Amma Theodora] also said that neither discipline, nor night watches nor any kind of suffering are able to save, only true humility can do that. There was a hermit who was able to banish the devils. He asked them, "What makes you flee? Is it fasting?" They replied, "We do not eat or drink." "Is it watching?" They replied, "We do not sleep." "Is it separation from the world?" "We live in the deserts." "What power sends you fleeing then?" They said, "Nothing can overcome us, but only humility." "Do you see how humility conquers even the devils?"

[Sayings of the Mothers of the Desert]
Amma Theodora, ascetic in the desert near Alexandria, Egypt,
c. fifth century

She [Amma Syncletica] also said, "Even as a person cannot build a ship unless he has some nails, so it is also impossible to be saved without humility."

[Sayings of the Mothers of the Desert]
Amma Syncletica, hermit in Egyptian desert,
caring for blind sister, d. 400

You then, Brother, do as we have said, and go find the person that God, whether in mystery by His own act, or exteriorly by His servant, will show you. Like Christ in person, you must see him and speak to him. You must honor him and thus you will learn from him what is useful for you. For example, you may hear him say: "Go forth from the land of your kinsfolk and from your father's house to a land that I will show you"; don't be undecided, don't be ashamed, don't let yourself be overcome by vanity. He says to you: "Come into the land of obedience that I will show you." Run, my brother, with all your strength, without giving sleep to your eyes nor bending your knee, which allows you to become lazy or careless. Perhaps it is here that God will manifest Himself to you, so that you may become father of many spiritual children and make you a gift of the promised land, the inheritance of the just alone. Or if he leads you to the mountain, climb with good heart because you will contemplate there, I am certain, the transfigured Christ, brilliant, as not even the sun shines, with the light of His divinity. Perhaps you will fall down, not being able to sustain the vision of that which you have never before contemplated, and you will hear from on high the voice of the Father. You will also see the cloud spread out its shadow, and the prophets from either side attest that this is He, the God of the living and the dead, the Lord. [*Theological Chapters*]

Saint Simeon the New Theologian, Eastern monk
and abbot of Studios, c. 949–1022

A humble and loving obedience to one in authority brings peace to the soul. It brings security to blind faith until the time when the Holy Spirit comes, giving understanding to what the ear has heard. . . . But if we refuse to obey one in authority at the beginning of our life of faith, we always take the wrong road, since we are following our own reason alone. [*Mirror of Faith*]

William of Saint-Thierry, Benedictine monk, 1085–1148

In many things he [St. Francis] had learned his own judgment from a revelation. Nevertheless conferring about it, he would place the ideas of others ahead of his own. He considered the advice of his companions surer, and the view of another seemed better than his own. He used to say that a brother had not given up all things for the Lord if he kept the purse of his own judgment. He preferred to hear blame spoken of himself rather than praise, for blame would lead him to amend his life, while praise could lead to a fall. . . .

Most carefully he searched for and religiously longed to know how, and by what way, and by what desire he might hold on perfectly to the Lord God according to his counsel and according to the good pleasure of his will. This was always his highest reasoning. This desire always burned within him while he lived, namely, to seek out from the simple, from the wise, from the perfect and imperfect, how he might reach the way of truth and come to the supreme good.

[Life of St. Francis of Assisi]
Thomas of Celano, thirteenth-century Franciscan poet
and biographer of Saint Francis of Assisi

As she [St. Gertrude] prayed for another person who desired Divine consolation, she received this response: "She is herself the impediment preventing her from receiving the sweetness of My Grace. When I draw My chosen one to Me by the interior attractions of My love, they who remain obstinate in the use of their own judgment place the same impediment to it as one would who closed his nose with his garment to prevent himself from smelling a fresh fragrance. But he who, for love of Me, gives up his own judgment to follow that of another, acquires a reward all the greater for acting contrary to his own tendency, because he is not merely humble, but a perfect success. The apostle says none will be crowned 'except he strives lawfully.' " *[The Life and Revelations of Saint Gertrude]*
Saint Gertrude the Great, German nun, 1256–1302

From humility comes obedience, for none can be inwardly obedient except the humble person. Obedience means humble, submissive, and a flexible mildness, and a will ready for all that is good. Obedience makes a person submit to the biddings, the forbiddings, and the will of God. It subordinates the senses and the animal powers to the higher reason, so that a person may live modestly and reasonably. It makes people submissive and obedient to Holy Church, to the sacraments, to the prelates and their teaching, to their commandments and their counsels, and to all the good customs practised by Holy Christendom. It also makes a person ready and pliant in his conversation with other people, in action and counsel, in spiritual and corporeal affairs, with prudent discretion, in a manner proper for each.

[The Adornment of the Spiritual Marriage]
Blessed John Ruysbroeck, secular parish priest
in Brussels and theologian, 1293–1381

Be certain that although you look diligently, you will not find any other way so sure nor so safe, in your search for the will of God, than that of humble obedience. We are so advised by all the saints, as was so well done by many of them, as the lives of the holy fathers give witness. Among them all there is held up as a very great sign of coming to spiritual perfection the fact that a person is subject to his wise counselor. Among the many good things that there are in religious orders, you will marvelously find it such a great good, that they all live under a wise person (superior) whom they obey, not only in exterior actions, but also by interior choice. If these religious have confidence and commitment to obedience, they will live a secure and peaceful life. *[Hear, O Daughter]*

Saint John of Ávila, Spanish diocesan priest, 1500–69

Our fasts, our prayers, our watchings, our intentions of duty, our frequent communions, and all exterior acts of religion, are to be guided by our superior, if he sees cause to restrain or modify any excess. For a wound may heal too fast, and then the tumor of the flesh is proud, not healthful. So also may the indiscretions of religion swell to vanity, when we think they grow towards perfection: but when we can endure the caustics and correctives of our spiritual guides in those things in which we are most apt to please ourselves, then our obedience is regular and humble, and in other things there is less danger. There is a story told of a very religious person, whose spirit, in the ecstasy of devotion, was transported to the clarity of a vision; and he seemed to converse personally with the holy Jesus, feeling from such conversation great spiritual delights and huge satisfactions. In the midst of these joys, the bell called to prayers; and he, used to the strictness and well instructed in the necessities of obedience, went to the church, and having finished his devotions, returned, and found the vision in the same posture of glories and entertainment: which also said to him, "Because you have left Me, you have found Me; for if you had not left Me, I would have left you immediately." Whatever the story be, I am sure it is a good parable; for the way to increase spiritual comforts is to be strict in the offices of humble obedience; and we never lose any thing of our joy, by laying it aside to attend a duty. [*Life of Christ*]

Jeremy Taylor, English Anglican bishop, 1613–67

Spiritual direction must be free as air, and fresh as the morning sun. Neither temptation nor scruple, neither mortification nor obedience, must be able to infuse into it one element of bondage. The moment they do, let us break the direction, and take the consequence. For the end of spiritual direction in all stages of the interior and mystical life is one and single and invariable, and it is liberty of spirit. The opposite doctrine does not belong to the wisdom of direction, but to the superstition of direction. [*Growth in Holiness*]

Frederick William Faber, Catholic priest
of the Oratory in England, 1814–63

Msgr. Charles Gay replies to a young man who wanted to obey him as a slave.

I shall not use, at least habitually, in spite of your desire, the approach about which you write. It seems to you that you would find peace. Perhaps, but a natural peace which is not what I desire for you. Such commands would free you from the burdens of life, but it is not good that you should not feel the weight of them. I will be for you as Cyrus the Cyrenian, nothing more. I will assist you, not substitute myself for you. Strong natures have need of obedience; weak ones, such as yours, have a gentleness which tends to laziness. It is necessary to give to each according to their needs. I do not want you to be a slave, the word is your own, an exaggerated and repulsive word. I wish you to be a son, and a reasonable son, enlightened by the counsels of his father . . . but walking as a man, not as a child.

[*Letters of Spiritual Direction*]
Msgr. Charles Gay, auxiliary bishop of Poitiers, 1815–92

Dostoevski describes the "elder" in a Russian monastery.

An elder was one who took your soul, your will, into his soul and his will. When you choose an elder, you renounce your own will and yield it to him in complete submission, complete self-abnegation. This novitiate, this terrible school of abnegation, is undertaken voluntarily, in the hope of self-conquest, of self-mastery, in order, after a life of obedience, to attain perfect freedom, that is, from self; to escape the lot of those who have lived their whole life without finding their true selves in themselves. This institution of elders is not founded on theory, but was established in the East from the practice of a thousand years. The obligations due to an elder are not the ordinary "obedience" which has always existed in our Russian monasteries. The obligation involves confession to the elder by all who have submitted themselves to him, and to the indissoluble bond between him and them.

[*The Brothers Karamazov*]
Feodor Dostoevski, Russian novelist, 1821–81

Direction does not necessarily demand obedience. It is an enlightened counsel to which we must pay attention according to prudence, consequently according to the value of the advice requested and of he who gives it. It would be very comforting not to have the responsibility of this personal discretion; but it is solely by exception that we must blindly resort to obedience. A habitual obedience of judgment would rather diminish us as persons. Direction is not a categorical imperative. The soul remains free. [*Letters of Direction*]

Léopold Beaudenom, French priest
and convent chaplain, 1840–1916

The director is not a superior in any official sense of the word. As a result, his authority does not have official force. It is not universal and does not oblige in virtue of obedience. Nevertheless we must not lose sight of the fact that direction should, before all things, safeguard liberty of soul. The obedience owed to a director is not of limitation. In obeying him the person does not lose her liberty; in obeying she remains free.

The person remains always her own master. The director was chosen freely and he can in no way restrain our liberty. By this decision the person has lessened her chances of error and consequently increased her true liberty, because submitting with her whole heart to her guide, she can walk more securely and easily towards her last end, which is holiness and God.

[The Christian Life and the Spiritual Life]
Père Yves Ernest Masson,
Dutch Dominican priest and scholar, 1883–1971

But there is still the good, strong traditional virtue of Holy obedience, which in no way contravenes Anglican liberties. The operative word is "Holy"; obedience is strictly amoral which can be good, bad, or indifferent according to what is obeyed and why. Holy obedience is the expression of that humility which convinces us that we might be wrong; that our thoughts, conscience, and especially feeling, might lead us astray. It is the principle behind my "lowest efficient method of going to Church." If despite distraction, boredom, inattention, and sluggishness, we go to Mass, we are adding something to the action of the Church simply by "being there." And we are adding something, however little, to our personal progress; given a modicum of good-will, what we lose in devotion we make up by obedience. We have shown that the life of the Christian is both corporate and personal, and both aspects are very closely related. The dictates of the Church, like being at Mass on certain days, are clear enough, there can be no doubt about our duty; but the personal decisions of everyday life can be much more complicated. Are we really doing enough by way of prayer? Is our Rule, or our penance, or our almsgiving, sufficient? We feel tired and listless and dull; shall we struggle on in prayer or have a little rest? Many moral decisions of life seem to consist of straight alternatives; which ought we to choose? And most difficult of all: was that experience in prayer true or false, does it mean this or that, am I being "led by the Spirit" or by something very very different indeed? *[Christian Proficiency]*

Martin Thornton, Anglican priest
and theology professor, b. 1915

The extreme difficulties that lie in the way of those who seek interior freedom and purity of love soon teach them that they cannot advance by themselves, and the Spirit of God gives them a desire for the simplest means of overcoming their own selfishness and blindness of judgment. And this is obedience to the judgment and guidance of another.

A spirit that is drawn to God in contemplation will soon learn the value of obedience: the hardships and anguish he has to suffer every day from the burden of his own selfishness, his clumsiness, incompetence and pride will give him a hunger to be led and advised and directed by somebody else.

His own will becomes the source of so much misery and so much darkness that he does not go to some other man merely to seek light, or wisdom, or counsel; he comes to have a passion for obedience itself and for the renunciation of his own will and of his own lights.

Therefore he does not obey his abbot or his director merely because the commands or the advice given to him seem good and profitable and intelligent in his own eyes. He does not obey just because he thinks the abbot makes admirable decisions. On the contrary, sometimes the decisions of his superior seem to be less wise: but with this he is no longer concerned, because he accepts the superior as a mediator between him and God and rests only in the will of God as it comes to him though the men that have been placed over him by the circumstances of his vocation. [*New Seeds of Contemplation*]

Thomas Merton, Trappist monk, 1915–68

Spiritual direction implies the recognition of a certain spiritual authority—at least in a few specific areas. The practice of obedience is to some extent inherent in your relationship with your Spiritual Director, who must be a person in whose sensitivity you have confidence. Your seeking a director indicates a willingness to be guided and to undertake new disciplines. For example, Evelyn Underhill accepted from her Spiritual Director, Baron Von Hügel, the somewhat distasteful suggestion that she lay aside temporarily her studies in mysticism and devote herself to ministering to the poor. . . .

Ordinarily spiritual direction is not a mutual relationship, though each person acting as a Spiritual Director should have direction. When the relationship becomes mutual it becomes one of spiritual companionship. While this is good, the element of authority in spiritual direction is lacking. [*Call to Commitment*]

> *Elizabeth O'Connor, Protestant author and member of*
> *the Church of the Savior in Washington, D.C., b. 1921*

If we have the humility to believe that we can learn from our brothers and sisters and the understanding that some have gone further into the divine Center than others, we can see the necessity of spiritual direction. As Virgil Vogt of Reba Place Fellowship has said, "If you cannot listen to your brother, you cannot listen to the Holy Spirit."

> [*The Celebration of Discipline*]
> *Richard J. Foster, American Quaker professor*
> *of pastoral theology, twentieth century*

There is however a special need of help for those who consciously and deliberately set out on this pilgrimage. Traditionally the aid that the pilgrim requires has been understood as spiritual direction. The term is not wholly satisfactory, for it smacks too much of an authoritarian style of pastoral care which few Christians could endure today. We do not value obedience for its own sake as did our Christian forefathers. No doubt obedience to another when given gladly and ungrudgingly fosters humility. But obedience rendered reluctantly and with resentment hinders the development of responsibility and makes growth out of childish immaturity more difficult. In the climate of today simple, wholehearted obedience is a great deal more difficult than in the past. The director today is rather a spiritual guide than one who gives directions to be obeyed and a rule to be followed. St. Teresa of Ávila who took for granted the importance of a spiritual director and received much help from some of her directors tells us that she received harm from bad and ignorant directors. The true director is and always has been the Holy Spirit, and the function of a human director is to help a person to recognise where the Holy Spirit is leading him, to give him encouragement, usually much needed, and the occasional word of warning. The fear of being given authoritative advice, unsuitable to the subtleties of their own case, deters from seeking spiritual help some who would value being able to talk over their spiritual problems with an experienced person who would listen with sympathy and understanding without giving "direction" at all. [*The Heart in Pilgrimage*]

Christopher Bryant, Anglican monk of the Society of
Saint John the Evangelist, twentieth century

The religious aspect of obedience has to do with the deeper self, with the need of the self to transcend itself. It is the "Yes!" to that within me which is more me than myself. To be fully human, we have to acknowledge the mystery within ourselves. St. Catherine of Genoa said: "My me is God, nor do I know my selfhood save in him." There, in a nutshell, is what a spiritual guide can show me. He or she places my sometimes wild thrashing about looking for "myself" in the ever-widening context of God's love. This love has specific shape and content in Jesus Christ. I discover that I become more "me" when my life is shaped and formed by him. Only by being obedient to God and to nothing and no one less, can I be liberated from lesser obediences: the slavery of moods, emotions, and preferences.

[*Exploring Spiritual Direction*]
Alan W. Jones, director of the Center for Christian Spirituality
and professor of ascetical theology
at General Theological Seminary, b. 1940

In the spirit of what has just been said about obedience, the responsibility of the director as a spokesman for God is very high. According to the tradition, the director becomes accountable to God for the directee.

What if a person, not from any personal decision, is expected to accept one or two disciples, and so to become the spiritual director of others as well? First, let him examine himself humbly, to see if he can teach them through his actions, more than by his words, placing his own life before them as a model of holiness. He must be careful that, through imitating him, they do not obscure the beauty of holiness with the hideousness of evil. He should also realize that he ought to work as hard for his disciples' salvation as he does for his own. Once he has accepted the responsibility for them, he will now be accountable to God for them as well as for himself. [*Ascetic Discourse*]

Saint Nilus the Elder, priest-monk in Ancyra, Galatia, d. 430

In their zeal these directors may be wrong with goodwill because they do not know any better. For this reason, however, they should not be excused for the advice they recklessly give, without first understanding the road and spirit a person may be pursuing, and for interfering in something they do not understand, instead of leaving the matter to one who does understand. It is no small concern or fault to cause a person to lose valuable goods and sometimes to do him real harm through bad advice.

One who recklessly makes a mistake will not escape a punishment corresponding to the harm he caused, for he was bound, as is everyone, to fulfill the function of his office well and not be in error. The ministry of God must be handled with great care and with open eyes, especially in so essential and sublime a matter as is that of these persons, where there is a heavenly reward in being right and almost an eternal failure in commiting an error. [*Living Flame of Love*]

> *Saint John of the Cross, Spanish cofounder (with Saint Teresa of Ávila) of the Discalced Carmelites, poet, 1542–91*

We will be satisfied to report in a few words a few dispositions that we have noticed in M. Olier and that he believed absolutely necessary in a spiritual director in order to properly direct persons and not lose himself in this hazardous ministry.

The first rule is not to meddle or interfere with, nor to push those who have the right to benefit from direction, but rather to wait until the direction and the will of God may be shown us by their own words. He regarded this so important that, of all the faults which can be in a director, he did not think there was one more dangerous either for the director or for others than this lack of vocation. It was in order to make us pay heed to it that he often told us, as M. de Bretonvilliers writes, "The directing of souls is the art of arts, the science of sciences, and the most difficult of all ministries in the Church. This burden was feared by all the Saints. It would be an unfounded boldness to exercise it before Our Lord entrusted it to us. It is, besides, a ministry which we cannot fulfill without a special grace, and God is not obliged to give it to those whom He does not call, as a master is not obliged to support his servant in things that he does without his approval and against his orders. . . "

He told us also that, far from introducing ourselves to this role, we should fear it and dread it after the example of the saints. If Christians themselves should always be in fear for their own salvation, although they had only one soul to save, spiritual directors should be in extreme fear, since they have as many persons upon whom their salvation depends as there were persons under their direction. He said that it was necessary to look at this role in a spirit of humility, regarding it much beyond our strength and recognizing in ourselves a total incapacity to perform it well. He also said that we should nevertheless accept it with confidence, because God would not fail to assist those whom he called, provided that they are faithful in praying without ceasing to Him in their needs. He also said that we would find there some powerful help to make us saints while sanctifying others.

> [*The Spirit of a Director of Souls*]
> *Jean-Jacques Olier, French priest and founder of*
> *the Society of Saint Sulpice, 1608–57*

Epilogue

Perhaps the most eloquent witness to the importance of spiritual direction is personal testimony to the transforming influence a spiritual director has had on an individual's life. Abbé Huvelin, as a spiritual director, profoundly influenced Baron Friedrich von Hügel, and he in turn directed and helped Evelyn Underhill. She, of course, affected many through her own writings, retreat leadership, and as a spiritual director. Father Daignault, S.J., directed Janet Erskine Stuart, who was to become superior general of the Society of the Sacred Heart. And there are many letters telling of Mother Stuart's influence on others. Letters and excerpts from other writings by the people involved in these two spiritual lineages are used in this epilogue to illustrate "how God can be good to someone through direction."

Baron Friedrich von Hügel wrote about Abbé Huvelin's influence on several occasions.

There is before my mind, with all the vividness resulting from direct personal intercourse and deep spiritual obligations, the figure of the Abbé Huvelin, who died only in 1910. A gentleman by birth and breeding, a distinguished Hellenist, a man of exquisitely piercing, humorous mind, he could readily have become a great editor or interpreter of Greek philosophical or patristic texts, or a remarkable Church historian. But this deep and heroic personality deliberately preferred "to write in souls," whilst occupying, during thirty-five years, a supernumerary, unpaid post in a large Parisian parish. There, suffering from gout in the eyes and brain, and usually lying prone in a darkened room, he served souls with the supreme authority of self-oblivious love, and brought light and purity and peace to countless troubled, sorrowing, or sinful souls. . . .

Thus, in the "Conferences on some of the Spiritual Guides of the Seventeenth Century," he says, . . . "God, who might have created us directly, employs, for this work, our parents, to whom He joins us by the tenderest ties. He could also save us directly, but He saves us, in fact, by means of certain souls, which have received the spiritual life before ourselves, and which communicate it to us, because they love us." [*Eternal Life*]

I had already in 1886 come under the grandly tonic influence of the Abbé Huvelin, that truly masculine saint who moved and trained so many a soul. There sanctity stood before me in the flesh, and this as the genuine deepest effect and reason of the Catholic Church; I could now utilize the sufferings of these hurricane years towards growing a little less unlike this mediator of Church and Christ and God.

[*Life of Baron von Hügel*]

There was the Abbé Huvelin—a rich and deep, a cultivated, above all an heroic soul, to whom I own incalculably much. A man full of vitality, the strongest passions and the deepest affections, the life of deliberate, irrevocable lifelong celibacy, entered upon by him in full manhood and with the clearest understanding of its meaning and range, was, I am very sure, profoundly costly. Yet he willed, used and loved this renunciation as an instrument, condition and price of the tenderest love of souls in God and of God in souls, right on to his end, in the seventies of his age.

[*Essays and Addresses on the Philosophy of Religion*]
Baron Friedrich von Hügel, lay Catholic theologian
and writer, 1852–1925

Evelyn Underhill describes her indebtedness to Baron Friedrich von Hügel as follows:

"He is the most wonderful personality I have ever known—so saintly, so truthful, sane and tolerant." "Under God, I owe him my whole spiritual life, and there would have been more of it than there is, if I had been more courageous and stern with myself, and followed his directions more thoroughly." Later she cherishes "the memory of an immense spiritual transcendence, . . . an Alpine quality, . . . the awe and passion which were felt when the Baron uttered the name of his God." [*The Letters of Evelyn Underhill*]

When I went to the Baron he said I wasn't much better than a Unitarian. Somehow by his prayers or something, he compelled me to experience Christ. He never said anything more about it—but I know, humanly speaking, he did it. It took about four months—it was like watching the sun rise very slowly—and then suddenly one knew what it was. . . . I seem to have to try as it were to live more and more towards him only. . . . The New Testament . . . now seems full of things never noticed—all gets more and more alive and compellingly beautiful. . . . . Holy Communion, which at first I did simply under obedience (to von Hügel), gets more and more wonderful too. It is in that world and atmosphere one lives. [*Life of Evelyn Underhill*]

Evelyn Underhill, Anglican married woman,
wrote on mysticism, 1875–1941

Father Daignault's direction of and friendship with Janet Erskine Stuart began in 1898 and only ended with her death in 1914. She often sought his counsel by letter as they were both frequently away from England. Here are portions of two letters expressing her gratitude and telling of his influence.

February, 1899
. . . Now let me tell you what use I made of the direction you were good enough to give me two months ago, and also thank you most gratefully for your letter of September 2nd. . . .

I recognise the truth of what you told me, that I have a tendency to draw things too fine, and so lose freedom of spirit and concentration of energy on the one thing necessary; also the tendency to judge too quickly and severely, though I do not think I hold those judgments when I reflect on them.

I have not been drowned once since I saw you, and hardly know myself, when I find firm ground under my feet, with no possibility of doubting. It is a great joy and I thank God with deep gratitude for putting my soul (as He did Himself, I think) into your hands. There is plenty of fighting, of course, but I am trying, exactly as you say, to laugh at what would have drowned me a short time ago. It is difficult sometimes and my act of confidence often consists of "I firmly hope because Father Daignault said it was all right. . . ."

[Life and Letters of Janet Erskine Stuart]

Roehampton: 7 September 1899

. . . This is not a letter that expects an answer, but only to express my most grateful thanks for yours of July 31. . . . It was a great joy in more ways than one, and brought me light and help, as your letters always do. . . . God has been so good to me through you that I have direction for life. . . .

Things have gone back now into their ordinary course, and the months in America are getting into perspective. As to the outside, they have taught me a great deal, made me feel older and more sure of things, not as if I had to feel my way so much. They have left me also a sense that life is hurrying on to its end, not with any particular thought of the nearness of death, but rather of the shortness of time and that one must work while it is day. . . .

[Life and Letters of Janet Erskine Stuart]

Three people wrote as follows about Janet Erskine Stuart's influence on them. The first is from an anonymous friend.

I felt a great attraction for Reverend Mother Stuart, even though I had never had any personal intercourse with her. Her writings and all I had heard of her drew me to her irresistibly. Sorrows, too great, I thought, to confide to any human heart, had entered my life. An inspiration came to me one day that they were not too great for her; she surely could help and sympathize. So I wrote, and with all confidence told her of my many and great needs. Her answer came quickly, and with the intuition and sympathy of the saints I found she understood all. Her words and prayers changed me at once, and the whole aspect of my life. . . . I feel her influence is ever with me brightening the way . . . so hard until the touch of her spirit changed my weakness to courage. *[Life and Letters of Janet Erskine Stuart]*

Speaking of her influence on people, one of her nuns writes as follows:

I find it difficult to express all that I owe to Reverend Mother Stuart. Through her I not only gave up a position which would have been full of danger and difficulty for me, but I also became a Religious. I saw her for the first time in October 1903, after a rough crossing during a stormy night, a picture of my life at that time. And like Our Lord she stood on the shore to receive me in the morning, at Roehampton. What a welcome she gave me, though I had never seen her before. From the first moment I was her child, as she often told me afterwards. I had no thought of the possibility of a religious vocation. For me there seemed to be but one way: to become an artist, and thus realise the great desires and designs which my parents had had upon this point. Mother Stuart knew all this. Our first interviews always ran on music. But little by little another note was touched, and then suddenly it dawned upon me that I had to exchange my musical career for a religious one. When I told her this, she asked me to put aside such thoughts, it was to soon. Only after many months of reflection, during which she was to me the kindest of mothers, did she receive me as a postulant.

[*Life and Letters of Janet Erskine Stuart*]

Another writes:

Reverend Mother Stuart seemed to be the very channel of God's grace to souls, or her prayer its condition. It happened that I was cut off from all intercourse with her at a period of great anguish of spirit. . . . One night I dreamt that she came to me: "What takes your soul straightest to God?" she asked. Power to speak failed me, so after a moment's pause she answered her own question: "Adversity; so courage, child, this trial is leading you to God." I awoke with the sense of joy that her words brought me. . . . At that very hour she had received Holy Communion at Roehampton and had prayed for me. At another time, with the pressure of her hand on my head, came to me the revelation of suffering before me and the grace to embrace it. [*Life and Letters of Janet Erskine Stuart*]

Janet Erskine Stuart, superior general of the Society of the Sacred Heart, 1857–1914

Bibliography and Index

This bibliography attempts to list many of the more significant persons and sources on the Christian ministry of spiritual direction, Anglican, Protestant, Roman Catholic, and Orthodox. Representative works from almost every period are included and listed alphabetically for easier reference. English translations are listed where available.

The works included (usually in the original language) were either actually used or were consulted in the preparation of this anthology—although not necessarily in the edition listed. Most of these works are available in theological libraries in the United States. The bibliography is meant to provide an extensive though not exhaustive list of references for anyone seriously interested in this Christian ministry.

For works quoted in this anthology we have indicated (in parentheses) the page number on which the selection may be found.

Aelred of Rievaulx, St. *Spiritual Friendship*. Migne, *PL* 195. (see p. 33)

———. *Spiritual Friendship*. Translated by M. E. Laker. Kalamazoo, Mich.: Cistercian Pubs., 1974.

Albert the Great, St. *Opera omnia*. "Commentary on Luke." Edited by Auguste Borgnet. 38 vols. Paris: L. Vivès, 1890–99. Vol. 23. (see p. 21)

Álvarez de Paz, Diego. *Opera Jacobi Alvarez de Paz*. Edited by Louis Vivès. 6 vols. Vol. 3, book 4. Paris: L. Vivès, 1875–76. (see p. 29)

Amvrosy, Staretz. *Hiermonk Amvrosy and His Writings*. Edited by Arch. Agapit. 2 vols. Moscow, 1900. (see pp. 154, 167)

———. *Letters to Religious*. 2 vols. N.p. :|Sergiev Posad, 1908–09.

Angela of Foligno, Bl. *The Book of the Visions and Instructions of Blessed Angela of Foligno*. Translated by A. P. J. Cruikshank. Leamington: Art & Book, 1888. (see p. 126)

———. *Le Livre des visions et instructions*. Translated by Ernest Hello. 5th ed. Paris: A. Tralin, 1914.

Anselm, St. *Eadmeri Historia Novorum in Anglia, et opuscula duo de Vita Sancti Anselmi et quibusdam miraculis ejus.* Edited by Martin Rule. London: Longman, 1884. (see p. 125)

———. *Life of St. Anselm,* by Eadmer. Translated by R. W. Southern. London: Thomas Nelson, 1962.

Anthony of Florence, St. *Opera a ben vivere.* Edited by Francesco Palermo. Florence: M. Cellini, 1858. (see p. 30)

Anthony, St. *Life of St. Anthony,* by St. Athanasius. Migne, *PG* 18. (see pp. 124, 183)

Apophthegmata Patrum (The Sayings of the Fathers). Migne, *PG* 65.71–440, and Migne, *PL* 73.739–1066. (see pp. 2, 50, 51, 170, 171)

———. *The Sayings of the Desert Fathers.* Translated by Benedicta Ward. Kalamazoo, Mich.: Cistercian Pubs., 1975. (see pp. 23, 24, 42, 48, 49, 64, 91, 121, 125, 141)

Arndt, Johann. *True Christianity.* Translated by Peter Erb. New York: Paulist Press, 1979.

Augustine, St. *Sermons.* Migne, *PL* 39. (see p. 149)

———. *Letter #130 to Proba.* Migne, *PL* 33.493–507.

———. *Letters.* Translated by Sr. Wilfrid Parsons. Fathers of the Church, vol. 13. New York: Fathers of the Church, 1956.

———. *Christian Instruction.* Migne, *PL* 34.17–18.

Aumann, Jordan. *Spiritual Theology.* Huntington, Ind.: Our Sunday Visitor, 1980. (see p. 100)

Baker, Augustine. *Holy Wisdom.* Edited by Serenus Cressy. New York: [Benziger] 1890. (see pp. 27, 43, 130)

Barat, Madeleine Sophie, St. *Conferences.* 2 vols. London, 1900.

———. *Lettres choisies.* 11 vols. London and Rome, 1920–65.

———. *Pensées et maximes.* 2d ed. Rome, 1940.

———. *St. Madeleine Sophie: Her Life and Letters.* Edited by Margaret Williams. New York: Herder & Herder, 1965. (see pp. 30, 144)

Barry, William A. and Connolly, William J. *The Practice of Spiritual Direction.* New York: Seabury, 1982. (see p. 139)

Barsanuphius and John. *Barsanuphe et Jean de Gaza; correspondance.* Sable-sur-Sarthe: Abbaye Saint-Pierre de Solesmes, 1972. (see pp. 17, 160, 164)

Basil, St. *The Long Rule.* Migne, *PG* 31. (see pp. 63, 79)

———. *The Short Rule.* Migne, *PG* 31.

———. *On Renunciation of the World.* Migne, *PG* 31. (see p. 41)

———. *Ascetical Works.* Fathers of the Church, vol. 9. Washington, D.C.: Catholic University Press, 1962.

Beaudenom, Léopold. *Spiritual Progress.* 2 vols. Baltimore: Carroll Press, 1950. (see p. 7)

————. *Lettres de direction.* Paris: Lethielleux, 1920. (see p. 176)

Bede, Ven. *Homily on St. James' Epistle.* Migne, *PL* 93.39. (see p. 79)

Bellarmine, Robert, St. *Letters.* Vol. 1. (in Provinciae Siculae S.J. Ortus et Res Gestae) P. Aquilera, ed. Panormi, 1740, Part II. (see p. 69)

Benoît, J. D. *Direction spirituelle et protestantisme, étude sur la légitimité d'une direction protestante.* Paris: Alcan, 1940.

————. *Calvin, Directeur d'âmes.* Strasbourg: Éditions Oberlin, 1947.

Bernard, St. *Five Books of Consideration.* Migne, *PL* 182. (see pp. 31, 129)

————. *Sermons.* Migne, *PL* 183. (see p. 31)

————. *Letters.* Migne, *PL* 184.

————. *Five Books on Consideration: Advice to a Pope.* Translated by J. D. Anderson and E. T. Kennan. Kalamazoo, Mich.: Cistercian Pubs., 1976.

Bérulle, Pierre Cardinal de. *Œuvres complètes.* Paris: Migne, 1856. (see p. 92)

————. *Le Mémorial de Direction pour les Supérieurs.* Edited by Claude Taveau. Paris: Desclée, de Brouwer, 1933. (see pp. 21, 89)

————. *Opuscules de piété.* Edited by Gaston Rotureau. Paris: Aubier, Éditions Montaigne, 1944.

————. *Correspondance du cardinal Pierre de Bérulle.* Edited by Jean Dagens. Paris: Desclée, de Brouwer, 1937–39. (see p. 90)

Boccardo, Can. Luigi. *Confessione e direzione.* 3 vols. Turin: Istituto per Ciechi, 1921.

Bona, John Cardinal. *Manductio ad coelum.* Brussels: F. Foppens, 1664. (see p. 24)

————. *Cursus vitae spiritualis.* Rome, 1674.

————. *Opuscula ascetica selecta Ioannis Cardinalis Bona.* "De discretione spirituum." Freiburg: Herder, 1911. (see p. 131)

————. *A Treatise of Spiritual Life.* Translated by D. A. Donovan. New York: Pustet, 1901. (see pp. 5, 66)

Bonaventure, St. *The Works of Bonaventure: Cardinal, Seraphic Doctor, and Saint.* Translated by José de Vinck. Vol. 3. Paterson: St. Anthony Guild Press, 1960.

Bonhoeffer, Dietrich. *Life Together.* Translated by John W. Doberstein. New York: Harper, 1954. (see p. 86)

Bossuet, Jacques. *Letters of Spiritual Direction.* Translated by Geoffrey Webb and Adrian Walker. London: Mowbray, 1958.

Bruno, J. "La Direction spirituelle dans le christianisme." *Hermes* 4 (1967).

Bryant, Christopher. *The Heart in Pilgrimage: Christian Guidelines for the Human Journey*. New York: Seabury, 1980. (see pp. 103, 108, 179)

Cagnac, Moïse. *Les Lettres spirituelles en France*. 2 vols. Paris: Gigord, 1929.

Callistus II of Xantoupulus. *Ascetic Conferences*. Migne, *PG* 147. (see p. 18)

Calvin, John. *Joannis Calvini opera selecta*. Edited by Peter Barth and W. Niesel. 5 vols. Munich: Kaiser, 1926–62. (see pp. 160, 166)

———. *Calvin: Institutes of the Christian Religion*. Edited by J. T. McNeill. 2 vols. Library of Christian Classics. Philadelphia: Westminster, 1960.

Cameli, Joseph. "Spiritual Direction for Priests." *Crux,* 15 November 1976.

Carter, Edward. *The Spirit Is Present*. Canfield, Ohio: Alba House, 1973. (see pp. 45, 55, 87, 131)

Cassian, John. *Institutes*. Migne, *PL* 49. (see p. 23)

———. *Conferences*. Migne, *PL* 49. (see pp. 2, 64, 128)

———. *The Works of John Cassian*. Translated by Edgar Gibson. A Select Library of Nicene and Post-Nicene Fathers of the Christian Church, 2d ser., vol. 11. New York: Christian Literature, 1894.

Catherine of Genoa, St. *Les Œuvres de Sainte Catherine de Gênes, précédé de sa vie*. 6th ed. Paris: A. Tralin, 1926. (see p. 11)

———. *Catherine of Genoa: Purgation and Purgatory, the Spiritual Dialogue*. Translated by Serge Hughes. New York: Paulist Press, 1979.

———. *The Life and Sayings of Saint Catherine of Genoa*. Translated and edited by Paul Garvin. Staten Island, N.Y.: Alba House, 1964.

Catherine of Siena, St. *Libro della divina dottrina*. Edited by Matilde Fiorilli. 2d ed. Bari: Laterza et Figli, 1928.

———. *Saint Catherine of Siena as Seen in Her Letters*. Translated and edited by V. D. Scudder. London: J. M. Dent, 1905. (see page 165-66)

———. *Catherine of Siena: The Dialogue*. Translated and edited by Suzanne Noffke. New York: Paulist Press, 1980.

Caussade, Jean Pierre de. *Abandonment to Divine Providence*. Exeter: Catholic Records Press, 1921.

Chantal, Jane Frances de, St. *Saint Jane Frances Frémyot de Chantal: Her Exhortations, Conferences and Instructions*. Rev. ed. Chicago: Loyola University Press, 1928

Chapman, Dom John, O.S.B. *The Spiritual Letters of Dom John Chapman, O.S.B., Fourth Abbot of Downside*. Edited by Roger Hudleston. 2d ed. London: Sheed & Ward, 1946. (see pp. 31, 157)

Chautard, Dom John Baptist. *L'Âme de tout apostolat*. Paris: Office français du livre, 1945. (see p. 83)

———. *The Soul of the Apostolate*. Techny, Ill.: Mission Press, 1946.

Choisy, Eugène. *Calvin, éducateur des consciences.* Neuilly: Éditions de "La Cause," 1925.

Climacus, John, St. *The Ladder of Divine Ascent.* Rev. ed. Boston: Holy Transfiguration Monastery, 1978.

Cloud of Unknowing, The. (Many good editions are available.) (see pp. 91, 104)

Connolly, William J. "Contemporary Spiritual Direction." *Studies in Spirituality of Jesuits* # 7 (1975). (see p. 97)

Corcoran, Sr. Donald. *Abba: Guides to Wholeness and Holiness East and West.* Edited by John R. Summerfeld. Kalamazoo, Mich.: Cistercian Pubs., 1982. (see pp. 61, 115)

Cropper, Margaret. *Life of Evelyn Underhill.* London: Mowbrays, 1958. (see p. 185)

Daniélou, Jean Cardinal. "La direction spirituelle dans la tradition ancienne de l'Église." *Christus* 7 (1960).

Dorotheos of Gaza, St. *Œuvres spirituelles.* Edited and translated by Lucien Regnault and Jacques de Préville. Sources chrétiennes, vol. 92. Paris: Éditions du Cerf, 1963 (or Migne, *PG* 88). (see p. 3)

———. *Dorotheos of Gaza: Discourses and Sayings.* "On Need of Consultation." Translated by E. P. Wheeler. Kalamazoo, Mich.: Cistercian Pubs., 1977.

Dostoevski, Feodor. *The Brothers Karamazov.* New York: Grosset & Dunlap, n.d. (see p. 176)

Doyle, Charles Hugo. *Guidance in Spiritual Direction.* Westminster, Md.: Newman Press, 1958. (see pp. 101, 107)

Dupanloup, Félix Antoine. *Lettres de direction.* Edited by Msgr. Chapon. Paris: Lethielleux, n.d. (see p. 82)

———. *Un Grand Évêque.* Paris: Hachette, 1914.

Eckhart, Meister Johann. *Deutsche Mystiker des vierzehnten Jahrhunderts.* Edited by Franz Pfeiffer. 4th ed. Göttingen: Vandennoeck & Reprecht, 1924. (see pp. 3, 164)

Edwards, Jonathan. *A Treatise Concerning Religious Affections in Three Parts.* Boston: S. Kneeland & T. Green, 1746. (see p. 137)

———. *Works.* New York: Daniel Appleton, 1835.

Edwards, Tilden. *Spiritual Friend: Reclaiming the Gift of Spiritual Direction.* New York: Paulist Press, 1980. (see p. 97)

English, John. *Spiritual Freedom: From an Experience of the Ignatian Exercises to the Art of Spiritual Direction.* Guelph, Ontario: Loyola House, 1973. (see p. 77)

Faber, Frederick William. *Growth in Holiness: or, The Progress of the Spiritual Life.* "The Office of Spiritual Director." Baltimore: Murphy, 1854. (see pp. 32, 175)

Fedotov, G. P., ed. *A Treasury of Russian Spirituality.* New York: Sheed & Ward, 1948.

Fénelon, François. *Œuvres complètes.* "Spiritual Letters." 10 vols. Paris: J. Leroux et Juby, 1848–52. (see pp. 153, 154)

———. *Letters to Men and Women.* Edited by Derek Stanford. Westminster, Md.: Newman Press, 1957.

———. *Letters of Love and Counsel.* Translated by John McEwen. New York: Harcourt, 1964.

Fenhagen, James C. *Ministry and Solitude: The Ministry of Laity and Clergy in Church and Society.* New York: Seabury, 1981. (see p. 133)

Fleming, David. "Beginning Spiritual Direction." *Review for Religious* 33 (1974). (see p. 56)

Foster, Richard J. *The Celebration of Discipline: Paths to Spiritual Growth.* San Francisco: Harper & Row, 1978. (see p. 179)

Foucauld, Charles de. *Père de Foucauld, abbé Huvelin; correspondance inédite.* Tournai: Desclée, 1957. (see p. 72)

———. *Œuvres spirituelles; anthologie.* Paris: Éditions du Seuil, 1958. (see p. 8)

———. *Pensées et maximes.* Paris: La Colombe, 1953.

———. *Lettres à Mme de Bondy, de la Trappe à Tamanrasset.* Paris: Desclée, de Brouwer, 1966.

———. *Lettres à mes frères de la Trappe.* Paris: Le Cerf, 1969.

———. *Directoire.* Paris, Éditions du Seuil, 1928. (see p. 37)

Fox, George. *The Journal.* Edited by Thomas Ellwood. N.p., 1964.

———. *The Journal of George Fox.* "Appendix." Revised and edited by Norman Penney. London: J. M. Dent, 1924.

Francis of Assisi, St. *Opuscula sancti patris Francisci Assisiensis sec. codices mss. emendata et denuo edita a pp. Collegii s. Bonaventurae.* Edited by Leonhard Lemmens. Quaracchi: Collegium s. Bonaventurae, 1904.

Francis de Sales, St. *Œuvres.* "Treatise on the Love of God." Annecy: Abry Libr., 1893. (see pp. 137, 141)

———. *Œuvres,* "Introduction to the Devout Life." Annecy: Abry Libr., 1893. (see p. 25, 36, 44, 62, 82)

———. *Œuvres.* "Letters." Annecy: Abry Libr., 1893. (see p. 40, 58, 152)

———. *Introduction to the Devout Life.* Edited and translated by Allan Ross. London: Burns, Oats & Washbourne, 1948.

———. *Selected Letters.* Translated by Elizabeth Stopp. London: Faber & Faber, 1960.

Frost, Dom Bede. *The Art of Mental Prayer*. 4th rev. ed. London: Philip Allan, 1932. (see pp. 26, 75, 89)

Garrigou-Lagrange, Réginald. *The Three Ages of the Interior Life, Prelude of Eternal Life*. Translated by Sr. M. T. Doyle. St. Louis: Herder, 1947.

Gay, Msgr. Charles. *Lettres de direction spirituelle*. 4 vols. Paris: Oudin, 1906. (see pp. 162, 175)

Gerson, John. *Opera omnia*. "De probatione spirituum"; "De examinatione doctrinarum"; "De distinctione verarum visionum a falsis"; "De tentationibus diaboli diversis"; "De conscientia scrupolosa." Antwerp: Sumptibus Societatis, 1706.

Gertrude the Great, St. *Œuvres spirituelles*, Sources chrétiennes, vols. 127, 139, 143, and 255. Paris: Éditions du Cerf, 1967–78.

———. *The Life and Revelations of Saint Gertrude, Virgin and Abbess, of the Order of St. Benedict*. Westminster, Md.: Newman Press, 1949. (see pp. 88, 173)

Godinez, Miguel, Fr. *Praxis theologiae mysticae*, Book VIII. Translated by E. I. de La Reguera. Paris: Lethielleux, 1921. (see p. 32)

Grandmaison, Léonce de. *Écrits spirituels*. 25th ed. 3 vols. Vol. 1. Paris: Beauchesne, 1953. (see p. 54)

———. *Écrits spirituels*. 26th ed. 3 vols. Vol. 2. Paris: Beauchesne, 1954.

Gratton, Carolyn. *Guidelines for Spiritual Direction*. Denville, N.J.: Dimension Books, 1980. (see p. 77)

Gregory the Great, St. *Rules for Pastoral Care*. Migne, *PL* 77.

———. *Pastoral Care*. Translated by Henry Davis. Westminster, Md.: Newman Press, 1950. (see p. 28)

———. *Dialogues*. Translated by O. J. Zimmerman. Fathers of the Church, vol. 39. New York: Fathers of the Church, 1959. (see p. 10)

Gregory Nazianzen, St. *Select Orations and Select Letters*. Translated by C. G. Browne and J. E. Swallow. A Select Library of Nicene and Post-Nicene Fathers of the Christian Church, 2d ser., vol. 7. New York: Christian Literature, 1894. (see p. 91)

———. *Orationes*. Migne, *PG* 35.

Gregory of Nyssa, St. *Life of Moses; On Virginity*. Migne, *PG* 46. (see pp. 27, 51)

———. *Ascetical Works*. Translated by Virginia W. Callahan. The Fathers of the Church, vol. 58. Washington, D.C.: Catholic University of America Press, 1967.

Gregory of Sinai, St. *Rules for Hesychasts*. Migne, *PG* 150. (see p. 42)

Grou, Jean. *Manuel des âmes intérieures, suite d'opuscules inédits du P. Grou*. Paris: Meyer, 1833. (see pp. 67, 82)

———. *Manual for Interior Souls*. Edited by Donald O'Sullivan. London: Burns & Oates, 1955.

————. *Spiritual Maxims*. Edited and translated by Monk of Parkminster. Springfield, Ill.: Templegate, 1961 (see p. 13)

Guibert, Joseph De. *Theologia spiritualis, ascetica et mystica; quaestiones selectae in praelectionum usumo*. Rome: Gregorian University, 1939. (see p. 40)

————. *The Theology of the Spiritual Life*. Translated by Paul Barrett. New York: Sheed & Ward, 1953.

Guilloré, Francis. *La Manière de conduire les âmes dans la vie spirituelle*. Paris: de Guyot frères, 1853. (see p. 93)

Hadewijch of Antwerp, Bl. *Mediaeval Netherlands Religious Literature*. Translated and edited by Eric Colledge. New York: London House & Maxwell, 1965. (see p. 3)

Harton, F. P. *The Elements of the Spiritual Life*. London: S.P.C.K., 1964. (see pp. 47, 83, 90, 113)

Hildegarde, St. *Life and Visions of St. Hildegarde*. Edited by F. M. Steele. St. Louis: B. Herder, 1915.

Hilton, Walter. *The Goad of Love*. Edited by Clare Kirchberger. London: Faber & Faber, 1952.

————. *The Scale of Perfection*. Edited by Evelyn Underhill. London: J. M. Watkins, 1923.

Honnay, Abbé. *L'Art de la direction*. 4th ed. Arras: Brunet, 1922.

Hügel, Baron Friedrich von. *Eternal Life: A Study of Its Implications and Applications by Baron Friedrich von Hügel*. Edinburgh: Clark, 1912.

————. *Essays and Addresses on the Philosophy of Religion*. London: J. M. Dent, 1928. (see pp. 8, 183)

————. *Spiritual Counsel and Letters*. Edited by Douglas V. Steere. New York: Harper & Row, 1964. (see pp. 148, 155)

————. *Letters from Baron Friedrich von Hügel to a Niece*. Edited by Gwendolen Green. London: J. M. Dent, 1928. (see pp. 113, 147, 156)

Hulst, Maurice d'. *Lettres de direction*. Edited by Msgr. Alfred Baudrillart. Paris: Poussielgue, 1908. (see p. 14)

Huvelin, Abbé Henri. *Quelques directeurs d'âmes au XVIIᵉ siècle. Saint François de Sales. M. Olier. Saint Vincent de Paul. L'Abbé de Rancé. Causeries*. Paris: J. Gabalda, 1911.

————. *Échos des entretiens de l'abbé Huvelin aux femmes chrétiennes et de quelques homélies*. Paris: Rublot, 1916.

————. *Écrits spirituels et paroles de l'abbé Huvelin*. Edited by M.-T. Louis Lefebvre. Paris: Lethielleux, 1959.

————. *Some Spiritual Guides of the Seventeenth Century*. Translated by M. Joseph Leonard. New York: Benziger, 1927.

Isaac of Nineveh, St. *Book on Contempt of the World*. Migne, *PG* 86a.869. (see p. 52)

———. *Mystic Treatises*. Translated by A. J. Wensinck. Wiesbaden: Martin Sandig, 1969.

Isabel, Damien. *The Spiritual Director*. Chicago: Franciscan Herald, 1976. (see pp. 87,118,128)

Isidore of Pelusium, St. *Letters*. Migne, *PL* 78. (see p. 52)

John of Avila, St. *Obras completas del santo maestro Juan de Avila*. "Audi, filia." Edited by L. S. Balust and F. M. Hernandez. Biblioteca de autores cristianos, vols. 313, 315. Rev. ed. Madrid: Editorial católica, 1970. (see pp. 4, 18, 62, 135, 174)

John of the Cross, St. *Vida y obras*. Biblioteca de autores cristianos, vol. 15. 4th ed., Madrid: Editorial católica, 1960. (see pp. 4, 5, 56, 92, 105, 106, 107, 110, 111, 119, 136, 181)

———. *Collected Works*. Translated by Kieran Kavanaugh and Otilio Rodriguez. Garden City, N.Y.: Doubleday, 1964.

Jones, Alan. *Exploring Spiritual Direction: An Essay on Christian Friendship*. New York: Seabury, 1982. (see p. 180)

Jones, Rufus M. *The Flowering of Mysticism: The Friends of God in the Fourteenth Century*. 1940. Reprint. New York: Hafner, 1971. (see p. 138)

———. *Rufus Jones Speaks to Our Time*. Edited by Harry E. Fosdick. New York: Macmillan, 1961.

Jordan of Saxony, Bl. *Love among the Saints: The Letters of Blessed Jordan of Saxony to Blessed Diana of Andalò*. Translated by Kathleen Pond. London: Bloomsbury, 1958.

Juliana of Norwich. *Revelations of Divine Love*. Reprint of Cressy 1670 ed. Leicester, 1845. (see p. 122)

———. *Showings*. Translated by Edmund Colledge and James Walsh. New York: Paulist Press, 1978.

Keane, Philip S. "Discernment of Spirits: A Theological Reflection." *American Ecclesiastic Review* 168 (1974): 52–53. (see p. 124)

Keble, John. *Letters of Spiritual Counsel*. 2d ed. London: James Parker, 1870. (see p. 67)

Kelsey, Morton T. *The Other Side of Silence: A Guide to Christian Meditation*. New York: Paulist Press, 1976. (see p. 44)

La Colombière, Claude de. *Œuvres complètes du vénérable Père Claude de la Colombière*. 6 vols. Grenoble: Imprimerie Notre-Dame, 1900–1901. Vol. 6. (see p. 142)

Lacordaire, Henri-Dominique. *Vie intime et religieuse*. Edited by B. Chocarne. Paris, 1866. (see p. 63)

Lallemant, Fr. Louis. *The Spiritual Doctrine of Father Louis Lallemant of the Society of Jesus*. Edited by A. G. McDougall. Westminster, Md.: Newman Press, 1946.

Laplace, Jean. *The Direction of Conscience*. Translated by J. C. Guinness. New York: Herder & Herder, 1967. (see p. 76)

Laurence Justinian, St. *Sancti Laurentii Justinianni proto-patriarchae Veneti opera omnia in duos tomus distincta, et ad meliorem harmoniam nunc primum redacts, atque aucta.* "On Contempt of the World"; "On Monastic Obedience." 2 vols. Venice: Baptista Albritius & Joseph Rusa, 1751. (see p. 18)

Law, William. *A Serious Call to a Devout and Holy Life*. Edited by P. G. Stanwood. New York: Paulist Press, 1978.

Lawrence, Brother. *La Pratique de la présence de Dieu*. Edited by L. Van den Bossche. Paris, 1934. (see p. 71)

———. *The Practice of the Presence of God*. Nashville: Abingdon Press, 1975.

Leech, Kenneth. *Soul Friend: The Practice of Christian Spirituality*. San Francisco: Harper & Row, 1980. (see p. 10)

Le Gaudier, Anthony. *De perfectione vitae spiritualis*. Edited by A. M. Michelletti. 3 vols. Vol. 2, part 5. Rome: Taurinorum, 1903.

Lehodey, Dom Vital. *The Ways of Mental Prayer*. Dublin: M. H. Gill, 1955. (see p. 54)

Leo XIII, Pope. *Testem Benevolentiae*. Rome: Vatican Polyglot Press, 1899. Pars. 7 & 8. (see p. 13)

Libermann, Ven. Francis. *Écrits spirituels du vénérable Libermann, premier supérieur général de la congrégation du Saint-Esprit et du Saint-Cœur de Marie*. Paris: Lecoffre, 1891.

———. *Lettres spirituelles du vénérable Libermann, premier supérieur général de la congrégation du Saint-Esprit et du Saint-Cœur de Marie.* 3 vols. Paris: Poussielgue, 1888–91. (see p. 94)

Liguori, St. Alphonsus de. *Lettere di S. Alfonso Maria de' Liguori*. 8 vols. Rome: Società S. Giovanni, 1887–90. Vol. 1. (see p. 59)

———. *The Complete Works of Saint Alphonsus de Liguori*. Cent. ed. 22 vols. New York: Benziger, 1886–92.

Louf, Andre. *Teach Us to Pray*. Translated by H. Hoskins. Chicago: Franciscan Herald, 1974. (see p. 21)

Loyola, Ignatius de, St. *Obras completas*. Edited by Ignacio Iparraguirre. Biblioteca de autores cristianos, vol. 86. Madrid: Editorial Católica, 1952. (see p. 134)

———. *Letters of St. Ignatius of Loyola*. Translated by William J. Young. Chicago: Loyola University Press, 1959.

———. *The Spiritual Exercises*. (Many good editions in English.)

Lucie Christine. *Spiritual Journal of Lucie Christine (1870-1908)*. Edited by Auguste Poulain. London: Kegan Paul, 1920.

Luther, Martin. *D. Martin Luther's Werke; kritische Gesammtausgabe.* "Sermon 8 at Wittenberg"; "Letters of Spiritual Counsel." Weimar: H. Böhlau, 1883–19–. (see pp. 79, 150)

————. *Letters of Spiritual Counsel.* Translated and edited by T. H. Tappert. Library of Christian Classics, vol. 18. Philadelphia: Westminster Press, 1956.

Macarius the Great, St. *Spiritual Homilies.* Migne, *PG* 34.

————. *Fifty Spiritual Homilies.* 1921. Reprint. Translated by A. J. Mason. Willits, Calif.: Eastern Orthodox Books, 1974.

Macarius Ivanov. *Letters to Monks.* Moscow, 1861. (see p. 167)

————. *Russian Letters of Direction.* Translated and edited by Julia de Beausobre. New York: St. Vladimir Seminary, 1975.

McBrien, Richard P. *Catholicism.* 2 vols. Minneapolis: Winston Press, 1980. (see p. 123)

Marie of the Incarnation, St. *Écrits spirituels et historiques.* Edited by Albert Jamet. 4 vols. Quebec: L' Action Sociale, 1929–39. (see p. 65)

————. *Lettres de la révérénde mère Marie de l' Incarnation (née Marie Guyard) première supérieure du monastère des ursulines de Québec.* 2 vols. Tournai: Casterman, 1876. (see p. 5)

————. *Spiritual Teaching of Mary of the Incarnation.* Translated by M. Herman. New York: Sheed & Ward, 1963.

————. *The Autobiography of Venerable Marie of the Incarnation, O.S.U., Mystic and Missionary.* Translated by J. J. Sullivan. Chicago: Loyola University Press, 1964.

Maritain, Raïssa. *Adventures in Grace.* Translated by Julie Kernan. New York: Longmans, Green, 1945.

Mark the Ascetic, St. *Spiritual Discourses.* Migne, *PG* 65.

Marmion, Dom Columba. *Abbot Columba Marmion: A Master of the Spiritual Life.* "The Spiritual Director." St. Louis: Herder, 1942.

Martin, Paul. *Un Directur spirituel au XVIe siècle; étude sur la correspondance de Calvin.* Montauban: J. Granié, 1886.

Masson, Yves E. *Vie chrétienne et vie spirituelle; introduction à l' étude de la théologie ascétique et mystique.* Paris: Bloud & Gay, 1929. (see pp. 33, 68, 99, 176)

————. *The Christian Life and the Spiritual Life: Introduction to the Study of Ascetical and Mystical Theology.* Translated by Sr. M. Hyacinth. St. Louis: Herder, 1930.

Maximus the Confessor, St. *The Ascetic Life: The Four Centuries on Charity.* Translated and annotated by Polycarp Sherwood. Ancient Christian Writers, vol. 21. Westminster, Md.: Newman Press, 1955.

Menéndez-Reigada, Ignacio. *De dirección espiritual.* Salamanca: Edit. Fides, 1934.

Merton, Thomas. *Spiritual Direction and Meditation*. Collegeville, Minn.: Liturgical Press, 1960. (see pp. 15, 21)

———. *The Climate of Monastic Prayer*. Kalamazoo, Mich.: Cistercian Pubs., 1969.

———. *New Seeds of Contemplation*. New York: New Directions, 1962. (see p. 178)

———. *Contemplation in a World of Action*. Garden City, N.Y.: Doubleday, Image, 1973. (see p. 9)

———. *Thomas Merton, Monk: A Monastic Tribute*. Edited by Patrick Hart. Garden City, N.Y.: Doubleday, Image, 1976. (see p. 127)

Molinos, Miguel de. *The Spiritual Guide Which Disentangles the Soul*. Edited by Kathleen Lyttelton. 6th ed. London: Methuen, 1950.

Nagolkin, Leonid. *Counsel of Father Leonid*. St. Petersburg, 1939. (see p. 68)

Neff, Félix. *Lettres de direction spirituelle inédites*. Dieulefit: Nouvelle Société de'éditions de Toulouse, 1934.

Neri, St. Philip. *La vita di San Filippo Neri libri tre,* by Alfonso Capecelatro, 4th ed. Rome: S. Giovanni, 1901. (see pp. 49, 50)

Newman, John Cardinal. *Cardinal Newman's Best Plain Sermons*. "Hidden Presence of Christ." Edited by V. F. Blehl. New York: Herder, 1964.

———. *Sermons Bearing on Subjects of the Day*. "Dangers to Penitent." London: Longmans, Green, 1918. (see p. 6)

Nicodemus the Hagiorite, St. *Writings from the Philokalia on Prayer of the Heart*. Translated by E. Kadloubovsky and G. E. H. Palmer. London: Faber & Faber, 1978.

Nilus the Elder, St. *Ascetical Discourses*. Migne, *PG* 79.747–750. (see pp. 24, 51, 180)

Nouwen, Henri J. M. *The Living Reminder: Service and Prayer in Memory of Jesus Christ*. New York: Seabury, 1981. (see p. 10)

———. *Reaching Out: The Three Movements of Spiritual Life*. Garden City, N.Y.: Doubleday, 1975. (see p. 40)

———. *Genesee Diary: Report From a Trappist Monastery*. Garden City, N.Y.: Doubleday, 1976.

O'Connor, Elizabeth. *Call to Commitment*. New York: Harper & Row, 1963. (see pp. 38, 58, 76, 90, 178)

Origen. *Homily on Psalm 37*. Migne, *PG* 12.1386. (see p. 78)

Olier, Jean-Jacques. *Vie de M. Olier, fondateur du séminaire de Saint-Sulpice,* by Abbé Faillon. 4th ed. 3 vols. Paris: Poussielgue, 1873. (see p. 89)

———. *Œuvres Completes*. "L'Esprit d'un Directeur des Âmes." Paris: Migne, 1856. (see p. 112, 181)

————. *Lettres de M. Olier.* Edited by Louis Tronson. Rev. ed. 2 vols. Paris: Lecoffre, 1885. (see p. 65)

Pachomius, St. *Life of St. Pachomius.* Migne, *PG* 73.238–239. (see p. 22)

Parente, Pascal Prosper. *The Ascetical Life.* St. Louis: Herder, 1944. (see pp. 29, 33, 99, 132)

————. *Spiritual Direction.* Rev. ed. New York: St. Paul Pubs., 1961.

Penington, Isaac. *The Works of the Long-Mournful and Sorrowfully Distressed Isaac Penington.* 2d rev. ed. 2 vols. London: Clark, 1761. (see p. 152)

Peyriguère, Albert. *Voice from the Desert.* Translated by A. M. Forsyth and A. M. de Commaille. New York: Sheed & Ward, 1967. (see pp. 96, 156)

Pinamonti, Giovanni Pietro. *Il direttore, ovvero metodo da poterse Tenere per ben regolare l'anime nella via della perfezione Cristiana.* Venice: Albrizzi, 1724.

Plus, Raoul. *La Sainteté catholique.* Paris: Bloud & Gay, 1928.

————. *La Direction d'après les maîtres spirituels.* Paris: Éditions Spes, 1933.

Poselyanin, E. *Russian Ascetics of the Nineteenth Century.* St. Petersburg, 1910.

Puente, Luis de la. *Du Directeur spirituel, extrait du "Guide spirituel" du V. P. Louis Dupont.* Lille: Desclée, de Brouwer, 1896.

Richard of Saint-Victor. *Benjamin Minor, Benjamin Major.* Migne, *PL* 196. (see pp. 121, 129)

————. *Richard of St. Victor: The Twelve Patriarchs, the Mystical Ark Book, Three of the Trinity.* Translated and edited by G. A. Zinn. New York: Paulist Press, 1979.

Rodriguez, Alphonsus. *Practice of Perfection and Christian Virtues.* Vol. 3. Chicago: Loyola University Press, 1929.

Rolle, Richard, of Hampole. *The Fire of Love.* Baltimore, Md.: Penguin, 1972.

————. *The Form of Living.* Translated by G. Heseltine. New York: Longmans, Green, 1930.

Ruysbroeck, Bl. Jan van. *The Adornment of the Spiritual Marriage, The Sparkling Stone, The Book of Supreme Truth.* Translated by C. A. Wynschenk. New York: Dutton, 1916. (see pp. 173)

————. *The Spiritual Espousals.* Translated by Eric Colledge. New York: Harper, 1953.

Saudreau, Auguste. *Les Degrés de la vie spirituelle; méthode pour diriger les âmes suivant leurs progrès dans la vertu.* 6th ed. 2 vols. Angers: Éditions de l'Ouest, 1935. (see pp. 25, 98, 101)

————. *The Degrees of the Spiritual Life: A Method of Directing Souls according to Their Progress in Virtue.* Translated by Dom Bede Camm. New York: Benziger, 1907.

———. *Manuel de spiritualité*. 3d rev. ed. Paris: P. Téqui, 1933.

Scaramelli, Fr. John Baptist. *The Director Asceticum; or Guide to the Spiritual Life*. Translated and edited by William Eyre. 4 vols. Dublin: W. B. Kelly, 1870–71.

———. *Le Discernement des esprits pour le bon règlement de ses propres actions et de celles d'autrui, ouvrage spécialement utile aux directeurs des âmes*. Paris: Walzer, 1893.

Schaller, Jean-Pierre. *Direction spirituelle*. Paris: Éditions Beauchesne, 1978.

Schneiders, Sr. Sandra. *Spiritual Direction*. Chicago: National Sisters Vocations Conference, 1977.

Schram, Dominikus. *Institutiones theologiae mysticae ad usum directorum animarum, ex S. Scriptura, conciliis, ss. patribus, mysticis primariis, ac theologicis ratiociniis adornatae*. New ed. 2 vols. Vol. 2. Paris: Baldeveck, 1868. (see p. 57)

Schutz, Prior Roger. *The Rule of Taizé*. Taizé: Les Presses de Taizé, 1967.

———. *Introduction à la vie communautaire*. Geneva: Labor et Fides, 1944. (see p. 19)

Scupoli, Lawrence. *The Spiritual Combat, and a Treatise on Peace of the Soul*. Westminster, Md.: Newman Bookshop, 1945.

Seelaus, Sr. Vilma, O.C.D. "New Approaches and Needs for Women in Spiritual Direction." *Crux*, 27 June 1977. (see pp. 38, 41)

Ségur, Msgr. Louis-Gaston de. *Lettres à ses filles spirituelles*. Paris: Retaux, 1876–99. (see p. 145)

Seraphim of Sarov, St. *The Spiritual Instructions of Saint Seraphim of Sarov*. Edited by Franklin Jones. Los Angeles: Dawn Horse Press, 1973.

———. *Conversations with Seraphim of Sarov*. Paris: V. N. Iliin, 1930. (see p. 47)

———. "An Ikon of Orthodox Spirituality," by Paul Evdokimov. *The Ecumenical Review* 15 (1963). (see pp. 43, 62, 64)

Sergieff, Fr. John. *Thoughts and Counsels of Father John*. Edited by Cyril Bickersteth and Agnes Illingworth. Oxford: Mowbray, 1899.

———. *Spiritual Counsels of Father John of Kronstadt*. Translated and edited by W. Jardine Grisbrooke. London: Clarke, 1967. (see p. 80)

Seton, St. Elizabeth. *Personal Notes*. Edited by Srs. J. P. King and E. M. North. Mt. St. Joseph Archives, Ohio: Private Publication, 1960. (see p. 13)

Spiritual Direction. A series of articles in *Dictionnaire de spiritualité ascétique et mystique, doctrine et histoire*. Paris: Beachesne, 1957.

Steere, Douglas Van. *On Listening to Another*. Edited by C. Glenne Hinson. New York: Harper, 1955. (see p. 85)

Stockman, Msgr. Polydore J. *Manual of Christian Perfection. Especially Designed for the Instruction of Novices Who Sincerely Desire to Enter a Religious Community.* New York: Paulist Press, 1921.

Stuart, Sr. Janet Erskine. *Life and Letters of Janet Erskine Stuart,* by Maud Monahan. London: Longmans, 1960. (see pp. 50, 145, 146, 185, 186, 187)

Surin, Jean Joseph. *Guide spirituel pour la perfection.* Edited by Michel de Certeau. Collection Christus, no. 12. Paris: Desclée, de Brouwer, 1963. (see p. 57)

———. *Les Fondements de la vie spirituelle, tirés du livre de l' Imitation de Jésus-Christ.* Paris: Spes, 1930. (see p. 92)

———. *Spiritual Letters of Father Surin, S. J.* Translated by Sr. M. Christopher. London: Derby, 1875. (see p. 12)

Suso, Bl. Henry. *The Exemplar: Life and Writings of Blessed Henry Suso, O.P.* Translated by Sr. M. Ann Edward. Dubuque: Priory Press, 1962.

Symeon the New Theologian. *Catéchèses.* Edited by Basile Krivochéine. Sources chrétiennes, vol. 96. Paris: Éditions du Cerf, 1963. (see pp. 11, 18, 36, 172)

———. *Chapitres théologiques, gnostiques et pratiques.* Edited by J. Darrouzès. Sources chrétiennes, vol. 51. Paris: Éditions du Cerf, 1957.

———. *The Discourses.* Translated by C. J. de Catanzaro. New York: Paulist Press, 1980.

Tanquerey, Adolphe. *The Spiritual Life.* 2d rev. ed. Tournai: Desclée, 1930.

Tauler, John. *The Sermons and Conferences of John Tauler, of the Order of Preachers, Surnamed "the Illuminated Doctor"; Being His Spiritual Doctrine.* Translated by Walter Elliott. Washington, D.C.: Apostolic Mission House, 1910. (see pp. 25, 28)

———. *Spiritual Conferences.* Translated and edited by Eric College and Sr. M. Jane. St. Louis: Herder, 1961. (see p. 11, 112)

Taylor, Jeremy. *The Whole Works of the Right Rev. Jeremy Taylor.* Edited by Reginald Heber. 10 vols. "Life of Christ," vol. 2. "Sermons," vol. 4. London: Longman, 1850–54. (see p. 174)

Teresa of Ávila, St. *Œuvres complètes.* Translated by R. P. Grégoire. Paris: Éditions du Seuil, 1949. (see pp. 42, 46, 102, 109, 110, 122, 132)

———. *Obras completas.* Edited by Silverio de Santa Teresa. 5th ed. Madrid: Aguilar, 1945.

———. *The Collected Works of St. Teresa of Avila.* Translated by Kieran Kavanaugh & Otilio Rodriquez. Washington, D.C.: Institute of Carmelite Studies, 1976.

Theophane the Recluse. *The Art of Prayer.* Edited by Igumen Chariton of Valano. London: Faber & Faber, 1976. (see pp. 53, 75)

Thérèse of Lisieux, St. *Histoire d'une âme, écrite par elle-même. Lettres et poésies.* Calvados: Carmel de Lisieux, 1910. (see p. 163)

———. *Manuscrits autobiographiques*. Lisieux: Office central de Carmel, 1957.

———. *Lettres*. Collection Interférences. Paris: Association Philippe Neri, 1967.

———. *Derniers entretiens avec ses sœurs, Mère Agnès de Jésus, Sœur Geneviève, Sœur Marie du Sacré-Cœur, et témoignages divers*. "Novissima Verba." 2 vols. Paris: Éditions du Cerf, 1971.

———. *Conseils et souvenirs de Ste. Thérèse de l'Enfant'-Jésus*. Edited by Sr. Geneviève de la Sainte-Face. 4th ed. Paris: Éditions du Cerf, Desclée de Brouwer, 1973.

———. *The Story of a Soul: The Autobiography of Saint Thérèse of Lisieux*. Translated by Michael Day (Revision). Westminster, Md.: Newman Press, 1952.

———. *Collected Letters*. Edited by Abbé Combes. Translated by F. J. Sheed. New York: Sheed & Ward, 1949.

Thomas of Celano. *Legenda Prima Sancti Francisci*. Edited by Edward Alencon.'Rome, 1906. (see p. 172)

Thornton, Martin. *Christian Proficiency*. London: S.P.C.K., 1959. (see pp. 37, 53, 55, 114, 132, 177)

Thurian, Max. *La Confession*. 3d ed. Neuchâtel: Delachaux et Niestlé, 1966. (see pp. 26, 96)

———. *Confession*. Translated by Edwin Hudson. London: SCM Press, 1958.

Tikhon of Zadonsk, St. *Saint Tikhon Zadonsky, Inspirer of Dostoevsky*, by Nadejda Gorodetzky. London: S.P.C.K., 1951. (see p. 143)

———. *Collected Works*. 6th ed. 5 vols. Moscow, 1898–99.

Tournier, Paul. *To Understand Each Other*. Atlanta: John Knox, 1962. (see p. 121)

Tourville, Henri de. *Piété confiante. Lettres*. "Letters of Counsel." Edited by Abbé F. Klein. Paris: Lecoffre, 1905.

———. *Letters of Direction: Thoughts on the Spiritual Life from the Letters of Abbé de Tourville*. Edited by Evelyn Underhill. Translated by Lucy Menzies. Westminster, Md.: Dacre Press, 1939. (see p. 30)

Tronson, Louis. *Œuvres complètes*. "De l'obéissance envers le directeur." Edited by J. P. Migne. Paris: Migne, 1857. (see pp. 5, 73)

Underhill, Evelyn. *The Letters of Evelyn Underhill*. Edited by Charles Williams. New York: Longmans, 1943. (see pp. 158, 159, 184, 185)

Vandenbroucke, François. *Direction spirituelle et hommes d'aujourd'hui*. Paris: Beauchesne, 1956.

Van Kaam, Adrian. *The Dynamics of Spiritual Self-Direction*. Denville, N.J.: Dimension Books, 1976. (see p. 96)

Velichkovsky, Paisius, Bl. *Bl. Paisius Velichkovsky, Life and Ascetic Labors*, (Schema-monk Metrophanes), Platina, Calif.: St. Herman of Alaska Brotherhood, 1976.

Vincent de Paul, St. *Correspondance, entretiens, documents.* Edited by Pierre Coste. 14 vols. Paris: Librairie Lecoffre, 1920–25. (see pp. 166)

———. *Conferences of St. Vincent de Paul to the Sisters of Charity.* Translated by Joseph Leonard. 4 vols. Christian Classics. Westminster, Md.: Newman Press, 1952.

———. *The Holiness of Vincent de Paul,* by V. D. Jacques Delarue. "Spiritual Direction." Translated by Suzanne Chapman. New York: P. J. Kenedy, 1960.

Vincent Ferrer, St. *Treatise on the Spiritual Life.* Translated by T. A. Dixon. Westminster, Md.: Newman Book Shop, 1944.

Voillaume, René. *Lettres aux fraternités.* 3 vols. Paris: Éditions du Cerf, 1960–66.

———. *Ce que croyait Charles de Foucauld.* Paris: Mame, 1971.

———. *Brothers of Men: Letters to the Petit Frères.* Edited by Lancelot Sheppard. Translated by A. Manson. London: Longman, 1966. (see p. 34)

Ward, Reginald Somerset. *A Guide for Spiritual Directors, by the Author of the Way.* London: A. R. Mowbray, 1957. (see p. 29)

Ware, Kallistos. "The Spiritual Fathers in Orthodox Christianity." *Cross Currents,* Summer-Fall, 1974. (see pp. 120, 127)

Way of a Pilgrim, The. *The Way of a Pilgrim; and the Pilgrim Continues His Way.* Translated by R. M. French. 2d ed. New York: Seabury, 1968. (see pp. 9, 39)

Weil, Simone. *The Simone Weil Reader.* Edited by G. A. Panichas. New York: McKay, 1977. (see p. 14)

Wesley, John. *A Plain Account of Christian Perfection.* New ed. London: Epworth Press, 1968. (see p. 6)

———. *John Wesley; an Autobiographical Sketch of the Man and His Thought, Chiefly from His Letters.* "Letters to Mrs. Chapman." Edited by Ole E. Borgen. Textus minores, vol. 35. Leiden: E. J. Brill, 1966. (see p. 143)

William of Saint-Thierry. *Golden Epistle.* Migne, PL 184. (see p. 24)

———. *Mirror of Faith.* Migne, PL 184. (see p. 172)

———. *Golden Epistle.* Translated by Theodore Berkeley. Spencer, Mass.: Cistercian Pubs., 1971.

———. *Le Miroir de la Foi.* Edited by Charles Beyaert. Bruges, 1946.

Woolman, John. *The Works of John Woolman. In Two Parts.* "A Journal of the Life, Gospel Labours, and Christian Experiences of that Faithful Minister of Jesus Christ, John Woolman." Philadelphia: J. Crukshank, 1774.

———. *The Journal and Major Essays of John Woolman.* Edited by Phillips P. Moulton. New York: Oxford University Press, 1971. (see p. 162)

Wulf, Friedrich. "Spiritual Direction," *Sacramentum Mundi* (rev. ed.), Karl Rahner, ed., New York: Seabury Press (1975), 1640. (see p. 76)

Yungblut, John. *Rediscovering Prayer*. New York: Seabury, 1972. (see p. 80)

Zosima, Verkhovsky, Father. *Life and Sayings*. Moscow, 1889. (see p. 68)